SURVIVING THE AI JOB ECONOMY

Hayden Van Der Post

Reactive Publishing

CONTENTS

PREFACE

We stand at the dawn of a revolution—a convergence of technology and human ambition that is reshaping our workplaces, our industries, and our lives. The age of artificial intelligence has arrived, ushering in transformative challenges and unprecedented opportunities. Whether you're a seasoned professional facing the evolving demands of AI, a lifelong learner eager to stay ahead of the curve, or an entrepreneur ready to harness the power of innovative technologies, this book is your essential guide to surviving—and thriving—in the AI job economy.

In crafting this guide, we recognized that today's workforce is not merely adapting to change; it is experiencing a seismic shift. The narrative of work is being rewritten, and so too must our strategies for success. Throughout these pages, you will discover a comprehensive roadmap designed not only to navigate but also to capitalize on the ongoing transformation of our work environments. We delve into historical contexts, emerging trends, and the future horizons of industries touched by AI, providing both critical insights and actionable strategies.

This journey begins by exploring the evolution of AI in workplaces—tracing its early adoption, the resistance it initially encountered, and the transformative role it now plays across sectors. As the lines between human and machine blur, the skills once taken for granted are being redefined. The book offers an in-depth look at the essential skills required in this brave new world, from technical prowess to the irreplaceable value of emotional intelligence, creativity, and lifelong learning. You will learn how to pivot your career with confidence, build robust professional networks, and embrace the flexibility necessary in today's job market.

Yet, this guide is much more than a manual for survival—it is a call to action, a source of empowerment for anyone willing to step into the future with an informed and proactive mindset. We examine every facet of the AI-driven transformation, from remote work and the gig economy to the ethical dilemmas and societal shifts that demand our attention. Chapters dedicated to entrepreneurship offer inspiration and practical advice for leveraging AI to launch and scale new ventures, while others provide tools and resources for continuous personal and professional development.

What makes this book truly unique is its multidisciplinary approach—merging insights from industry experts, case studies of both success and failure, and a forward-looking perspective on global and ethical implications. Our aim is to prepare you for the long-term impacts of AI, offering strategies to overcome barriers, address economic inequality, and foster a culture of resilience and adaptability in your career and organization.

This guide is an invitation to engage with the future—to rise to the challenge of a world where the human spirit and artificial intelligence coexist to create new frontiers. As you turn the pages, you will find that every chapter is crafted to equip you with the tools, the knowledge, and the inspiration you need to build the career and life you desire. We encourage you to embrace this journey with an open mind, to challenge old paradigms, and to harness the boundless possibilities that lie ahead.

Welcome to a transformational guide for navigating the AI job economy. Together, let's shape a future where technology and humanity not only coexist but thrive in mutual innovation and growth.

Your future begins here.

INTRODUCTION

In today's rapidly changing work environment, the emergence of artificial intelligence (AI) represents more than just a passing trend; it signifies a transformative shift with significant implications. AI is reshaping job roles, altering workplace dynamics, and reimagining the concept of employment itself. This transformation is not a distant prospect—it's occurring right now. The urgency to adapt has never been more pressing, prompting both individuals and organizations to reassess their strategies for navigating an AI-driven economy.

Take the retail sector as a prime example of this change. Here, AI has revolutionized customer engagement. Businesses are harnessing predictive analytics to anticipate purchasing trends and employing chatbots for 24/7 customer service, thereby enhancing operational efficiency and enriching user experiences. Companies like Amazon illustrate this well by using advanced algorithms to recommend products based on past purchases, which not only boosts sales but also personalizes the shopping journey. That's why, retail professionals are compelled to shift away from traditional sales methods towards more tech-savvy approaches that prioritize data literacy and digital engagement.

However, this evolution also brings a wave of anxiety. Many workers fear that AI could render their jobs obsolete.

According to a report from the McKinsey Global Institute, up to 375 million workers worldwide may need to transition to different occupational categories by 2030 due to automation. This alarming statistic highlights the urgent need for proactive measures—acquiring new skills and embracing flexibility have become essential rather than optional.

Navigating this landscape strategically is key. Skills that once seemed adequate may no longer suffice in a world where technology advances at breakneck speed. While technical proficiency in software applications remains important, the ability to analyze data trends and make informed decisions based on those insights is increasingly sought after across various sectors. To thrive amidst these changes, professionals must adopt a mindset of continuous learning and adaptability.

Real-world examples underscore the importance of this journey toward adaptation. Consider Sarah, a mid-career marketing professional who recognized the growing significance of AI-driven digital marketing tools. By enrolling in online courses focused on data analytics and machine learning applications in marketing, she not only secured her position but also advanced to a leadership role where she now guides her team through data-informed strategies. Sarah's experience illustrates how embracing new technologies can turn perceived threats into opportunities for growth.

As we delve deeper into this book, we will explore practical strategies for flourishing in this evolving environment. Whether it's developing essential skills or building connections that open new doors, our focus will remain on actionable insights grounded in real-world applications. Each chapter will build on these themes, equipping you with tools and resources designed to empower your journey through the complexities of an AI-augmented workforce.

This journey is not solely about survival; it is also about leveraging change as a catalyst for personal and professional development. As we embark on this exploration together, remember that every challenge posed by technological advancements also carries with it untold opportunities for those who are ready to adapt and evolve.

· Understanding the AI Job Economy

To truly grasp the dynamics of the AI Job Economy, it's essential to explore the driving forces behind this transformation and its implications for workers across various sectors. Essentially of this shift lies a redefinition of work, productivity, and job satisfaction. Companies now prioritize not just employees who can complete tasks, but those who can effectively collaborate with AI systems to boost efficiency, creativity, and problem-solving.

A prime example of this evolution is seen in the healthcare sector. Here, AI tools process vast amounts of patient data, aiding doctors in making more accurate diagnoses than ever before. Take this example, AI algorithms can analyze medical images to detect early signs of diseases like cancer, often surpassing traditional methods. That's why, healthcare professionals are expected to not only possess clinical expertise but also to interpret insights generated by these technologies. This integration of AI into healthcare demands that practitioners develop both technical skills and strong interpersonal abilities.

The rise of the gig economy adds another layer of complexity to this landscape. As businesses increasingly seek flexibility without the commitment of full-time employment, freelancers and contractors are becoming more prevalent. Platforms like Upwork and Fiverr illustrate this trend, enabling individuals to offer their services on-demand. While these platforms create opportunities, they also foster a competitive environment where success hinges on effective self-promotion and agility in adapting to shifting demands.

In this context, understanding economic factors becomes

paramount. Economic downturns or rapid technological advancements can result in job displacement for many workers. Research from Oxford University indicates that up to 47% of jobs in the U.S. may be at high risk of automation within the next two decades. This looming threat highlights the importance for workers to stay informed about industry trends and actively engage in upskilling efforts to maintain their relevance in a changing job market.

Businesses are also adapting their hiring practices in response to these shifts. Many organizations now seek candidates who possess a blend of technical expertise and interpersonal skills—often referred to as "T-shaped" professionals. These individuals have deep knowledge in one area while also being able to collaborate across disciplines. As such, job seekers must demonstrate not only their qualifications but also their adaptability and eagerness to learn.

Real-world examples illustrate these shifts vividly. Consider John, a graphic designer who initially relied on traditional design software. Recognizing that automation tools could enhance his workflow, he proactively pursued training in new design technologies that integrate AI capabilities. This way, he positioned himself as an innovator in his field rather than becoming obsolete due to technological advancements. John's proactive approach exemplifies how individuals can navigate the complexities of an evolving job market by embracing new tools and methodologies.

As we examine these realities, it becomes clear that understanding the nuances of the AI Job Economy is crucial for anyone aspiring not just to survive but to thrive within it. A willingness to adapt—whether through reskilling or redefining one's professional narrative—can turn challenges into opportunities.

With every shift in industry standards and expectations comes an invitation for growth. Embracing this invitation means remaining open-minded about learning new technologies while nurturing connections that extend beyond traditional networks. By cultivating both hard skills—rooted in technology—and soft skills such as communication and emotional intelligence, professionals can thrive alongside AI innovations instead of being sidelined by them.

This exploration of the AI Job Economy aims not only to provide survival strategies but also to equip you with approaches that foster resilience and innovation amid ongoing change—a path marked by adaptability leading toward personal empowerment in your professional landscape.

- **Purpose of the Book**

The primary aim of this book is to equip readers with actionable strategies and insights that will empower them to navigate the complexities of the AI job economy effectively. As this landscape continues to evolve, many professionals grapple with uncertainty, wondering how they can remain relevant and competitive. This guide seeks to alleviate those concerns by offering practical tools and frameworks that can be immediately applied in various contexts.

Understanding the rapid advancements in artificial intelligence is crucial. AI is more than just a trend; it has become a transformative force reshaping industries and influencing everything from hiring practices to employee expectations. By examining these changes closely, we clarify which skills and competencies are essential for success in this new environment. For example, data analytics has shifted from a niche skill to a fundamental requirement across many roles, including those traditionally deemed non-technical.

In addition to technical abilities, this book emphasizes the importance of emotional intelligence and adaptability. While technical skills can help open doors, it is often the ability to connect with others that sustains a career during turbulent times. Throughout this guide, we highlight professionals like Sarah, a project manager who cultivated her soft skills alongside her technical training. Her journey demonstrates how fostering relationships and enhancing communication can lead to significant opportunities, even when technology disrupts established pathways.

Another key theme is the necessity of continuous learning. In a world where knowledge quickly becomes outdated, adopting a mindset geared towards lifelong education has become essential rather than optional. The proliferation of online platforms offering courses—from coding boot camps to business management seminars—shows that accessible resources are available for those willing to invest time in their growth. Each chapter will highlight specific resources and strategies readers can use to upskill or pivot into new areas.

Resilience amid change is also vital. Embracing challenges as opportunities rather than obstacles characterizes many successful careers today. We explore techniques for building mental resilience and adapting to shifting market demands through real-world examples of individuals who have successfully navigated their own career pivots in response to AI developments.

And, this guide does not shy away from examining the ethical dimensions of AI integration into the workplace. Understanding how technology impacts society—particularly concerning issues like bias and privacy—is crucial for future leaders committed to responsible innovation. The book offers insights into how professionals can advocate for ethical practices within their organizations while contributing positively to societal discussions surrounding AI.

our goal is not just survival but thriving in this evolving landscape. By blending practical advice with inspirational stories from those who have successfully adapted, we provide a roadmap for readers determined to embrace their potential in an AI-driven economy.

As you explore each section, consider how these strategies align with your own professional journey. Reflect on your strengths and identify growth opportunities—each insight shared here serves as a stepping stone toward navigating your unique path in a world shaped by artificial intelligence. Engaging with this material can transform potential uncertainties into empowered actions as you move forward.

- **Key Themes and Concepts**

Navigating the complexities of the AI job economy reveals several key themes that are vital for professionals aiming to thrive in this evolving landscape. At the forefront is the importance of adaptability, which has become the cornerstone of career success. As AI technologies progress, the demands on individuals across various fields also shift. This adaptability goes beyond merely being open to change; it entails a proactive approach to skill development and career planning. Take Alex, for example—a marketing specialist who successfully transitioned from traditional advertising strategies to data-driven campaigns. By embracing new tools and methods, Alex not only enhanced his value within his company but also emerged as a leader in a rapidly transforming industry.

Closely linked to adaptability is the concept of lifelong learning. The urgency to continuously update one's skill set has never been more pressing. Traditional educational pathways often struggle to keep pace with technological advancements, making self-directed learning through online courses, webinars, and industry workshops essential. Consider Lisa, who recognized her need for digital marketing skills. While working full-time, she enrolled in several online courses, dedicating her weekends to mastering SEO and analytics. This commitment not only transformed her career trajectory but also led her to a role where she advises companies on integrating AI into their marketing strategies.

Another crucial theme is emotional intelligence, which plays a significant role in fostering personal growth and strengthening professional relationships. In today's workplace, technical proficiency alone is insufficient; effectively collaborating with diverse teams is equally vital. Take Rahul, a software engineer who found that his technical skills were often overshadowed by his struggles to communicate ideas clearly. By concentrating on developing his emotional intelligence—actively listening and empathizing with colleagues—he improved team dynamics and became an integral part of cross-functional projects that incorporated AI solutions into software development.

Equally important is the need to embrace ethical considerations in AI practices. As technology advances at an unprecedented pace, understanding the implications of AI on privacy, bias, and societal norms becomes essential for today's leaders. Professionals must champion ethical frameworks that guide AI integration within their organizations. Take this example, Emily, a compliance officer at a tech firm, took the initiative to implement training sessions focused on ethical AI use among her team. This proactive approach not only fostered responsible innovation but also bolstered her company's reputation and compliance standing.

Resilience is yet another critical attribute in this dynamic environment. The capacity to endure setbacks and view challenges as opportunities for growth can profoundly influence career longevity and satisfaction. James' journey exemplifies this principle; after being laid off due to automation in his role as an administrative assistant, he reframed this setback as a chance to pivot into project management by acquiring new skills through targeted online courses and mentorship.

Finally, building networks in an increasingly digitized world serves as a powerful strategy for career advancement. The connections professionals cultivate can lead to collaborations and opportunities that might otherwise remain elusive. Sarah capitalized on connections made at industry conferences to secure a partnership with a tech startup exploring AI applications in healthcare—a move that opened multiple avenues for innovation within her organization.

· How to Use This Guide

Effectively utilizing this guide is essential for anyone looking to navigate the dynamic AI job economy. Each section is designed not only to inform but also to equip you with practical strategies that can be put into action right away.

Begin by immersing yourself in the key themes presented in this book: adaptability, lifelong learning, emotional intelligence, ethical engagement, resilience, and networking. These concepts are woven throughout the text and will serve as the foundation of your professional journey. As you read, take notes on how these themes relate to your personal situation. Take this example, if adaptability resonates with you, think about ways to enhance this trait in your career. Setting personal milestones can help you track your progress as you adopt new skills or technologies.

As you move through each chapter, engage actively with the material. Rather than simply absorbing information, create action plans based on the strategies discussed. If a chapter focuses on emotional intelligence, for example, consider implementing a practice like weekly reflections on your interactions with colleagues. Ask yourself what went well and where you could improve in terms of communication and empathy.

The real-world examples provided throughout the text serve as case studies for analysis and inspiration. Reflect on these stories: What strategies did Alex or Lisa implement that you might replicate? Are there aspects of their journeys that resonate with your own experiences? By connecting these narratives to your life, you can extract actionable insights tailored to your unique circumstances.

To deepen your understanding and facilitate self-assessment, make use of the worksheets and exercises included in the guide. Completing these will reinforce your learning and clarify your career goals. Take this example, when considering ethical implications in AI practices, use the provided frameworks to analyze how they apply to your current role or industry. This reflection will help foster a sense of ownership over your learning process.

Additionally, take advantage of the resources recommended in each chapter—whether online courses, books, or networking opportunities. Develop a personal growth plan that outlines specific courses or certifications you want to pursue based on both your interests and market demand. This structured approach will keep you proactive in advancing your career rather than reactive.

Keep in mind that this guide is not just about acquiring knowledge; it's about cultivating a mindset focused on growth and resilience. Be prepared for setbacks along the way; they are often stepping stones to success. If you encounter challenges similar to those faced by individuals highlighted in the book —like James' transition after losing his job—view them as opportunities to pivot and redefine your career path.

Finally, connect with others who are also navigating this landscape. The guide emphasizes the importance of networking; reach out to peers from various industries or join professional organizations centered on AI integration. Sharing experiences can lead to collaborations that enrich both your understanding and network.

By engaging deeply with this guide and its insights, you position yourself not just to survive but to thrive in an AI-driven economy. The tools provided are designed to empower you as an active participant in shaping your future career—

one where continuous adaptation and lifelong learning are vital for success. Embrace this journey with intention and curiosity; the rewards await those willing to take action and forge their own paths amid change.

CHAPTER 1: THE DAWN OF AI-DRIVEN WORKPLACES

*Historical Context of AI
in the Workplace*

T he story of artificial intelligence (AI) in the workplace unfolds over several decades, rooted in the vision of machines enhancing human capabilities. Its origins trace back to the 1950s, when pioneers like Alan Turing and John McCarthy laid the groundwork for what would become a transformative force across various industries. In those early days, the potential applications of AI were largely theoretical, yet they ignited imaginations and spurred research that gradually evolved into practical uses.

By the late 20th century, we began to see significant integration of AI into business processes, with the manufacturing sector leading the charge. Automation technologies revolutionized assembly lines, dramatically boosting productivity while cutting labor costs. The introduction of computer-aided design (CAD) systems enabled engineers to innovate at unprecedented speeds. This wave of technological advancement created a ripple effect; as efficiency improved, so did expectations for speed and quality across industries.

The rise of personal computing in the 1980s marked another pivotal moment. As computers became more accessible, businesses tapped into data like never before. This influx of information gave rise to decision-making algorithms capable of analyzing trends and patterns, further enhancing operational efficiency. Rather than displacing workers, these technologies transformed roles, fostering collaboration between humans and machines.

However, this technological progress was not without its challenges. Many employees harbored fears about job displacement due to automation, leading to a wave of resistance among workers concerned about dehumanization in the workplace. These sentiments intensified during economic downturns when job security became a pressing issue. In response, some companies approached AI adoption cautiously, opting for hybrid systems that emphasized close collaboration between humans and AI tools.

Despite this resistance, certain industries wholeheartedly embraced AI. The finance sector serves as a prime example; algorithmic trading transformed investment decision-making by leveraging AI's capacity to process vast amounts of data at remarkable speeds. As finance firms adapted to this new landscape, they attracted a new generation of talent skilled in data science rather than traditional financial expertise.

The healthcare sector experienced its own AI renaissance in the 2010s as diagnostic tools and treatment planning software transitioned from research labs to clinical environments. Medical professionals gained access to predictive analytics that could analyze patient data and suggest personalized treatment options. In these instances, AI did not replace clinicians; instead, it augmented their decision-making capabilities, allowing them to focus more on patient care.

Yet this evolution brought challenges and ethical dilemmas surrounding data privacy and algorithmic bias—issues that continue to provoke heated debates today. Take this example, if an AI system inadvertently favors certain demographics over others due to biased training data, it risks perpetuating inequality rather than alleviating it.

Entering the 2020s, the COVID-19 pandemic unexpectedly accelerated AI adoption across various fields. With remote work becoming the norm, organizations sought solutions that streamlined virtual communication and collaboration. Companies rapidly integrated AI tools into their workflows; chatbots provided customer service support while machine learning algorithms optimized supply chains strained by pandemic-related disruptions.

Today's workplace is characterized by a deep embedding of AI into daily operations—ranging from automating repetitive tasks to enhancing complex analytical processes that require human intuition combined with machine efficiency. This synergy has redefined job descriptions across sectors; roles are evolving as workers are expected to adapt swiftly to changing technologies while mastering new skills to remain relevant.

Understanding this historical context not only highlights how far we've come but also prepares us for what lies ahead in our increasingly automated world. Recognizing patterns of adaptation—and resistance—equips professionals with insights essential for navigating future transformations effectively. With this knowledge in hand, individuals can better position themselves for success amid ongoing changes driven by artificial intelligence—an evolution that is no longer a distant prospect but an immediate reality shaping our professional lives today.

Early AI Adoption and Resistance

The story of early AI adoption in the workplace is

characterized by a blend of excitement and apprehension. As businesses began to integrate artificial intelligence into their operations, they faced a dual challenge: tapping into the immense potential of these technologies while addressing the skepticism and fears that often accompanied them. The arrival of AI tools sparked both enthusiasm for innovation and concerns about job security, creating a complex landscape for employers and employees alike.

Initially, industries such as manufacturing led the way in AI integration. The introduction of robotics not only revolutionized production lines but also altered labor dynamics. Workers found themselves collaborating with machines designed to enhance efficiency rather than replace human effort. However, this transition faced resistance from those who feared that automation would threaten their jobs. Companies had to navigate these concerns delicately, often opting for gradual implementation strategies that prioritized retraining workers over immediate displacement.

This hesitance wasn't just a reaction to technological change; it was also shaped by historical precedents where innovation resulted in job losses. The rise of computers in the 1980s had already unsettled many industries, leading to widespread anxiety about obsolescence. In light of this, many businesses recognized the importance of fostering an environment where employees felt secure and supported—an essential factor for successful AI integration.

Despite the unease, certain sectors embraced AI with enthusiasm. The financial industry serves as a prime example; algorithmic trading platforms emerged as powerful tools capable of analyzing vast datasets far beyond human capability. This shift not only optimized trading strategies but also required a new kind of workforce—data scientists adept at leveraging these advanced systems. So, companies began to adjust their hiring practices, moving away from traditional finance roles in favor of data-centric positions.

Healthcare followed a similar trajectory as it gradually integrated AI into its practices during the 2010s. Diagnostic tools powered by machine learning began assisting physicians in evaluating patient data, leading to more accurate diagnoses and personalized treatment plans. Instead of perceiving AI as a threat to their expertise, healthcare professionals increasingly saw it as an ally—one that could enhance their decision-making capabilities and improve patient outcomes.

However, this shift brought significant ethical considerations regarding data usage and privacy. The challenge extended beyond merely deploying technology; it involved ensuring that such systems operated fairly and transparently. Take this example, if predictive algorithms inadvertently favored specific demographics due to biased training data, they risked reinforcing existing disparities in care rather than alleviating them.

As we moved into the 2020s, external factors like the COVID-19 pandemic accelerated AI adoption across various sectors. Organizations quickly sought solutions that facilitated remote work while maintaining productivity levels amid disruptions. From virtual meeting platforms with intelligent features to customer service chatbots managing inquiries around the clock, companies rapidly integrated AI into everyday workflows—often out of necessity rather than foresight.

This swift integration underscored both opportunities and challenges inherent in technology-driven change. While many organizations thrived through enhanced efficiency and communication, others encountered implementation hurdles —from technical issues to employee resistance rooted in past experiences with automation.

Today's workplace landscape reflects a deep embedding of AI technologies across diverse sectors, automating mundane tasks while enhancing complex analytical processes that require human judgment paired with machine capabilities. Job roles are evolving rapidly; today's professionals must continuously adapt and acquire new skills relevant in an ever-changing technological environment.

This historical perspective on early AI adoption not only highlights how far we've come but also provides valuable lessons for navigating future transformations effectively. By acknowledging patterns of resistance alongside enthusiasm, individuals gain insights necessary for thriving in an era defined by artificial intelligence—a reality that is reshaping our professional lives more dramatically than ever before.

Key Industries Transforming Rapidly

As industries navigate the transformative effects of artificial intelligence, some sectors are evolving at an unprecedented pace, fundamentally reshaping the nature of work and the skills needed for success. Each industry adapts to AI in distinct ways, leveraging its potential to drive efficiency, foster innovation, and improve outcomes.

The healthcare sector serves as a prime example of this transformation. AI technologies have become essential in diagnostics, enabling algorithms to analyze medical images and patient data with remarkable accuracy. Take this example, IBM's Watson Health illustrates how AI assists oncologists by rapidly processing vast amounts of clinical data to recommend personalized treatment plans. Instead of being replaced, radiologists now collaborate with these intelligent systems, enhancing their diagnostic skills through the insights provided by AI tools. This partnership not only improves patient care but also alleviates some of the pressures healthcare professionals face amid increasing caseloads.

Similarly, education has experienced significant changes driven by advancements in AI. Intelligent tutoring systems now tailor learning experiences based on individual student performance and engagement levels. Companies like Knewton utilize data analytics to customize educational content to meet each learner's unique needs, fostering a more personalized approach that enhances comprehension and retention. So, teachers have transitioned from merely delivering content to becoming facilitators who leverage technology to better support diverse learners. This shift underscores the move away from traditional teaching methods toward innovative models that empower both educators and students.

In the finance sector, AI adoption has fundamentally altered investment strategies. Machine learning algorithms analyze market trends in real-time, enabling traders to make data-informed decisions that were once beyond human capabilities. Firms like BlackRock employ these technologies not only for trading but also for risk management and compliance—areas where precision is critical. That's why, there is a growing demand for employees who can interpret these complex algorithms and translate their findings into actionable business strategies.

Retail is another industry experiencing rapid transformation driven by AI integration. Machine learning enables businesses to analyze customer behavior effectively and personalize shopping experiences. Take this example, Amazon's recommendation engine employs sophisticated algorithms that suggest products based on previous purchases and browsing history. This level of personalization not only enhances customer satisfaction and loyalty but also drives sales growth—highlighting the importance of understanding data-driven insights in retail operations.

Manufacturing processes have similarly evolved, with AI capabilities streamlining supply chains and optimizing production lines. Robotics equipped with AI can now perform complex tasks alongside human workers—automating repetitive functions while improving precision in assembly processes. Companies like Tesla exemplify successful implementation of AI-powered robots that enhance efficiency and reduce error rates in manufacturing operations.

While these industries showcase the dynamic changes brought about by artificial intelligence, each transition presents challenges that must be navigated thoughtfully. Workers often feel uncertain as roles shift or transform due to technological advancements, leading to anxiety over job security or skill relevance. However, organizations increasingly recognize that fostering a culture of continuous learning is crucial for alleviating resistance to change.

Amid this rapid evolution across industries, investing in employee reskilling programs is essential. By providing training opportunities tailored to emerging technologies and new operational paradigms, companies empower their workforce to adapt rather than feel threatened by progress. For example, IBM's SkillsBuild program offers resources aimed at preparing individuals for careers in tech-driven fields—taking a proactive approach to address potential skills gaps before they widen further.

And, collaboration between sectors is becoming increasingly vital as organizations seek innovative solutions amid competitive pressures intensified by globalization and technological advancements. Partnerships between tech companies specializing in AI development and traditional firms pursuing digital transformation can yield mutual benefits: enhanced capabilities for businesses while accelerating innovation cycles for technology providers.

Understanding how key industries are rapidly transforming through AI offers valuable insights for navigating one's career path in this evolving landscape. Embracing change involves recognizing the opportunities created by new technologies —whether through upskilling initiatives or collaborative efforts across various sectors—and adapting accordingly ensures sustained relevance in an ever-changing job market increasingly influenced by artificial intelligence innovations.

As we delve deeper into these transformations across multiple sectors impacted by AI integration strategies, it becomes clear that how we engage with these changes today will shape our professional landscapes tomorrow. By inspiring proactive engagement rather than passive observation, we can navigate the technological evolution unfolding around us at breakneck speed.

The Role of Automation

The rise of automation represents a pivotal shift in the evolution of work, fundamentally redefining roles, responsibilities, and the structure of entire industries. Rather than simply replacing human labor, automation enhances capabilities, optimizes processes, and drives efficiencies that were once deemed unattainable. As we navigate this evolving landscape, it's essential to recognize both the opportunities and challenges that automation brings to the workplace.

In manufacturing, for example, automation is closely linked to increased productivity. Modern assembly lines are equipped with advanced robotics that not only handle repetitive tasks but also collaborate seamlessly with human workers. This partnership creates a more dynamic production environment where machines manage heavy lifting while humans concentrate on quality control and problem-solving. A noteworthy illustration of this is Ford's use of robotic arms in vehicle assembly, which boosts speed and precision without compromising safety. The clear implication is that as machines take over monotonous tasks, the demand for skilled human oversight increases—workers must adapt by developing competencies in areas such as system management and data analysis.

The impact of automation is also evident in the service industry, particularly through customer-facing technologies. Automated kiosks and AI-driven chatbots have become commonplace in retail and hospitality, streamlining operations and enhancing customer experiences. Take this example, McDonald's introduction of self-service kiosks empowers customers to control their orders while reducing wait times. That's why, employees in these settings have transitioned from order-taking roles to focusing on enriching customer interactions—underscoring the growing importance of interpersonal skills alongside technical expertise.

In logistics, automation is transforming supply chain management through intelligent systems that predict demand fluctuations and optimize inventory levels. Companies like Amazon have made significant investments in robotics to enhance warehouse efficiency. By employing autonomous vehicles and drones for deliveries, they not only accelerate shipping processes but also minimize human error. However, this transition requires a workforce adept in data analytics and logistics management to effectively interpret the systems' outputs.

Healthcare too is undergoing significant change due to automation. Robotics are now integral to surgical procedures, providing precision that improves patient outcomes and reduces recovery times. The advent of robotic surgery systems allows surgeons to perform complex procedures with minimal invasiveness. Yet this technological advancement demands continuous training; healthcare professionals must stay abreast of these innovations to leverage their full potential safely.

Despite these advancements, concerns about job displacement due to automation remain prevalent. Many workers worry that their roles may become obsolete as machines become increasingly capable. This anxiety highlights the necessity for proactive engagement from both employers and employees in fostering a culture of continuous learning and adaptation. Organizations can help alleviate these concerns by investing in reskilling programs that prepare their workforce for shifting demands.

Take this example, Siemens has initiated programs aimed at upskilling employees to work effectively alongside automated systems. These initiatives focus on imparting new technical skills while also emphasizing adaptability—ensuring that workers are not only prepared for current challenges but also equipped to pivot as future needs emerge.

And, addressing the implications of automation requires broader industry conversations about workforce development policies and educational frameworks. Collaboration among businesses, educational institutions, and government agencies can create a talent pipeline skilled in both technology and the soft skills necessary for navigating an automated landscape.

automation presents an opportunity to reimagine work rather than merely displace it. The key lies in recognizing how these technologies can augment human capabilities rather than replace them outright. Embracing this perspective allows professionals to adapt effectively within their careers while fostering an innovative spirit within organizations.

As we reflect on automation's role in shaping our professional futures, it becomes clear that adaptability is essential. Engaging thoughtfully with technology—whether through continuous learning or strategic collaboration—will empower individuals to thrive amid change rather than merely survive it. This mindset not only positions workers favorably in an evolving job market but also stimulates broader economic growth driven by technological advancement.

The Shift in Job Descriptions

The evolution of job descriptions in response to AI and automation reflects a significant shift in how we define roles, skills, and expectations in the workplace. As these technologies gain traction across various industries, organizations are rethinking the competencies and qualities they seek in candidates. The emphasis is moving away from rigid, task-oriented descriptions toward dynamic profiles that prioritize adaptability, creativity, and collaboration.

Take the marketing field as an example. Traditionally, job descriptions outlined specific responsibilities like managing campaigns or creating content. However, as AI tools automate many of these tasks—such as data analysis and customer segmentation—the focus has shifted toward strategic thinking and innovation. Marketers are now required to interpret insights generated by AI systems and leverage those insights to craft compelling narratives. This evolution demands a broader skill set that merges analytical abilities with creative storytelling—a combination that is not always easy to find.

Similarly, project management has seen a transformation from traditional metrics to advanced analytics provided by AI-driven tools. Today's project managers not only coordinate teams but also need to understand how to interpret complex data outputs that inform decision-making processes. Platforms like Monday.com and Trello are integrating AI features to identify bottlenecks and predict project timelines based on historical data. That's why, job descriptions now highlight the importance of organizational skills alongside technical proficiency with these new tools.

In the healthcare sector, we observe another striking example of this shift. The rise of telemedicine and health monitoring technologies has redefined traditionally stable roles. Physicians must now be familiar with digital health platforms in addition to their medical expertise. Instead of solely diagnosing conditions through physical examinations, they engage with patients via virtual consultations— an approach that demands strong communication skills coupled with technical know-how. So, job postings for healthcare professionals increasingly emphasize familiarity with telehealth applications as essential criteria.

The integration of AI also affects hiring practices beyond skill sets; it shapes the qualities sought in candidates. Organizations are beginning to recognize the growing importance of emotional intelligence (EQ) as human interactions evolve alongside technology. Customer service roles now seek individuals who excel in empathy and conflict resolution because while machines can handle routine inquiries, they lack the human touch needed for more nuanced situations. This evolution is particularly evident in call centers: while basic queries can be managed by chatbots, complex issues still require empathetic human intervention.

And, this transformation extends beyond established sectors; emerging industries rooted in technology demand an agile workforce that can adapt quickly to new methodologies and tools. Startups often prioritize candidates who demonstrate a willingness to learn rapidly over those with extensive experience tied solely to traditional roles.

Companies like Google have recognized the necessity for flexibility by implementing hiring strategies that value soft skills alongside technical proficiencies. They assess potential employees' ability to embrace change—an increasingly vital trait in an unpredictable job market where roles may continue to evolve dramatically due to technological advancements.

Additionally, incorporating diversity into job descriptions enhances creativity within teams tasked with tackling complex challenges posed by rapid technological growth. Diverse teams bring unique perspectives that drive innovation; therefore, organizations are reconfiguring their hiring practices not only around qualifications but also around inclusivity.

However, this progression raises important questions about equity and access within the workforce landscape affected by AI adoption. Job seekers must adapt to these new definitions while navigating existing barriers related to educational disparities or socioeconomic status that may limit access to relevant training resources.

As organizations refine their approach to job descriptions influenced by advancements in AI, it becomes clear that a multifaceted perspective on candidate profiles will shape recruitment strategies for years to come. Emphasizing skills like adaptability will better prepare individuals for fulfilling careers amid ongoing change while fostering workplaces defined by collaboration rather than competition.

we are entering an era where conventional job titles may become obsolete as employers seek holistic representations of candidate potential instead of straightforward metrics tied to past experiences or educational achievements alone. Recognizing this paradigm shift empowers both employers and prospective employees—not just to survive but to thrive through newfound opportunities shaped by evolving demands in our increasingly automated world.

AI as a Tool vs. AI as a Threat

The conversation about artificial intelligence (AI) often swings between viewing it as a catalyst for progress and perceiving it as a looming threat. This duality highlights the complexity of incorporating such powerful technology into our daily lives and workplaces. At the heart of this discussion is our approach to AI's role: should we embrace it as a facilitator of human potential, or view it with apprehension as a challenge to job security?

Consider how AI enhances productivity in various industries. In manufacturing, for instance, robotics has transformed production lines, boosting efficiency and minimizing human error. Companies that implement AI-driven systems frequently report significant cost savings and increased output. These advancements can foster job creation in sectors dedicated to maintaining and developing these technologies. Yet, the same technology raises concerns about redundancy for workers engaged in repetitive tasks now performed by machines. This paradox illustrates how perceptions of AI can vary dramatically based on individual experiences.

And, the narrative surrounding AI as a tool is deepened by its capacity to augment human abilities rather than replace them entirely. In healthcare, for example, professionals are increasingly utilizing AI-assisted diagnostic tools to improve patient care. These tools analyze vast datasets to uncover patterns that might escape even the most experienced practitioners, resulting in more accurate diagnoses and personalized treatment plans that ultimately benefit patients. However, this evolution necessitates that healthcare workers acquire new skills, merging clinical expertise with technological proficiency. This requirement underscores the importance of adaptation in harnessing AI's advantages.

A compelling case study arises from the legal sector, where AI has streamlined processes such as document review and legal research. Advanced algorithms can sift through vast amounts of data more rapidly than any human team could manage. While some fear this technology will render junior lawyers obsolete, others argue that it liberates them from mundane tasks, enabling them to concentrate on higher-level strategic thinking and client interaction—areas where emotional intelligence is vital. That's why, integrating AI into legal practices reveals transformative potential; rather than eliminating jobs, it reshapes their very essence.

However, a significant challenge remains: addressing the disparities in access to technology and training. For individuals from lower socioeconomic backgrounds or underrepresented communities, the apprehension surrounding AI adoption is palpable. If these groups lack access to education or resources necessary for upskilling into new roles created by technology, they risk falling further behind in an already competitive job market. This dilemma raises critical questions about equity—how can we ensure that advancements benefit all segments of society instead of exacerbating existing inequalities?

As organizations navigate these complexities, they must also reflect on their internal cultures during the integration of AI solutions. A company culture that promotes open dialogue about automation-related fears can lead to more thoughtful implementations of technology. By encouraging employee input and acknowledging concerns about job security, businesses can not only reduce resistance but also cultivate an environment where innovation thrives.

Additionally, proactive engagement is essential for bridging the gap between traditional roles and emerging opportunities shaped by AI advancements. Educational institutions play a crucial role in this process; they must adapt curricula to prepare students for future jobs while also offering mentoring programs to support those currently in the workforce facing displacement due to automation.

On a broader scale, policy interventions are equally important in steering the narrative from fear toward empowerment regarding AI's impact on employment landscapes. Governments can enact policies that promote lifelong learning initiatives and support programs tailored for individuals whose jobs are at risk due to technological disruptions.

whether one views AI as a tool or a threat largely depends on perspective—and proactive engagement with its implications can significantly reshape outcomes. By embracing AI's potential while acknowledging its challenges, individuals can position themselves not merely as passive observers but as active participants in crafting an inclusive future defined by collaboration between human ingenuity and technological advancement. The focus must remain on leveraging this powerful tool for societal betterment while building resilience against any threats it may present along the way.

Predictions for the Future Workforce

The future workforce is poised for significant transformation as artificial intelligence (AI) advances rapidly. This evolution will likely revolve around the emergence of new job types, the demand for specific skills, and changes in work structures. To successfully navigate this evolving job landscape, it is essential to understand these key elements.

One major prediction is the rise of hybrid job roles that combine traditional responsibilities with advanced technological skills. For example, data analysts are becoming increasingly vital as organizations recognize the importance of interpreting vast datasets. These professionals require not only analytical skills but also a solid understanding of AI tools that aid in data manipulation. That's why, educational programs will need to incorporate AI-related content into their curriculums. Students and professionals must be ready to engage with learning platforms offering courses in data science, machine learning, and related fields to remain competitive.

As new roles emerge, the need for continuous reskilling becomes paramount. Many experts assert that lifelong learning will be essential in the workforce of tomorrow. In customer service, for instance, chatbots and AI-driven systems are taking over routine inquiries, allowing human agents to focus on more complex issues that require empathy and nuanced communication. To adapt, employees must develop soft skills such as emotional intelligence, critical thinking, and effective problem-solving strategies. Organizations that promote a culture of continuous learning— through workshops or online courses—will not only enhance their workforce's capabilities but also improve morale and retention rates.

How X works work is also expected to shift dramatically towards greater flexibility. The pandemic has accelerated trends toward remote work, leading many companies to adopt hybrid models where employees split their time between home and office environments. Studies indicate that flexibility can increase productivity and job satisfaction, indicating a lasting change in how businesses operate. Companies like Slack and Zoom have reported heightened usage among teams utilizing these tools for seamless collaboration across distances. Embracing technology will thus be crucial for facilitating this new way of working.

While many anticipate positive outcomes from these changes, potential challenges loom large. As automation becomes more prevalent, concerns about job displacement—especially in sectors reliant on routine tasks—are growing. If left unaddressed, these fears can stifle innovation. A collaborative effort between industry leaders and policymakers can help create pathways for displaced workers through retraining initiatives and economic support systems.

Equity is another critical consideration as we look toward the future workforce. Predictions highlight the risk of widening disparities if access to AI education and training isn't equalized. Individuals from marginalized communities may struggle to acquire the necessary skills for emerging job markets unless targeted efforts are made to bridge these gaps. Initiatives providing scholarships for tech boot camps or community-based training programs could empower underrepresented groups to seize opportunities presented by AI advancements.

As organizations prepare for an AI-driven future, they must cultivate an inclusive environment that values diversity in thought and background. Companies like Salesforce have begun implementing diversity training alongside their AI initiatives, recognizing that diverse teams foster better decision-making and innovation. By nurturing an inclusive workplace culture, organizations can attract a broader talent pool while enhancing creativity in problem-solving.

And, organizations should leverage data analytics not just for operational efficiency but also for gaining insights into employee needs. Tools measuring employee engagement and satisfaction can help identify areas for improvement before they escalate into larger issues like turnover or dissatisfaction.

The work landscape will undoubtedly evolve as AI continues to influence various sectors; however, this transformation offers opportunities alongside challenges. By anticipating changes and strategically adapting—whether through skill development, embracing flexibility, or prioritizing equity— individuals and organizations can effectively navigate this new terrain.

In summary, predictions about the future workforce reveal a complex interplay between technological advancement and human capability enhancement. As we stand on the brink of this evolution, proactive engagement with emerging trends will shape individual careers and organizational success in an increasingly interconnected world defined by AI integration. Embracing these shifts enables us not only to survive but to thrive in an exciting new era of work.

CHAPTER 2: SKILLS FOR THE NEW ECONOMY

Identifying Essential Skills

I dentifying essential skills in the evolving landscape of the AI job economy is vital for professionals who wish to stay relevant and competitive. As the nature of work transforms, understanding which skills to prioritize can significantly impact career progression and personal satisfaction.

Technical skills are at the forefront of this shift. The demand for proficiency in AI tools and technologies is skyrocketing, making familiarity with programming languages such as Python and R a considerable asset. Python, in particular, is renowned for its simplicity and versatility, widely used in data analysis and machine learning. Professionals who can write scripts to automate data collection or manipulate datasets will find themselves ahead of the curve. A practical approach to mastering these languages includes enrolling in coding boot camps or leveraging online platforms like Codecademy or Coursera, which offer interactive courses tailored to various skill levels.

Equally crucial are analytical skills. The ability to interpret data, draw meaningful conclusions, and make informed decisions based on evidence distinguishes professionals in today's job market. Companies increasingly rely on data-driven strategies, highlighting the importance of effectively analyzing trends. For example, a marketing analyst skilled in using statistical software like Tableau to visualize consumer behavior can significantly influence a company's strategic direction. Participating in analytics workshops or certification programs can further enhance these capabilities.

While technical and analytical skills are essential, the importance of soft skills cannot be overlooked. Emotional intelligence (EI) emerges as a key attribute in an AI-driven world. Understanding emotions—both one's own and those of others—and responding appropriately is crucial in collaborative environments where machines handle routine tasks. Employees who excel in EI can navigate complex interpersonal dynamics, guiding teams through transitions with empathy and insight. To build these competencies, individuals might seek mentorship, engage in group projects requiring collaboration, or attend workshops focused on communication and conflict resolution.

And, creativity is an often-overlooked skill that becomes increasingly vital as automation takes over repetitive tasks. With machines managing mundane activities, human creativity will be the driving force behind innovation within organizations. In industries like advertising, professionals who can craft compelling narratives that resonate emotionally with audiences will always be in demand. Techniques such as brainstorming sessions or design thinking exercises can help cultivate this creative mindset.

In addition to these specific skills, adaptability is paramount. The rapid pace of change requires professionals to remain open-minded and committed to continuous learning. This adaptability extends beyond mastering new tools; it involves embracing change itself and rethinking one's approach to challenges. Those who thrive during organizational shifts—whether adopting new technologies or adapting to hybrid work environments—often view change as an opportunity rather than a threat.

Networking plays a pivotal role in identifying essential skills within your industry or field of interest. Connecting with peers through platforms like LinkedIn or attending industry conferences provides valuable insights into emerging trends and required competencies. Engaging with thought leaders can reveal which skills are gaining traction and which may soon become obsolete.

Finally, cultivating a growth mindset is crucial. This philosophy emphasizes viewing challenges as opportunities for growth rather than insurmountable obstacles. Individuals who embrace this mindset actively seek out new learning experiences and demonstrate greater resilience in the face of setbacks.

By focusing on these key areas—technical abilities, analytical prowess, soft skills like emotional intelligence and creativity, adaptability, networking opportunities, and fostering a growth mindset—professionals can position themselves favorably in an ever-changing job market shaped by AI advancements.

While the path ahead may seem uncertain, those who invest actively in their skill development will not only survive but thrive amid these changes. Embracing continuous learning will be essential for success as we navigate this evolving economic landscape together.

Soft Skills vs. Hard Skills

In today's job market, understanding the interplay between soft skills and hard skills is essential, particularly as AI fundamentally reshapes our work landscape. While technical expertise serves as the foundation for many roles, it is increasingly the soft skills that set candidates apart and drive success.

Hard skills are specific, teachable abilities that can be quantified and measured. Examples include programming languages like Python, proficiency in data analysis tools such as Excel or Tableau, and a solid grasp of machine learning algorithms. These skills are typically gained through formal education or specialized training programs. Take this example, a data scientist needs to master statistical methods and coding techniques to effectively analyze large datasets. Professionals can enhance these technical capabilities by enrolling in relevant courses or workshops.

In contrast, soft skills involve interpersonal attributes that affect how individuals interact and collaborate with others. Key examples include communication, emotional intelligence, teamwork, and problem-solving abilities. Unlike hard skills, which can often be assessed through tests or certifications, soft skills are more nuanced and usually develop over time through experience. For example, while a project manager might excel in organization, they may struggle to motivate their team without strong interpersonal skills.

The relationship between hard and soft skills is not merely additive; these two skill sets complement each other in significant ways. A programmer may excel at coding but find it challenging to convey complex findings to a non-technical audience. On the other hand, a marketing professional with outstanding interpersonal skills might lack the analytical capability needed to make data-driven strategic decisions. The integration of both hard and soft skills creates well-rounded professionals who can navigate complex workplace dynamics effectively.

Real-world scenarios highlight this synergy vividly. Take a

tech startup where collaboration is crucial for innovation: developers must not only write code but also work closely with designers and marketers to ensure the final product aligns with user expectations. Here, emotional intelligence becomes invaluable; it enables team members to appreciate each other's perspectives and fosters constructive feedback loops. Engaging in team-building exercises or actively seeking feedback from peers can strengthen these vital interpersonal connections.

Creativity also emerges as an essential soft skill in an era increasingly influenced by automation. In fields like design and marketing, the ability to generate innovative ideas often distinguishes successful individuals from their peers. Take this example, an advertising executive must blend creative storytelling with analytical insights from consumer data to craft campaigns that resonate emotionally while meeting business objectives. Workshops focused on creative thinking or cross-disciplinary collaboration can help enhance these abilities.

Adaptability stands at the crossroads of hard and soft skills—especially crucial when navigating technological advancements or organizational changes. Professionals who exhibit both technical proficiency with new tools and the flexibility to adjust their approaches are well-positioned for growth. For example, during recent shifts towards remote work due to global events, those who quickly adapted by mastering collaboration tools like Zoom or Slack flourished compared to those who resisted change.

Incorporating networking strategies can further enhance understanding of essential skill sets within specific industries or roles. Connecting with industry professionals through events or platforms like LinkedIn provides valuable insights into which skills employers prioritize and where there may be opportunities for development. This exchange of knowledge is vital for recognizing trends that influence both hard and soft skill requirements.

Finally, cultivating a growth mindset empowers professionals to continuously evolve their skill sets—both technical and interpersonal—in response to changing demands. This mindset encourages individuals to embrace new challenges rather than shy away from them due to fear of failure. Those who adopt this philosophy often achieve better outcomes in personal development and career advancement.

As professionals evaluate their competencies through the lens of both hard and soft skills, they strategically position themselves for success in an AI-driven job market. Emphasizing both realms not only enhances individual capabilities but also promotes collaborative environments where innovation can thrive amid technological change. Balancing these competencies will be vital as we navigate an exciting future defined by continuous learning and adaptation.

The Value of Emotional Intelligence

Emotional intelligence (EI) has become a vital component of success in today's workplace, particularly as artificial intelligence transforms roles and responsibilities. More than just a soft skill, EI is a powerful competency that enhances interpersonal relationships, drives teamwork, and builds resilience amid change. In an era where technical skills alone may no longer suffice, understanding and cultivating emotional intelligence can significantly influence one's career trajectory.

At its essence, emotional intelligence involves recognizing, understanding, and managing our own emotions while also empathizing with others. This dual focus on self-awareness and social awareness equips individuals to navigate complex workplace dynamics more effectively. Take this example, consider a project manager who can sense team members' frustrations before they escalate into conflict.

By addressing concerns proactively, this leader fosters an environment where collaboration thrives rather than falters. Such an approach not only boosts morale but also enhances productivity by ensuring that every team member feels heard and valued.

The relationship between emotional intelligence and communication is particularly crucial in today's fast-paced work environments. Effective communication hinges on an understanding of emotions—both one's own and those of colleagues. Take the example of a sales professional receiving critical feedback from their supervisor. A person with high EI processes this information constructively rather than defensively; they might seek clarification, demonstrate understanding, and ultimately leverage the feedback to refine their approach. This adaptable mindset strengthens relationships with peers and superiors alike, paving the way for personal growth and career advancement.

Real-world examples illustrate the tangible benefits of emotional intelligence across various industries. In healthcare, providers with high EI often build stronger rapport with patients, leading to improved health outcomes and greater patient satisfaction. A nurse who empathizes with patients during difficult moments not only provides comfort but also encourages adherence to treatment plans. Similarly, in technology sectors, teams characterized by high emotional intelligence frequently display enhanced creativity and innovation driven by their collaborative spirit.

For professionals looking to enhance their emotional intelligence, practical steps abound. Self-reflection serves as a powerful starting point; keeping a journal to document daily interactions can help individuals identify emotional triggers and recognize patterns in their responses. Seeking feedback from trusted colleagues offers valuable insights into how one's emotions impact teamwork dynamics. Additionally, workshops focused on EI training are increasingly available across industries; participating in these programs can equip individuals with tools for managing stress, improving communication skills, and fostering empathy.

Creating an emotionally intelligent workplace culture requires commitment from both leadership and individual employees. Leaders who model vulnerability by acknowledging their own emotional struggles foster a safe space for others to do the same. This openness cultivates an atmosphere of trust where team members feel comfortable expressing concerns or asking for help without fear of judgment.

As we navigate the evolving landscape shaped by AI advancements, the significance of emotional intelligence becomes even clearer. While AI excels at optimizing processes and analyzing data rapidly, it lacks the innate human capacity for empathy—an essential quality for understanding customer needs or addressing employee concerns effectively. Organizations that prioritize EI alongside technical expertise will be better equipped to adapt to the changes ushered in by technology.

In summary, fostering emotional intelligence is not merely beneficial but essential in today's job economy, where human connection holds increasing importance amid rising automation. Those who invest time in developing this skill set are likely to gain a competitive edge—whether through improved workplace relationships or enhanced leadership capabilities—ultimately contributing to both personal fulfillment and organizational success. Although mastering emotional intelligence may take time, the profound rewards extend beyond the individual level; they enrich entire teams and organizations striving for excellence in a world that increasingly values both technology and humanity alike.

Upskilling and Reskilling

Upskilling and reskilling have evolved from mere buzzwords to essential strategies for survival in today's fast-changing job market, largely influenced by artificial intelligence. As technology advances at an unprecedented pace, the workforce must adapt and refine their skill sets to remain relevant. For professionals eager to succeed in an AI-driven economy, grasping the nuances of these concepts is crucial.

Upskilling involves enhancing existing skills to improve proficiency in current roles or industries. This process deepens expertise and can significantly impact performance. Take this example, a marketing professional might pursue training in advanced analytics tools, allowing them to interpret data more effectively and make informed, data-driven decisions that enhance campaign outcomes. By elevating individual capabilities, upskilling also contributes to broader organizational objectives, fostering a skilled and adaptable workforce.

In contrast, reskilling focuses on acquiring new skills to transition into entirely different roles or industries. As automation threatens traditional jobs, such as those in manufacturing, workers may need to pivot toward tech-oriented positions. For example, a factory worker who enrolls in coding courses for Python or JavaScript can open new doors in software development, positioning themselves as vital contributors in an increasingly digital landscape.

The urgency of upskilling and reskilling cannot be overstated. Industries are constantly evolving, and skills that were once highly sought after may quickly become obsolete, while new competencies arise. The World Economic Forum predicts that by 2025, 85 million jobs could be displaced due to shifts between humans and machines, but 97 million new roles may emerge better suited to this new division of labor. These figures underscore the necessity of continuous education; relying on outdated skills can lead to career stagnation.

For those looking to embark on their upskilling or reskilling journey, several actionable steps can facilitate this process.

Online learning platforms like Coursera, Udemy, and LinkedIn Learning offer a wealth of courses tailored to various professions. For example, a financial analyst might take courses in machine learning applications relevant to finance, positioning themselves as an expert capable of leveraging AI for predictive analytics.

Establishing clear career goals is equally important. By identifying specific areas for development, professionals can select the most appropriate courses or training programs. Creating a personalized learning plan—detailing target skills, timelines for acquisition, and available resources—can provide structure and motivation throughout the learning journey.

Networking also plays a crucial role in effective upskilling and reskilling efforts. Engaging with industry peers on platforms like LinkedIn or attending workshops can offer valuable insights into emerging trends and necessary skill sets within specific fields. Connecting with mentors who have successfully navigated similar transitions can provide guidance and encouragement during this process.

Organizations also share the responsibility of fostering a culture of continuous learning. By implementing robust training programs, companies demonstrate their commitment not only to employee development but also to long-term organizational success. For example, Amazon has invested heavily in upskilling initiatives for its employees, providing access to educational resources and partnering with universities to ensure its workforce remains competitive as job functions evolve.

The benefits of effective upskilling and reskilling extend beyond individual professionals; they also enhance organizational agility by creating teams capable of adapting swiftly to changes in technology and market demands. Companies that invest in their employees' growth are likely to experience higher engagement and retention rates while maintaining a competitive edge over rivals that may overlook skill development.

As artificial intelligence continues to reshape industries from healthcare to finance, both individuals and organizations must wholeheartedly embrace the necessity of upskilling and reskilling. The journey ahead may present challenges but is rich with opportunities for those prepared to adapt proactively rather than reactively. In this transformative landscape, investing time in personal development is not merely optional; it is essential for ensuring that talent remains relevant amid rapid technological advancements.

Lifelong Learning Strategies

In today's world, increasingly shaped by artificial intelligence, the importance of lifelong learning has become a fundamental pillar for success. This is not merely a passing trend; it is essential for navigating a constantly evolving job market. Professionals are called to adopt a mindset centered on continuous improvement and adaptability, seamlessly integrating learning into their daily routines.

Lifelong learning extends far beyond traditional education. It embodies a proactive approach to acquiring knowledge and skills throughout one's career. The conventional model of education—where learning is confined to the classroom—is rapidly becoming outdated. Instead, professionals are encouraged to explore various avenues for growth, such as online courses, workshops, podcasts, and industry events. Take this example, a seasoned project manager might enhance their expertise by enrolling in courses focused on agile methodologies or mastering digital tools like Trello and Asana. These initiatives not only sharpen their existing skills but also prepare them for future roles that demand advanced project management capabilities.

Incorporating learning into daily life can be quite

manageable. Setting aside specific time blocks each week for skill development promotes consistency and accountability. Whether it's dedicating an hour every Wednesday evening to delve into the latest AI advancements or committing to read one industry-related book each month, these small yet impactful actions can collectively lead to significant professional growth over time.

Collaboration also plays a vital role in fostering lifelong learning. Engaging with colleagues in knowledge-sharing sessions can create an environment where continuous education thrives. For example, initiating "lunch and learn" sessions allows team members to present on various topics —from new software tools to the latest developments in AI —cultivating a culture of curiosity and collective growth. When everyone contributes their insights, the organization transforms into a hub of innovation.

Additionally, mentorship enriches the lifelong learning experience by providing opportunities to learn from seasoned professionals who have successfully navigated career challenges. Gaining insights from a mentor can offer valuable guidance tailored to individual aspirations and help reshape perspectives on change and growth.

As we reflect on technological advancements, it becomes clear that adaptability is crucial. Industries are no longer static; they evolve rapidly due to innovations fueled by AI and automation. Take this example, healthcare professionals must consistently update their knowledge regarding telemedicine technologies as they redefine patient care delivery methods. A nurse might pursue certifications in remote monitoring systems or data analysis to better support patients while collaborating effectively with IT teams.

A robust lifelong learning strategy also involves leveraging technology as an educational tool. Many platforms offer personalized learning experiences powered by AI algorithms that adapt content based on individual progress and preferences. For example, tools like Duolingo provide tailored language lessons that evolve with users' skills, while platforms such as Codecademy offer interactive coding exercises suitable for learners at any level.

While pursuing educational opportunities is essential for personal growth, organizations play a critical role in nurturing an environment conducive to lifelong learning. Companies should prioritize creating educational pathways that align employee interests with business needs—this could involve offering tuition reimbursement programs or internal training initiatives focused on emerging technologies relevant to organizational goals.

Investing in employee development brings tangible benefits: organizations that prioritize continuous learning experience improved employee satisfaction and retention rates alongside heightened productivity levels. A well-trained workforce is better equipped to respond dynamically to the changes driven by AI advancements, ensuring job security for employees while providing sustained competitive advantages for employers.

embracing lifelong learning strategies equips professionals with the resilience necessary to thrive amidst constant technological change. By fostering habits that prioritize ongoing skill acquisition—whether through formal coursework or informal peer interactions—individuals position themselves favorably within an ever-evolving job market.

In this transformative era driven by artificial intelligence, commitment to personal growth transcends traditional boundaries; it embodies an agile mindset ready to seize opportunities while navigating potential challenges—a crucial foundation for success in any professional journey today.

Critical Thinking and Problem Solving

The ability to think critically and solve problems effectively is a cornerstone of success in the modern workforce, particularly as AI technologies become increasingly prevalent. Navigating the complexities of today's job market requires not only knowledge but also a flexible and analytical mindset. Critical thinking enables individuals to assess situations, make informed decisions, and devise innovative solutions—skills that are essential in the face of the rapid changes introduced by AI.

Take, for example, a marketing professional facing declining engagement metrics. Rather than simply reacting by launching another ad campaign, a critical thinker will analyze the data from multiple perspectives. They might examine user demographics, evaluate the effectiveness of current strategies, or investigate competitor actions. By synthesizing this information, they can develop a strategic plan that goes beyond superficial fixes—perhaps by shifting focus toward content personalization or exploring entirely new platforms.

In an AI-influenced environment, problem-solving often demands creative approaches. Traditional methods may not suffice when confronted with unique technological challenges. Take this example, a logistics manager might identify inefficiencies stemming from outdated software systems. While a conventional response could involve merely replacing these systems, a true problem solver would step back to consider how AI integration might streamline processes —potentially using machine learning algorithms to predict demand fluctuations or optimize routing based on real-time traffic data.

To cultivate critical thinking and problem-solving skills, professionals should engage in exercises that stimulate analytical thought. One effective technique is the "Five Whys," which encourages individuals to dig deeper into the root causes of an issue by repeatedly asking "why" until they uncover underlying factors. For example, if production is delayed, exploring the reasons can lead to an examination of supplier performance and reveal further inefficiencies or communication barriers.

Collaboration with diverse teams also significantly enhances problem-solving capabilities. Different perspectives can lead to creative solutions that one individual alone might overlook. Imagine a tech company brainstorming ideas for a new app feature; input from engineers, designers, marketers, and end-users fosters innovation while ensuring comprehensive consideration of potential pitfalls and advantages.

Learning from past experiences enriches critical thinking abilities as well. Analyzing case studies—both successful strategies and failures—provides valuable insights into what works in practice. Consider how companies like Nokia once dominated the mobile market but struggled to adapt quickly enough to smartphone trends; this serves as a vital lesson in flexibility and foresight.

Integrating AI tools can further enhance critical thinking by providing data-driven insights that inform decision-making processes. Platforms that analyze large datasets allow professionals to focus on interpreting results rather than becoming bogged down in raw numbers. For example, business intelligence software can quickly visualize industry trends, enabling users to navigate complexities with greater confidence by leveraging these tools alongside their reasoning skills.

Educators and employers play crucial roles in fostering critical thinking within their environments. Programs designed around real-world challenges encourage students and employees alike to engage in thoughtful analysis while applying knowledge practically. Simulations or role-playing exercises help participants experience scenarios requiring decisive action, reinforcing theoretical concepts through hands-on engagement.

Additionally, cultivating an inquisitive mindset enhances overall problem-solving capabilities. Encouraging oneself—and others—to ask questions can spark deeper discussions that unveil unforeseen opportunities for growth or improvement. An environment that celebrates curiosity fosters innovation, allowing teams to collectively explore potential avenues for development.

As we integrate these practices into our daily routines—whether through formal training programs or informal team dialogues—the potential for enhancing critical thinking grows exponentially. Embracing diverse viewpoints combined with disciplined analytical techniques creates an atmosphere ripe for creativity and effective problem resolution.

honing these skills positions professionals as adaptable workers and strategic leaders within their organizations—individuals capable of steering teams through uncharted waters shaped by technological advancement and evolving job demands. The journey toward excellence in critical thinking and problem-solving is ongoing but undeniably essential for thriving amid the constant transformation of today's job economy influenced by artificial intelligence.

Digital Literacy and Technological Competence

In today's job market, digital literacy and technological competence have become essential rather than optional. As industries transform under the influence of artificial intelligence, professionals face the challenge of navigating a complex landscape of tools and technologies to stay relevant and effective. Mastering these resources not only enhances individual capabilities but also drives organizational success.

Take the role of a data analyst in a company shifting towards AI-driven decision-making. A skilled data analyst does more than just gather data; they actively work with advanced analytics software and machine learning models, interpreting intricate datasets to turn raw information into actionable insights. Take this example, by leveraging Python libraries like Pandas and NumPy, an analyst can efficiently manipulate large datasets to uncover trends or anomalies. Consider this simple code snippet:

```python
import pandas as pd

\#\# Load data
data = pd.read_csv('sales_data.csv')

\#\# Calculate average sales by region
average_sales = data.groupby('Region')['Sales'].mean()

print(average_sales)
```

This example illustrates how technology can simplify the analysis process, allowing professionals to focus on deriving meaningful conclusions instead of getting bogged down in data entry.

Developing digital literacy also means becoming familiar with various collaboration and productivity tools. Platforms like Slack, Trello, and Asana enhance project management and communication across teams, especially when members are located in different places. When professionals make it a habit to explore new features or attend workshops on best practices, using these tools becomes second nature, facilitating smoother project progression.

Technological competence also involves the ability to quickly adapt to new systems. For example, when a company introduces a customer relationship management (CRM) system such as Salesforce, employees need to efficiently learn its functionalities. A proactive approach might include utilizing available training resources—like online tutorials or internal sessions—to ensure everyone is up to speed. Hands-on workshops that simulate real-world scenarios within the system can deepen understanding and retention.

In this digital era, understanding cybersecurity is crucial. Professionals must be aware of potential threats and familiarize themselves with basic security protocols to protect sensitive information. Knowledge about phishing scams, secure password practices, and data encryption methods is essential. Companies can support their employees by implementing regular cybersecurity training sessions that keep staff informed about evolving threats while promoting best practices for safeguarding digital assets.

Fostering a culture of continuous learning further reinforces digital literacy within organizations. Encouraging employees to pursue certifications—such as Google Analytics or Microsoft Azure—not only provides them with credentials but also boosts their confidence in their skills. These achievements empower individuals while simultaneously equipping organizations with a more knowledgeable workforce capable of leveraging technology effectively.

Engagement in online communities can also enhance technological competence. Platforms like GitHub for developers or LinkedIn groups for marketing professionals offer valuable resources for learning from peers and sharing experiences. Participating in discussions about industry trends or seeking advice on challenges broadens perspectives and enhances skills through collaboration.

The practical applications of digital literacy extend beyond individual roles; they significantly impact team effectiveness. In software development, for example, adopting Agile methodologies supported by tools like Jira or Git fosters better communication and adaptability within teams, enabling quicker iterations based on feedback and changing requirements.

Navigating the ever-evolving technological landscape requires dedication but offers rich rewards for those willing to invest time in skill development. By integrating digital literacy into daily routines—whether through formal training programs or self-directed exploration—professionals learn to utilize technology as an asset rather than an obstacle.

digital literacy bridges traditional skill sets with modern workplace demands. As AI continues to shape job roles across sectors, the ability to navigate technology confidently will set successful professionals apart from their peers. Embracing this journey is not just about survival; it's about thriving amid rapid change—a commitment that yields significant benefits for personal growth and career advancement alike.

Cross-disciplinary Skills

In today's rapidly evolving work environment, heavily influenced by artificial intelligence, cross-disciplinary skills have emerged as a vital asset. Professionals who can blend knowledge and methods from various fields tend to be more adaptable, innovative, and effective. This ability to connect ideas across disciplines allows individuals to tackle problems from broader perspectives, often leading to solutions that might remain hidden when viewed through a single lens.

For example, consider a marketing specialist working alongside data scientists. The marketer's insights into consumer behavior, when combined with the data scientist's analytical expertise, can produce outstanding results. By employing statistical models and machine learning techniques, they can uncover patterns in customer engagement that inform targeted marketing strategies. A practical illustration of this collaboration could involve analyzing website traffic data to evaluate the effectiveness of different campaigns. The marketer might utilize Google Analytics in tandem with R or Python to conduct regression analysis, ultimately optimizing their marketing efforts. Here's a brief demonstration using Python:

```python
import pandas as pd
import statsmodels.api as sm

\#\# Load marketing campaign data
data = pd.read_csv('campaign_data.csv')

\#\# Define independent and dependent variables
X = data[['Budget', 'Duration']]
y = data['Conversions']

\#\# Add constant for intercept
X = sm.add_constant(X)

\#\# Fit regression model
model = sm.OLS(y, X).fit()
print(model.summary())
```

This code snippet illustrates how the fusion of marketing insight and statistical analysis not only deepens the understanding of conversion rates but also guides future campaign investments based on predictive outcomes.

Cross-disciplinary skills also encompass essential soft

skills such as communication, leadership, and emotional intelligence. These competencies are crucial for effective collaboration among teams from diverse sectors. Take this example, a project manager with knowledge of both software development and user experience design can facilitate productive discussions between engineers and designers. Their expertise fosters better collaboration and innovation within the team while ensuring that product development aligns closely with user needs.

To cultivate these cross-disciplinary skills, professionals can engage in interdisciplinary projects or initiatives within their organizations. By volunteering for cross-functional teams or taking on roles that require a diverse knowledge base, they can broaden their perspectives while contributing to organizational goals. This proactive approach encourages an environment where different viewpoints converge, often resulting in creative problem-solving.

And, academic institutions are increasingly acknowledging the importance of cross-disciplinary training by offering programs that integrate fields such as business and technology or arts and sciences. For example, an MBA program that incorporates data analytics equips students to address real-world challenges by merging strategic thinking with technical skills.

Networking is another crucial element in developing cross-disciplinary expertise. Interacting with professionals from various fields at conferences or workshops fosters relationships that promote knowledge sharing. Take this example, a health tech conference might attract healthcare practitioners alongside IT specialists focused on AI applications in medicine. Conversations at such events can inspire innovative ideas that neither party may have considered independently.

The impact of cross-disciplinary skills on innovation is

significant across industries. In the automotive sector, for instance, collaboration between engineers knowledgeable about AI algorithms and designers focused on user experience has led to the development of smarter vehicles equipped with adaptive technologies—enhancing safety features while providing intuitive interfaces for drivers.

cultivating cross-disciplinary skills reshapes how individuals approach their careers in the face of technological change. Instead of confining themselves to traditional roles defined by singular expertise, professionals equipped with diverse knowledge are better positioned to navigate complexities and adapt swiftly to market demands while fostering innovation.

As AI continues to transform work environments globally, the ability to draw upon varied disciplines will become increasingly essential for success. Those who embrace this multifaceted approach will not only survive but thrive— leveraging their unique blend of expertise to drive personal growth and professional advancement alike.

The Importance of Creativity

Creativity is a cornerstone of innovation in today's AI- driven job economy. It goes beyond technical skills, enabling professionals to envision possibilities that break free from conventional limits. As artificial intelligence automates routine tasks, the human ability for original thought becomes increasingly valuable. Creativity inspires new ideas, fuels problem-solving, and enhances adaptability in the face of rapid technological change.

Consider the field of product development. An engineer may excel at coding algorithms or designing systems, but without a spark of creativity, these technical skills can lead to ordinary or inefficient solutions. When teams prioritize creativity in their approach to challenges, they can envision applications that utilize AI in transformative ways. For example, imagine a software developer collaborating with an artist to create an interactive application that adjusts its user interface based on emotional feedback. This synergy between engineering and creative vision not only enriches user experience but also establishes a new standard for engagement in digital products.

In the advertising industry, creativity similarly plays a pivotal role. Creative teams leverage AI tools to analyze consumer sentiment and behavior while weaving imaginative storytelling into their campaigns. Take this example, an advertising agency might use machine learning algorithms to identify trending themes and then combine these insights with creative brainstorming sessions. This collaboration can lead to campaigns that resonate profoundly with target audiences, illustrating how the interplay between creativity and data can enhance campaign performance—an essential factor in today's competitive landscape.

And, fostering creativity requires individuals to step outside their comfort zones. Participating in workshops or hackathons that encourage diverse ideation creates an environment where innovative thinking can thrive. A tech company, for example, might host regular innovation sprints where employees from various departments collaborate on projects free from the constraints of their usual roles. Such initiatives not only inspire fresh ideas but also dismantle silos that can stifle creativity.

To cultivate an organizational culture that values creativity, leadership must demonstrate commitment. Encouraging experimentation and accepting failure as part of the learning process empowers employees to explore uncharted territories without fear of repercussions. Companies like Google exemplify this philosophy through their "20% time" policy, which allows employees to dedicate part of their workweek to projects they are passionate about—often resulting in groundbreaking innovations like Gmail.

The link between creativity and emotional intelligence is

crucial as well. Professionals who can connect with their emotions and empathize with others are often more adept at fostering collaborative environments where ideas flourish. Team leaders with strong emotional intelligence are likely to inspire and engage their members effectively, creating an atmosphere conducive to creative breakthroughs. Techniques such as active listening and open feedback loops ensure diverse perspectives are integrated into problem-solving processes.

Educational institutions also play a vital role in nurturing creativity by emphasizing interdisciplinary learning and experiential education. Programs that blend liberal arts with technical training—such as those found in design thinking curricula—equip students not only with knowledge but also with the ability to synthesize information creatively. This holistic approach cultivates graduates who are skilled at navigating complexities and innovating beyond traditional frameworks.

In industries like healthcare or renewable energy, creative thinking has driven transformative advancements. For example, healthcare professionals employing design thinking principles have developed innovative patient care solutions by focusing on empathetic understanding and user experience design. These initiatives highlight how creative insight can lead to significant improvements in service delivery and operational efficiency.

As we navigate an evolving landscape shaped by AI, nurturing creativity becomes essential for both individual success and organizational growth. Professionals equipped with creative skills will not only adapt more readily but also contribute meaningfully to their fields' advancement. Embracing creativity is no longer optional; it is a vital strategy for thriving in an economy increasingly defined by technological evolution.

cultivating creativity reshapes our perception of our

roles within the workforce—transforming us from mere participants into pioneers who shape our futures through innovative thinking and imaginative solutions. Those who harness their creative potential will find themselves at the forefront of change, driving progress while inspiring others along the way.

Building a Personal Learning Network

Building a personal learning network is essential for navigating the complexities of the AI job economy. This network, composed of diverse professionals, mentors, and peers, serves as a dynamic resource for sharing knowledge and enhancing skills. Unlike traditional learning environments, which often deliver information in a one-way manner, personal learning networks thrive on collaboration and mutual growth.

To begin building your network, start by identifying key individuals within your field. Attending industry conferences or webinars where thought leaders share their insights can be incredibly beneficial. Engaging in conversations during these events can lead to valuable connections. Following up with personalized messages that reference specific topics discussed helps solidify these relationships and opens doors for future collaboration.

Participating in relevant online communities can further enrich your network. Platforms like Reddit and Discord host groups focused on various aspects of AI and technology. Actively engaging by asking questions or sharing experiences not only positions you as a contributing member but also exposes you to diverse perspectives that can broaden your understanding of the field. This exchange of ideas is crucial as technology evolves rapidly; staying informed through varied sources ensures you remain ahead of the curve.

Social media also plays a pivotal role in networking today. Platforms like Twitter are particularly effective for following industry trends and connecting with influencers shaping conversations around AI advancements. By curating your feed to include thought leaders and innovative companies, you create a continuous flow of information that keeps you updated on new developments and emerging best practices.

Another key component of your personal learning network is mentorship. Finding a mentor with experience navigating the AI landscape can provide invaluable guidance tailored to your career aspirations. This relationship offers not just technical expertise but also insights into the soft skills necessary for success in an increasingly automated world. To find a mentor, consider reaching out through professional associations or alumni networks, where shared experiences can facilitate meaningful connections.

As your network expands, it's important to give back by sharing your own knowledge and experiences. Teaching others solidifies your understanding while establishing you as a knowledgeable figure within your field. Hosting workshops or writing articles about your experiences can attract like-minded professionals eager to learn from you, while simultaneously enriching your own knowledge base through their inquiries.

Regular engagement with your network fosters ongoing development and ensures that you remain adaptable amid changes in technology and job roles. Consider scheduling monthly check-ins or discussions with different contacts— these touchpoints keep relationships warm and encourage collaborative exploration of new ideas.

To further enhance this process, utilizing digital tools designed for networking can streamline your connection-building efforts. Applications like MeetUp allow users to find local groups centered around specific interests, opening avenues for face-to-face interactions that deepen relationships beyond virtual settings.

building a personal learning network goes beyond merely expanding contacts; it's about cultivating relationships grounded in mutual growth and knowledge exchange. As industries evolve due to AI advancements, those equipped with robust networks will be better positioned to adapt and thrive amid these changes.

Fostering these connections transforms how we approach our careers, shifting from solitary endeavors to collaborative journeys where innovation flourishes through collective intelligence. By investing time in nurturing their networks, individuals not only benefit personally but also contribute significantly to advancing their fields, ensuring they remain integral players in the ever-evolving job economy driven by AI technologies.

CHAPTER 3: CAREER PIVOTING IN AN AI WORLD

Recognizing When to Pivot

Recognizing when to pivot in your career is essential in today's AI-driven job economy. The ability to assess your current trajectory, analyze external changes, and make informed decisions about new opportunities can distinguish between stagnation and growth. Many professionals find themselves at a crossroads as their roles evolve with technological advancements, and understanding these pivotal moments empowers proactive steps forward.

Take the case of a marketing professional who has relied on traditional methods for years. As AI tools increasingly dominate digital marketing strategies—automating tasks such as data analysis and customer segmentation—this professional must evaluate whether their skills still meet market demands. Acknowledging the need for new competencies, like familiarity with AI analytics platforms or content automation tools, can prompt a timely pivot. By staying attuned to industry trends, this marketer can identify opportunities for training or certification that enhance their value in a rapidly changing landscape.

Awareness of external signals is equally important. Economic shifts or company restructuring may signal changes in job security. When organizations begin investing in automation technologies, employees should consider how this might impact their roles. Staying informed through industry reports or news articles enables you to grasp broader market trends that could necessitate a shift in your career direction.

Self-assessment also plays a critical role in determining when it's time to pivot. Regularly evaluating your skills, interests, and values helps you gauge your satisfaction with your current position. If you find that your work no longer aligns with your passions or that you feel stagnant despite your efforts, it may be time to explore new avenues. Tools like SWOT analysis—assessing strengths, weaknesses, opportunities, and threats—can provide clarity on your current standing and future aspirations.

Engaging with mentors or industry peers can significantly enhance this process. Conversations about their experiences navigating change can offer valuable insights and illuminate potential paths forward. Mentorship provides accountability; discussing your goals with someone knowledgeable encourages thoughtful reflection on whether a pivot is necessary.

And, cultivating a growth mindset is essential for embracing change as it arises. This perspective allows you to view challenges as opportunities for learning rather than obstacles. Take this example, if an AI tool is introduced that replaces certain tasks within your role, instead of resisting the change, consider how you might adapt by learning the tool's new functionalities or proposing ways to integrate it into your workflow more effectively.

Networking within professional communities not only offers

insights into trends but also opens doors to alternative career paths. Regular interactions with peers facing similar challenges can lead to collaborations or job referrals that might not have been possible otherwise. Attending workshops or webinars on emerging technologies facilitates learning while simultaneously expanding your network.

recognizing when to pivot depends on being proactive rather than reactive. Monitoring industry shifts while continuously assessing personal goals creates a framework for timely transitions. Embracing change as an inherent aspect of your career journey fosters resilience against the uncertainties brought by technological advancements.

As we navigate the turbulent waters shaped by AI innovations, those equipped with the insight and readiness to pivot will emerge stronger and more adaptable in their careers. Embracing change becomes not just a survival tactic but a strategic advantage in the evolving job landscape.

Mapping Transferable Skills

Understanding transferable skills is essential for professionals navigating the evolving AI job economy. These versatile skills enable individuals to apply their expertise across various roles and industries, enhancing their marketability and empowering them to pivot effectively when necessary.

Take, for example, a project manager with years of experience in traditional sectors like construction or manufacturing. As businesses increasingly integrate AI tools into project management—such as predictive analytics and automated reporting—this manager may feel compelled to adapt. Rather than viewing AI as a threat, they can recognize that their transferable skills—leadership, organization, and communication—are vital for success in this new environment. By embracing the role of a facilitator who guides teams through technological transitions, this project manager can position themselves as an invaluable asset across any sector.

To begin identifying your own transferable skills, start with a thorough inventory of your professional experiences. Document key tasks and responsibilities from various roles. Take this example, if you've transitioned from customer service to sales, the ability to communicate effectively with clients remains a constant asset. The persuasive skills developed in sales can also prove beneficial when presenting ideas or proposals in different contexts.

Next, look for patterns among your tasks that highlight overarching competencies rather than specific job functions. Skills such as analytical thinking, problem-solving, and interpersonal communication are broad competencies applicable across industries. A software developer moving into product management might discover that their technical background provides the analytical skills necessary for market analysis or user experience design.

Real-world examples further illustrate this concept. Consider someone with a finance background exploring opportunities in data science. The analytical and quantitative skills honed in finance—such as statistical analysis and financial modeling—are highly relevant when analyzing data sets for insights in diverse fields like marketing or healthcare analytics. This cross-industry relevance emphasizes the importance of viewing your abilities through a broader lens.

Engaging with self-assessment tools can enhance your understanding of these transferable skills. Tools like the Holland Code or Myers-Briggs Type Indicator help clarify your strengths and preferences while providing insight into how these traits align with various career paths. Additionally, seeking feedback from colleagues or supervisors can reveal skills you may undervalue or overlook.

Networking is also crucial; discussions with peers from diverse backgrounds can open up pathways you hadn't considered before. Take this example, talking to someone who successfully transitioned from journalism to content strategy might inspire you to explore how your writing skills could translate into sectors like marketing or public relations.

Participating in skill-building workshops focused on transferable abilities serves as an excellent resource for practical development. Online platforms like Coursera or LinkedIn Learning offer courses aimed at enhancing various competencies—from leadership techniques to digital literacy —aligning growth opportunities with market demands.

Also, attending industry conferences not only exposes you to emerging trends but also facilitates interaction with professionals who have successfully navigated significant career shifts. Hearing their stories can provide inspiration and actionable insights into how they identified and leveraged their own transferable skills.

As you cultivate a comprehensive understanding of your skill set, keep in mind that adaptability is paramount in today's fast-changing job market characterized by rapid technological advancements. Approaching career shifts with a mindset that embraces lifelong learning ensures you're prepared to pivot when new opportunities arise.

mapping out your transferable skills empowers you with confidence during times of change, allowing you to creatively leverage past experiences across various roles and industries. Recognizing the inherent value within these competencies transforms uncertainty into opportunity—a critical mindset for anyone aspiring to thrive in an evolving workforce shaped by AI advancements.

Leveraging Existing Experience

Navigating the landscape of an AI-driven job economy requires more than just recognizing transferable skills; it also involves strategically leveraging your existing experiences to unlock your full career potential. This approach can be transformative, allowing you to present yourself as a versatile professional capable of thriving in various environments.

Take, for example, a seasoned marketing professional with years of experience in traditional media campaigns. As digital marketing and AI analytics redefine how businesses engage with customers, this individual encounters both challenges and opportunities. By acknowledging their strengths in consumer behavior, project management, and creative strategy, they can pivot into roles that emphasize data-driven decision-making. Combining their understanding of target audiences with AI tools for campaign optimization positions them as leaders at the intersection of creativity and technology.

To effectively leverage your own experiences, start by mapping out your career milestones. Create a list of significant projects or achievements from each role you've held. This exercise not only showcases your accomplishments but also reveals patterns that highlight your strengths. Take this example, if you have a background in human resources with successful employee engagement programs, those skills translate seamlessly into customer experience roles where an understanding of human behavior is vital.

Once you've mapped out your milestones, think about how to frame your experiences as compelling narratives. Emphasize adaptability and results in each past role. If you've led teams through significant changes—such as the adoption of new technologies—highlighting this ability will attract employers seeking candidates who can navigate uncertainty. Sharing specific anecdotes about overcoming obstacles or achieving successful outcomes will resonate during interviews.

Engaging in professional development is equally crucial. Enroll in courses that enhance your existing skills and bridge the gap between traditional methods and emerging technologies. For example, if you're transitioning from financial analysis to data science, taking classes in machine learning or predictive analytics not only bolsters your qualifications but also signals to potential employers that you are committed to evolving alongside industry trends.

Collaboration offers another powerful way to leverage your experience. Seek mentorship or partnerships in fields you want to explore further. If you're interested in the intersection of law and AI ethics but come from a technical background, connecting with legal professionals can provide valuable insights into how technological advancements impact regulatory frameworks. This cross-pollination enriches your understanding while expanding your network.

Networking should be approached proactively: attend events where thought leaders discuss trends relevant to both your current skill set and desired future roles. Engaging with these leaders provides knowledge and opens doors for potential collaborations or job opportunities that may not yet be publicly advertised.

Real-world application is essential as well; consider volunteering or taking on freelance projects that allow you to utilize your current skills in new contexts. For example, a project manager could offer services to startups looking to implement agile methodologies while integrating AI tools— broadening their portfolio while positioning themselves at the forefront of innovation across various sectors.

When it comes time to present this information on resumes or LinkedIn profiles, tailor each entry not just by job title but by illustrating how each role contributes to your overarching narrative of adaptability and expertise in leveraging technology for positive outcomes.

Lastly, maintaining an agile mindset regarding personal growth is vital when leveraging past experiences effectively. The workforce is increasingly shaped by rapid technological advancements; thus, embracing lifelong learning ensures you remain competitive while exploring beyond familiar domains.

Harnessing the power of existing experiences does more than build confidence—it illuminates pathways previously unseen within an ever-evolving job market influenced by AI innovations. With the right strategies in place, any professional can transform their journey into one marked by resilience and forward momentum amid change.

Embracing Flexibility

Flexibility has become a crucial necessity in today's job market, far beyond being just a buzzword. As the AI-driven economy evolves, professionals must cultivate adaptability not only in their skill sets but also in their mindsets. This embrace of flexibility enables individuals to navigate the increasingly complex and non-linear career paths that characterize modern employment.

Consider a software developer who has spent years specializing in traditional coding languages. With the growing demand for machine learning and artificial intelligence, the ability to pivot becomes essential. By dedicating time to learn new programming languages like Python or R—both highly regarded in data science—this developer can transform themselves into a valuable asset for organizations leveraging AI technologies. This proactive approach to learning can be the key difference between stagnation and thriving in a rapidly changing landscape.

Building on existing skills is vital for this transition. Reflecting on past experiences can unveil unexpected connections and opportunities. For example, a project manager with extensive experience guiding teams through project lifecycles may discover that their skills are transferable to managing AI-related initiatives, which require strong oversight and coordination among diverse teams. By contextualizing their past successes within agile methodologies or data-driven decision-making, they enhance their appeal to employers seeking leaders capable of steering tech-driven projects.

Taking action involves seeking opportunities to apply newfound knowledge and skills in practical settings. Internships, freelance gigs, or volunteering for projects related to AI implementation can provide invaluable hands-on experience that solidifies theoretical learning. A graphic designer interested in incorporating AI into their work might take on pro bono projects for nonprofits using design automation tools. This not only enriches their portfolio but also showcases their commitment to creatively integrating advanced technologies.

Networking is another critical component of embracing flexibility. Engaging with professionals across various industries can spark innovative ideas and collaborations. Attending workshops or seminars focused on emerging trends allows individuals to learn from those already thriving in the AI space while establishing valuable connections with peers who share similar aspirations. Building relationships with thought leaders offers insights into how flexible adaptation can lead to significant career advancement.

And, adopting an entrepreneurial mindset creates an environment where experimentation is encouraged. Professionals should feel empowered to test new concepts without the fear of failure—a fundamental driver of innovation across all fields. Take this example, an educator might explore integrating AI tools into lesson planning while sharing their findings with colleagues; this trial-and-error approach fosters adaptability and promotes continuous improvement.

It's also essential to consider self-care alongside professional development when discussing flexibility. Maintaining a balanced life helps manage stress during periods of change and uncertainty. Techniques such as mindfulness or regular physical activity bolster mental resilience, enabling individuals to tackle challenges with clarity and purpose.

Communicating one's flexible capabilities effectively is crucial during interviews and performance evaluations. Candidates should articulate how they have embraced change and adapted their strategies based on emerging needs or technological advancements—demonstrating not only a history of adaptability but also a willingness for continued growth.

embracing flexibility transforms professional journeys from rigid paths into dynamic explorations marked by resilience and innovation. Professionals equipped with this mindset not only enhance their own career prospects but also contribute positively to the organizations they serve, fostering environments where creativity thrives amid the rapid changes brought about by AI advancements.

As we explore further strategies for success within the AI job economy, remember that your ability to pivot effectively relies on your willingness to adapt, continuously learn, and seize opportunities as they arise. In this evolving landscape, flexibility is not merely beneficial; it is essential for survival and success.

The Role of Mentoring and Coaching

The role of mentoring and coaching in the AI job economy is crucial. As professionals navigate the evolving landscape of their careers, the support and guidance of experienced mentors can reveal opportunities that might otherwise go unnoticed. Mentors not only provide valuable insights but also act as catalysts for personal and professional growth, helping individuals recognize their strengths and areas for improvement while offering perspectives on industry trends and best practices.

Take this example, consider a mid-career marketing professional eager to explore AI-driven analytics. By engaging with a mentor who has successfully incorporated AI tools into marketing strategies, this individual can significantly shorten their learning curve. Regular discussions with the mentor can unveil practical experiences related to data analysis tools and algorithms, allowing for effective application of these technologies. This mentoring relationship creates an open environment where questions are encouraged, fostering a rich exchange of knowledge.

Complementing this mentorship is coaching, which focuses on skill enhancement and achieving specific goals. A coach can assist individuals in setting tailored objectives that align with the demands of the AI landscape—whether it's mastering machine learning techniques or understanding ethical implications in technology development. For example, an HR professional might collaborate with a coach to devise strategies for implementing AI-driven recruitment tools while addressing potential biases within algorithms. By breaking down complex objectives into manageable steps, coaching empowers individuals to make tangible progress toward their aspirations.

In addition to formal mentoring and coaching relationships, peer coaching offers valuable support within workplaces transitioning to AI integration. Colleagues can form small groups to share insights and tackle challenges related to new technologies. This collaborative approach not only fosters camaraderie but also enhances collective problem-solving. A project team facing difficulties in implementing an AI tool could benefit from regular brainstorming sessions that encourage diverse viewpoints, leading to innovative solutions that improve overall project outcomes.

Accountability plays a vital role in both mentoring and coaching relationships. Mentors should encourage their mentees to establish timelines and benchmarks for their learning or career progression. Take this example, a software engineer aiming to learn about neural networks might be encouraged to commit to completing specific online courses within set timeframes. Regular check-ins with a mentor help ensure steady progress while fostering a sense of responsibility for personal growth.

As industries adapt to the rise of AI technologies, it's essential for mentors to stay informed about current trends and innovations. This commitment to continuous learning ensures that they remain relevant and capable of providing informed guidance. The relationship becomes mutually beneficial; mentors gain fresh perspectives from their mentees' experiences while sharing their own knowledge gained over years in the field.

Consider a healthcare professional integrating AI into patient management systems. A mentor who has successfully navigated similar initiatives can offer invaluable insights on overcoming resistance from staff or patients. Drawing on firsthand experiences allows mentors to help mentees anticipate challenges and develop effective strategies for addressing them.

Another important aspect of mentoring is cultivating a growth mindset—the belief that skills and intelligence can be developed through effort and dedication over time. Encouraging this mindset helps individuals view challenges as opportunities for learning rather than setbacks. A mentee who learns to approach project failures as stepping stones—guided by their mentor's emphasis on resilience—can transform adversity into momentum for future success.

Incorporating diverse perspectives within mentoring relationships further enriches discussions. Mentors from varied backgrounds—whether related to gender, ethnicity, or professional experience—offer unique insights that challenge conventional thinking and stimulate creativity. Such diversity fosters innovation by inspiring mentees to consider alternative approaches when addressing complex problems arising from AI advancements.

As professionals continue adapting their careers in this dynamic environment, seeking mentorship or coaching should be seen not merely as an auxiliary resource but as essential components of success in the AI job economy. This commitment not only enhances individual capabilities but also strengthens organizations by cultivating talent equipped with cutting-edge skills and innovative mindsets.

nurturing these relationships empowers professionals to thrive amidst change, leveraging shared experiences and collective wisdom while forging pathways toward personal fulfillment and career advancement in an increasingly complex world driven by artificial intelligence.

Building a Multi-faceted Career

Navigating the complexities of today's job market demands a multi-faceted approach to career development, especially in an era increasingly influenced by artificial intelligence. Professionals are required to cultivate diverse skill sets that allow them to adapt to various roles and industries while drawing on their unique experiences. This adaptability not only enhances employability but also fosters resilience, empowering individuals to seize opportunities that emerge amidst rapid technological change.

Start by assessing your current skill set. Identify your core competencies and consider how they can be augmented with new skills relevant to emerging technologies. Take this example, a project manager skilled in resource allocation might gain a competitive edge by learning about data analytics tools that optimize team performance. Enrolling in online courses or workshops focused on AI applications in project management can broaden your knowledge and position you as a forward-thinking leader capable of steering projects toward innovative solutions.

Equally important is the value of cross-functional expertise. Professionals who have experience across different domains are often better equipped to identify synergies and integrate diverse perspectives into their work. A finance professional with insights into marketing, for example, can provide fresh perspectives when evaluating the financial impact of AI-driven marketing strategies. Embracing interdisciplinary learning fosters creativity and enables you to tackle problems from multiple angles—an essential trait in an AI-driven economy where traditional job boundaries are increasingly blurred.

Networking also plays a crucial role in building a well-rounded career. Engaging with professionals from various fields can uncover hidden opportunities and facilitate the sharing of knowledge. Attend industry conferences, participate in webinars, or join professional organizations focused on AI advancements that align with your interests. These interactions allow for the exchange of ideas with individuals from diverse backgrounds, inspiring new ways of approaching the challenges you face in your own career.

Mentorship further enriches your career development strategy. Establishing relationships with mentors who possess varied backgrounds provides valuable insights drawn from their experiences. A mentor in healthcare can guide you through ethical dilemmas related to AI, while a technology expert might share the latest developments shaping your industry. These relationships not only refine your skills but also build confidence as you navigate new challenges.

Personal branding is another vital component of this multi-faceted approach. Cultivating an online presence that showcases your diverse capabilities positions you as a thought leader in your field. Regularly sharing insights related to your areas of expertise—whether through blog posts, social media updates, or speaking engagements—enhances your visibility and establishes credibility within professional circles. By contributing valuable content, you invite discussions that deepen your knowledge while expanding your network.

A proactive attitude toward continuous learning is fundamental; it serves as the foundation for a resilient career. Make it a habit to stay informed about industry trends and technological advancements through podcasts, articles, or video tutorials related to your interests. Dedicate time each week to personal development—focusing on mastering software that leverages AI for improved productivity or exploring leadership techniques suited for managing diverse teams.

In this evolving landscape, resilience is more critical than ever; setbacks are integral to growth on a multi-faceted career path. Rather than viewing challenges as failures, reframe them as opportunities for learning and adaptation. For example, if an AI tool you implemented does not yield the expected results, take the time to analyze what went wrong and how similar issues might be avoided in future projects. Such reflective practices enhance problem-solving skills and build confidence in navigating complexities.

Creating a supportive community can further enhance your journey toward a diversified career path. Surround yourself with like-minded individuals who share similar goals yet possess different strengths; collaborating with such peers fosters mutual growth as everyone brings unique skills and perspectives to shared projects or discussions. Whether through informal study groups or structured mastermind sessions, these interactions enrich understanding and cultivate innovation.

Finally, embrace flexibility as a guiding principle in your career development efforts. The rapid pace of change demands adaptability; being open to pivoting roles or exploring new industries can lead to unexpected advantages while simultaneously expanding your network and skill set. For example, someone initially trained in graphic design might transition into user experience (UX) design roles due to their understanding of visual aesthetics—a shift supported by additional training focused on human-computer interaction principles.

In summary, building a multi-faceted career involves ongoing evolution informed by self-reflection and engagement across various disciplines, all aimed at enhancing personal effectiveness within dynamic work environments shaped by advancements in artificial intelligence. This comprehensive approach not only increases resilience but ultimately positions professionals at the forefront of innovation, enabling them to lead transformative initiatives across industries while adeptly navigating future challenges.

Evaluating New Opportunities

Identifying new opportunities in an AI-driven job economy requires a strategic approach that goes beyond traditional career paths. The key is to explore the intersection of your existing skills and the rapidly changing demands of various industries. As professionals face the accelerating pace of technological change, cultivating an agile mindset becomes essential. This mindset not only helps recognize emerging trends but also aligns personal aspirations with market realities.

Start by conducting a thorough market analysis, focusing on sectors where AI is making a significant impact. Industries such as healthcare, finance, and manufacturing are not merely adopting AI; they are undergoing profound transformations. Take this example, a healthcare professional might find opportunities in telemedicine or AI-assisted diagnostics, which require both clinical expertise and familiarity with data analytics tools. Staying updated on advancements through industry reports or specialized newsletters can help you identify areas that are ripe for exploration.

Networking is crucial for uncovering these hidden opportunities. Actively engage with professionals from diverse backgrounds on platforms like LinkedIn or in industry-specific forums. Informational interviews can provide valuable insights into the skills and qualifications currently in demand. For example, connecting with someone at the intersection of data science and marketing can reveal how companies leverage AI for customer segmentation and engagement strategies, highlighting potential roles you may not have previously considered.

Another effective strategy for evaluating new opportunities is skill-mapping. Begin by listing your current skills alongside emerging technologies that interest you. Consider how these technologies can enhance your strengths. A project manager, for example, might explore AI-driven project management tools that improve workflow efficiency or predictive analytics software that optimizes resource allocation decisions. Online platforms offering free trials or certifications can provide hands-on experience without significant financial commitment.

Adaptability is vital when considering new roles. This may involve pursuing additional training or obtaining certifications related to AI tools specific to your field. If you work in human resources, gaining proficiency in HR analytics software could open doors to roles focused on workforce optimization using AI insights. Free resources like Coursera or edX often host courses designed by top universities, keeping you informed of the latest developments.

Engaging in continuous learning fosters resilience against shifts in job requirements. Joining professional organizations or online communities centered around AI trends in your field can facilitate knowledge sharing with peers equally invested in adapting their careers. Collaborative discussions can inspire innovative ideas about leveraging technology creatively while reinforcing your understanding of its practical applications.

Evaluating opportunities also requires a readiness to take

calculated risks. The fear of venturing into unknown territories can inhibit growth, but reframing challenges as adventures empowers you to pursue uncharted paths confidently. Take this example, a software developer might explore entrepreneurial endeavors by creating niche applications tailored to specific audience needs identified through market research—transforming a passion project into a viable business opportunity.

Additionally, cultivating a growth-oriented mindset encourages openness to feedback and learning from experiences within new roles or projects. After embarking on an unfamiliar venture, reflecting on what worked well and what didn't creates valuable lessons that strengthen future decision-making processes. If an initiative doesn't yield the desired results—such as a marketing campaign driven by AI analytics—analyzing its performance can lead to deeper insights about target audiences and engagement strategies.

Support systems are also vital during these transitions; seek mentorship from individuals who have successfully navigated similar career pivots within tech-driven environments. Their guidance can illuminate best practices and inspire confidence during challenging transitions.

As you evaluate potential opportunities against personal interests and market needs, remember that passion plays an integral role in sustaining motivation throughout your career exploration journey. Balancing ambition with enjoyment enhances satisfaction as new pursuits unfold.

At its core, navigating the complexities of an AI-centric landscape requires an inquisitive approach supported by proactive networking, skill enhancement, and reflective practices that drive continuous improvement. By remaining adaptable and committed to lifelong learning, you position yourself not only as a participant in the evolving job market but also as an innovator ready to harness technology's transformative power for personal success while contributing meaningfully to broader economic progress.

Navigating Industry Changes

Adapting to changes in the industry requires a proactive mindset and a readiness to embrace uncertainty. As markets evolve due to advancements in technology, shifts in consumer behavior, and global economic pressures, professionals must cultivate agility. This agility goes beyond merely reacting to change; it involves anticipating future trends. Today, companies seek individuals who can navigate the complexities of an AI-driven landscape with foresight and strategic insight.

A deep understanding of your specific industry is crucial. Take the healthcare sector as an example. With the integration of AI, roles that once focused on manual data entry or basic administrative tasks are transforming into positions that demand data analysis and decision-making skills. Take this example, a medical administrative assistant may find their role evolving into that of a healthcare data analyst, highlighting the importance of upskilling. By identifying trends early—such as the growing reliance on telehealth solutions—professionals can pivot their careers toward these emerging opportunities.

Similarly, in manufacturing, the rise of AI and robotics is reshaping job descriptions. While automation has increased efficiency, it has also created a demand for skilled technicians capable of maintaining and troubleshooting advanced machinery. To remain relevant in this changing landscape, individuals should seek training programs that provide practical skills in robotics and automation technologies. For example, learning to program robotic process automation (RPA) tools can enhance an employee's value as companies increasingly automate routine tasks.

Networking is another critical component in navigating these changes effectively. Engaging with industry groups and attending conferences allows professionals to gain insights into future trends while connecting with like-minded individuals. Participating in webinars focused on AI's impact within your field can offer invaluable knowledge and introduce you to thought leaders who may provide guidance or mentorship.

A practical approach to navigating change includes developing a personal brand that showcases adaptability and expertise. Creating an online portfolio featuring relevant projects or certifications can attract potential employers or clients. Utilizing platforms like LinkedIn to share articles or insights related to your firsthand experiences with industry changes not only positions you as an authority but also helps expand your professional network organically.

Resilience is another essential trait for adapting to industry shifts. Embracing a growth mindset enables professionals to view challenges as opportunities for development rather than setbacks. Reflecting on past experiences where you successfully navigated change can bolster your confidence when facing new obstacles. For example, if you transitioned from a traditional marketing role to digital marketing amid technological advancements, sharing this journey with peers can inspire others while reinforcing your own adaptability.

It is equally important to continuously assess how external factors influence industry dynamics. Global events—such as economic downturns or pandemics—can dramatically shift priorities within sectors. Staying informed about news related to your industry helps guide decisions regarding career moves or skill development initiatives. Subscribing to industry newsletters or following influential analysts on social media provides ongoing insights that keep you well-informed.

successfully navigating industry changes requires a blend of continuous learning, strategic networking, and resilience. By understanding how technological advancements impact job roles and embracing an adaptable mindset, professionals can position themselves not just as survivors but as leaders in their fields. Embrace the journey of transformation with curiosity and confidence; every challenge presents an opportunity for growth and innovation in your career path.

CHAPTER 4:
NETWORKING
AND BUILDING
CONNECTIONS

The New Landscape of Networking

The landscape of networking has transformed significantly in the age of artificial intelligence. Traditional methods, once dominated by face-to-face meetings and business card exchanges, are now enhanced—if not replaced—by digital platforms that enable broader and more dynamic connections. For professionals aiming to thrive in this evolving environment, understanding this new terrain is essential.

Online networking has shifted from a mere trend to an absolute necessity. Platforms like LinkedIn have revolutionized the way we build and maintain professional relationships. Instead of only reconnecting with former colleagues, professionals can now engage with industry leaders, potential clients, and peers from around the globe. This expanded reach opens up opportunities to share insights, seek mentorship, and collaborate on projects that transcend geographical boundaries.

Creating an influential online presence involves more than just setting up a profile; it requires curating content that showcases your expertise while reflecting your personality and values. Sharing articles relevant to your field or offering thoughtful commentary on industry developments can establish you as a knowledgeable resource. For example, if you work in AI development, writing about recent breakthroughs or ethical considerations can position you as a thought leader. Engaging with others' content by commenting or sharing also fosters reciprocal relationships.

Active engagement goes beyond simply promoting your achievements. Participating in relevant discussions—whether through forums or social media groups—allows for deeper connections with professionals who share similar interests or challenges. Joining an AI-focused community, for instance, can lead to collaborative projects or partnerships that enhance your knowledge and broaden your network.

Networking extends beyond individual relationships; it also involves the creation of professional communities. Engaging with organizations or local meetups dedicated to emerging technologies provides valuable opportunities to connect with individuals facing similar challenges. These shared experiences foster an environment conducive to collective growth, where members can learn from one another's successes and setbacks.

Strategic networking tactics are crucial for navigating the complexities of modern job markets influenced by AI advancements. One effective approach is identifying key influencers within your industry—those whose opinions shape trends—and engaging with them directly. Whether by commenting on their posts or reaching out through private messages, initiating conversations with these individuals can lead to mentorship opportunities or collaborations that enhance your career trajectory.

Nurturing genuine relationships is also vital; it requires building trust and respect over time rather than focusing solely on transactional interactions. Adopting a mindset of giving before receiving—offering support, sharing resources, or providing insights without expecting immediate reciprocation—strengthens bonds and often leads to valuable connections when you need them most.

The role of social media in networking cannot be overstated; it serves as both a tool for connection and a platform for thought leadership. Utilizing channels like Twitter to participate in relevant hashtags amplifies your voice within professional circles and helps you connect with others who share similar interests.

As industries continue to evolve due to AI integration, our approaches to networking must adapt accordingly. Establishing thought leadership through insightful contributions is key to remaining visible amid the noise of competing voices. Effectively leveraging online platforms positions professionals not just as participants but as influential contributors shaping their respective fields.

mastering the new landscape of networking requires embracing digital tools while fostering authentic connections grounded in mutual growth and respect. By navigating this territory thoughtfully—balancing engagement across various platforms while cultivating lasting relationships—you'll expand your professional circle and pave the way for new opportunities that traditional frameworks may not offer. Adaptability is essential; every connection made today could lead to transformative collaborations tomorrow.

Building an Influential Online Presence

Creating an influential online presence begins with intentionality. In today's digital landscape, it's no longer enough to merely exist on various platforms; professionals must actively shape their narratives and establish authority in their fields. This journey starts with a thoughtfully crafted profile that clearly communicates your skills, experiences, and aspirations. Think of it as your digital business card— invest the time to create a compelling summary that not only highlights your qualifications but also reflects your unique personality.

As you build your online identity, content creation becomes a crucial element. Sharing insights, commentary, and relevant resources not only demonstrates your expertise but also engages others in meaningful dialogue. Take this example, you might consider writing a LinkedIn article on the impact of AI in specific industries or sharing innovative practices that have benefited your career. If you have experience in data analysis, discuss recent trends and tools you've adopted to enhance productivity. Doing so positions you as knowledgeable while inviting deeper conversations.

Engagement plays a vital role in this process; it's about more than just posting content—it involves interaction as well. By commenting on industry-related posts or participating in discussions within relevant groups, you can forge connections that may evolve into collaborative opportunities. Don't hesitate to express your opinions or ask questions; such interactions can lead to richer discussions that highlight your curiosity and willingness to learn from others. Joining online forums focused on machine learning, for example, allows you to engage with peers facing similar challenges while sharing valuable insights.

Equally important is the development of professional communities online. Platforms like Slack or Discord host groups where professionals can gather to discuss emerging trends or collaborate on projects. These communities not only provide a supportive network but also present opportunities for joint ventures or partnerships. The shared experiences within these groups create an environment ripe for knowledge exchange, significantly enhancing both personal and professional growth.

Identifying and connecting with key influencers in your field is another strategic move. Engaging with thought leaders can open doors to mentorship or collaboration that might otherwise remain inaccessible. When reaching out, consider sending direct messages with thoughtful questions or comments about their work. Authenticity is essential here —demonstrate genuine interest in their insights rather than merely seeking something in return.

Nurturing these relationships requires more than occasional exchanges; it's about building trust over time. Approach networking as a long-term investment rather than a transactional endeavor. Offer assistance where possible— whether it's sharing a resource, providing feedback on a project, or publicly celebrating someone's achievements—this generosity often pays off when you need support.

Social media serves not only as a connection tool but also as a platform for showcasing thought leadership. By effectively utilizing Twitter—joining conversations through trending hashtags related to AI or technology—you amplify your voice within the industry and attract followers who resonate with your ideas. This active participation boosts your visibility and positions you at the forefront of relevant discussions.

As AI continues to reshape various industries, adapting your networking strategies becomes crucial. With the digital space becoming increasingly crowded, establishing yourself as an authority requires consistent, insightful contributions that cut through the noise. By leveraging diverse online platforms while maintaining authenticity in your engagements, you position yourself not only as a participant in the industry but as an influential figure shaping its future.

building an influential online presence is about more than

just numbers; it's about cultivating genuine connections grounded in mutual respect and growth. The relationships you forge today could lead to significant collaborations tomorrow, making it essential to approach each interaction thoughtfully and strategically. Embrace the evolving landscape of digital networking; every post, comment, and shared resource contributes to the tapestry of your professional narrative— one that can open doors to new opportunities while driving personal success amid the complexities of the AI job economy.

Participating in Professional Communities

In today's professional landscape, engaging with communities relevant to your field is not just beneficial—it's essential for your growth. Connecting with like-minded individuals who share your interests and aspirations creates a supportive network that can significantly influence your career trajectory. These communities provide invaluable resources, insights, and opportunities that are often inaccessible when working in isolation.

One effective way to immerse yourself in these networks is through professional associations and groups specific to your industry. Many sectors have established organizations that offer tailored resources, workshops, and networking events for their members. Take this example, if you work in the tech field, you might consider joining organizations like the Association for Computing Machinery (ACM) or the Institute of Electrical and Electronics Engineers (IEEE). These groups frequently host local meetups, webinars, and conferences where members can learn from industry experts and share their own experiences.

In addition to formal associations, online platforms such as LinkedIn serve as excellent hubs for connecting with peers and thought leaders in your industry. Actively participating in discussions on these platforms enhances your visibility and credibility. Instead of merely scrolling through your feed, take the time to engage with content by liking, sharing, or offering thoughtful comments. If you come across an article about emerging AI technologies, for example, consider sharing your perspective or asking questions in the comments section. This approach not only highlights your engagement but also encourages others to interact with you.

Joining discussion groups on platforms like Facebook or specialized forums related to your profession can provide even deeper insights. These communities often concentrate on niche topics where members discuss challenges they face and share effective solutions. If you're navigating a specific technology stack in AI development, seek out forums dedicated to those tools. The collective knowledge within these groups can be a powerful resource for addressing problems.

Another important aspect of engaging with professional communities is the opportunity to give back. Consider sharing your expertise by leading a webinar or writing an article for an industry publication or community newsletter. Doing so positions you as a contributor and potential leader within the community. Your willingness to share insights fosters relationships based on mutual respect and collaboration.

Active participation in these circles also opens doors to mentorship opportunities. By connecting with seasoned professionals—whether through formal mentorship programs or casual interactions—you can gain invaluable guidance on navigating career challenges. Approaching potential mentors with specific questions about their career paths or seeking advice on particular issues can lead to meaningful exchanges that benefit both you and your mentor.

The landscape of networking has transformed dramatically with the rise of remote work and digital communication tools. Webinars, virtual conferences, and online workshops enable broader participation without geographical constraints. Take advantage of these formats by attending sessions that interest you; they provide excellent avenues for learning while also presenting opportunities to connect with speakers and fellow attendees through chat functions or social media.

Engaging actively in professional communities nurtures not only career advancement but also personal growth. Exposure to diverse perspectives broadens your understanding of industry trends while sharpening critical skills such as communication and collaboration. The exchange of ideas can ignite innovative thoughts that you might not have considered on your own.

While it can be easy to get caught up in daily responsibilities, prioritizing time for community engagement is crucial. Set aside moments each week dedicated solely to networking activities—whether that involves attending an event, participating online, or reaching out to peers for coffee chats (virtual or otherwise). This investment often yields significant dividends as you build relationships that will support your career journey.

being part of professional communities enriches both your personal network and professional skill set. The connections formed here frequently lead to unexpected opportunities— collaborations on projects, introductions to key players in various industries, or even job offers stemming from personal recommendations. Each interaction strengthens the fabric of your professional narrative while empowering you to navigate the complexities of an evolving job market with confidence.

As you immerse yourself in these vibrant ecosystems, remember: every connection made today could blossom into significant opportunities tomorrow. Your proactive engagement lays a strong foundation for resilience in a landscape increasingly shaped by technology and innovation.

Strategic Networking Tactics

Strategic networking is more than just exchanging business

cards or sending connection requests; it's about building meaningful relationships that can advance your career in the AI job economy. To create a strong professional network, you need to approach each interaction with intention and strategy, ensuring that every connection aligns with your overarching career goals.

A crucial first step is to identify key individuals within your industry who can offer valuable insights, mentorship, or collaboration opportunities. Begin by mapping out the landscape of your field: Who are the thought leaders? Which organizations are influencing industry standards? Platforms like LinkedIn enable you to connect with these individuals, follow their work, engage with their content, and participate in discussions they initiate. Take this example, if you're in healthcare technology, consider following leaders in digital health and contributing to conversations about AI's impact on patient care. This not only showcases your engagement but also positions you as an informed participant in essential dialogues.

After pinpointing influential figures, don't hesitate to reach out directly. Personalize your messages by highlighting shared interests or experiences—mentioning a recent article they wrote or a project that inspired you can create a meaningful connection. Genuine outreach fosters community and often leads to reciprocal exchanges of ideas. Think of each new connection as opening a door—what will you bring through it? Perhaps it's an innovative collaboration idea or insights from your own experiences that could benefit them.

Additionally, take advantage of industry conferences and seminars—both virtual and in-person—where networking opportunities abound. These events often feature breakout sessions designed for more intimate interactions. Actively participating allows for deeper conversations than what may occur in larger settings. Prepare thoughtful questions related to the speaker's presentation or current industry trends to spark further dialogue and strengthen connections.

Leveraging existing connections for introductions can also be an effective strategy. If a colleague knows someone whose expertise aligns with your interests, asking for an introduction can lead to more fruitful conversations than cold outreach alone, as it comes with an implicit endorsement from someone they trust.

To maximize your networking potential, consider setting specific goals for each event or interaction. Instead of vague objectives like "meet new people," aim for actionable targets such as "connect with three professionals in AI ethics" or "find one potential mentor." These focused intentions will help keep your efforts measurable and on track.

Follow-up is equally critical after initial meetings or interactions. Sending thank-you notes expressing appreciation for their time and insights—whether through email or social media—reinforces your engagement and demonstrates that you value the relationship beyond mere networking. Sharing any relevant resources discussed during your conversation can further solidify this bond.

Social media platforms can play a pivotal role in maintaining relationships over time. Regularly share relevant content that sparks discussion—be it articles on AI advancements or thoughtful commentary on industry news—to ensure you're present in the minds of your connections even when direct interaction isn't possible.

Remember that networking isn't solely about personal gain; it's also about reciprocity. Look for opportunities to assist others within your network by sharing knowledge, providing introductions, or supporting projects they're passionate about. This spirit of generosity strengthens relationships and encourages others to return the favor when needed.

Participating in local community initiatives related to technology not only offers networking potential but also allows you to give back. Whether volunteering at events aimed at bridging the digital divide or mentoring students interested in AI careers, these experiences enrich your professional life while broadening your influence.

Lastly, embrace vulnerability in networking situations; don't shy away from discussing challenges you face on your career path. Sharing these experiences invites authentic connections based on common ground rather than purely transactional interactions driven by ambition.

By consistently applying these strategic tactics, you'll cultivate a vibrant professional network capable of supporting your aspirations amidst the complexities introduced by AI advancements across various industries. Each relationship represents a potential avenue for collaboration, learning, and growth—essential elements for thriving in a rapidly changing landscape.

In this evolving job market shaped by technological advances like artificial intelligence, proactive networking equips you with the tools necessary not just for survival but for success —a nurtured network today translates into opportunities realized tomorrow.

The Role of Social Media in Networking

As you explore the world of networking, it becomes evident that social media is a powerful ally in building and nurturing professional relationships. Far more than just a platform for personal updates, it is a vibrant space where ideas circulate, expertise is shared, and connections thrive. In today's AI-driven job market, effectively leveraging social media can set you apart from your peers and help position you as a leader in your field.

To fully capitalize on social media for networking, start by optimizing your profiles. A polished and professional image, combined with a clear expression of your career goals and skills, lays the groundwork for meaningful connections. Take this example, tailor your LinkedIn profile to not only showcase past experiences but also highlight projects that reflect your engagement with AI technologies. Including links to presentations or articles you've authored can serve as concrete evidence of your expertise.

Engagement is crucial on social media platforms. Regularly contribute to discussions relevant to your field by commenting on posts from thought leaders or sharing insights on recent trends in AI. For example, if an influential figure discusses ethical AI practices, add your perspective on how these principles could be implemented in real-world scenarios. This approach not only demonstrates your knowledge but also increases your visibility among peers and industry experts.

Joining specialized groups on platforms like LinkedIn or Facebook can also enhance your networking efforts. These groups often consist of professionals who share similar interests and face common challenges. Actively participating in discussions—whether by asking questions or offering advice based on your own experiences—can foster a sense of community and lead to valuable connections beyond traditional networking events.

Consider utilizing Twitter as a dynamic networking tool. The platform's fast-paced environment allows you to engage with industry trends in real-time. By following prominent figures in AI, you gain insights into their perspectives while also having opportunities to interact through retweets or replies. Sharing insightful articles or thoughts related to their tweets creates touchpoints that can initiate deeper conversations later on.

A compelling example is Sarah, an emerging data scientist who skillfully navigated her career transition from marketing to tech using social media. She began curating content related to AI developments and analytics trends on her Twitter account, which resonated with followers interested in these topics. By engaging in conversations with industry leaders through hashtags like #DataScience and #AIethics, she attracted the attention of hiring managers who appreciated her proactive approach and depth of knowledge.

Maintaining these relationships requires consistent effort; therefore, having a strategic follow-up plan is essential after establishing initial connections. Set reminders to reach out periodically—not just when you need something—but also to share relevant articles or congratulate others on their achievements. This ongoing communication strengthens bonds that go beyond superficial interactions.

As you navigate this landscape, remember that collaboration often stems from shared goals or challenges. If you discover common ground with someone regarding project aspirations or industry trends, consider exploring ways to collaborate —whether through co-authoring an article or participating in webinars together. Such initiatives not only deepen connections but also enhance visibility for both parties within professional circles.

Additionally, embrace storytelling on social media; share narratives that highlight lessons learned from setbacks or breakthroughs in your journey within AI industries. Authentic stories resonate well with audiences, fostering dialogue and attracting individuals who value vulnerability and sincerity in professional interactions.

At its core, effective networking through social media goes beyond simply increasing numbers; it's about cultivating genuine relationships built on mutual respect and shared aspirations. Each interaction presents an opportunity for personal and professional growth, creating a support system capable of navigating the complexities introduced by advancements in artificial intelligence.

By engaging intentionally and authentically within these

digital spaces, you'll not only expand your professional network but also solidify your position as an informed contributor in the evolving landscape of the AI job market—an invaluable advantage as we move into an uncertain future shaped by innovation.

Establishing Thought Leadership

Establishing thought leadership in the AI-driven job economy involves more than just expertise; it requires a proactive commitment to sharing insights, nurturing connections, and making a lasting impact on your industry. Thought leadership is about shaping conversations, influencing decision-making, and guiding others through the complexities of technology integration.

To begin, identify your niche within the expansive landscape of AI. Reflect on the unique perspectives you can offer: Are you passionate about ethical implications, practical applications, or technological advancements? Defining your area of focus enables you to curate content that resonates with your audience. Take this example, if AI ethics sparks your interest, start by writing articles or blog posts that delve into current debates on bias in AI systems and suggest frameworks for responsible use. This positions you as a knowledgeable voice in an important conversation.

High-quality content creation is vital for building credibility. Whether through blog posts, videos, podcasts, or social media updates, your contributions should not only reflect your expertise but also demonstrate a commitment to continuous learning. For example, if you've recently attended a conference on machine learning, share key takeaways or actionable insights from the event. This not only showcases your engagement with the field but also serves as a valuable resource for others seeking knowledge.

Engaging with established thought leaders can significantly enhance your visibility. Start by following and interacting with influencers in your niche on platforms like LinkedIn and Twitter. When they share insights or initiate discussions, add thoughtful comments that expand their points or introduce new ideas. This engagement can lead to collaboration opportunities or mentorship. Take this example, if an influential figure discusses the future of AI in healthcare, you might comment on how integrating patient data analytics could improve outcomes—potentially sparking a dialogue that captures their attention.

Networking through speaking engagements can further solidify your status as a thought leader. Look for opportunities to present at industry conferences, webinars, or workshops where you can share findings and engage directly with an audience. Prepare engaging presentations featuring case studies or practical examples from your experiences. If you're focused on AI's role in marketing automation, demonstrate how specific algorithms have transformed consumer engagement strategies—real-world applications resonate more deeply than theoretical discussions.

Building an online presence is another critical aspect of thought leadership. Create a personal website or portfolio that showcases your work and achievements while providing valuable resources for visitors. Include links to articles you've written, projects you've contributed to, or curated lists of recommended readings related to AI trends. A well-maintained website serves as a hub for those interested in learning from you and positions you as an accessible expert.

As you establish yourself within professional circles, remember to share stories that highlight personal experiences and lessons learned along the way. Authenticity fosters connections—people are drawn to narratives that reflect vulnerability and perseverance. For example, discussing challenges you've faced when integrating AI solutions into traditional business models can resonate with others navigating similar obstacles.

Consider contributing to industry publications or platforms dedicated to AI discourse as well. Writing guest posts for reputable blogs or participating in collaborative whitepapers enhances credibility while exposing your ideas to broader audiences beyond your immediate network.

Engaging with educational institutions can also strengthen your reputation as a thought leader. Offer guest lectures or workshops at universities focusing on emerging technologies and their implications across various industries. Collaborating with academia not only builds community ties but also allows you to tap into fresh perspectives from aspiring professionals eager to learn from experienced voices.

Finally, always be open to feedback and willing to adapt based on evolving conversations within the field of AI. Staying current with trends ensures that your insights remain relevant while also demonstrating a commitment to ongoing growth—a hallmark of effective thought leadership.

Becoming a thought leader is an ongoing journey requiring dedication and strategic effort in both personal branding and community engagement. By generously sharing knowledge and fostering relationships rooted in mutual respect, you'll cultivate influence not only within traditional networking circles but throughout the ever-expanding realm of AI innovation—an essential component for thriving amid change in today's job economy.

Coordinating With AI-related Professional Societies

Collaborating with AI-related professional societies is a strategic way to enhance your career and broaden your network within the AI-driven job economy. These societies act as hubs for knowledge, innovation, and collaboration, offering invaluable resources that support skill development and industry engagement.

To get started, identify societies that align with your

professional goals and interests. Each organization has a unique focus: some emphasize ethical considerations in AI, while others prioritize technical advancements or industry applications. For example, the Association for the Advancement of Artificial Intelligence (AAAI) is ideal if you're looking to deepen your technical expertise in AI technologies. In contrast, the IEEE Global Initiative on Ethics of Autonomous and Intelligent Systems caters to those interested in the ethical implications of AI.

After identifying relevant societies, immerse yourself in their activities. Many host regular events such as conferences, webinars, and workshops where professionals share insights and present research findings. Participating in these gatherings not only enhances your understanding but also positions you alongside thought leaders and innovators. Take this example, attending an annual conference can provide you with insights from leading experts on the latest trends in machine learning or data ethics.

In addition to attending events, consider taking on active roles within these organizations. Volunteering for committees or special interest groups can strengthen your professional reputation while allowing you to contribute to meaningful projects. This involvement could range from organizing events to collaborating on research initiatives—experiences that can be highlighted on your resume or LinkedIn profile. A member of the AI Ethics Lab exemplifies this; their active participation led to co-authoring a paper presented at a prominent conference, significantly boosting their visibility in academic circles.

Networking plays a crucial role when engaging with professional societies. Building relationships with fellow members can unlock mentorship opportunities and collaborative projects. Approach this process authentically; focus on fostering genuine relationships based on mutual interests rather than simply seeking personal gain. Scheduling informal coffee chats or virtual meetings with other members whose work resonates with you can provide valuable insights into their career paths while helping you clarify your own goals.

The rise of online platforms has made it easier than ever to connect with societies beyond geographical boundaries. Many organizations maintain active social media channels where they share news about upcoming events and opportunities for engagement. Follow these channels closely—participating in online discussions can increase your visibility within these communities without requiring physical attendance at every event. Thoughtfully engaging in comments or discussions about recent publications can demonstrate your knowledge and help expand your network organically.

Additionally, take advantage of the educational resources these societies offer. They often provide access to exclusive research papers, webinars, tutorials, and toolkits tailored to specific areas of AI expertise. Regularly engaging with these materials keeps you informed and allows you to apply new insights directly within your professional context—a key aspect of continuous learning.

Consider establishing or joining local chapters of these professional societies as well; this localized approach often fosters stronger community ties while providing more personalized networking opportunities. Such chapters frequently organize smaller gatherings that may feel less intimidating than larger conferences but still offer valuable connections and knowledge-sharing experiences.

As you deepen your engagement with these organizations, don't hesitate to share what you're learning within your broader network—whether through blog posts discussing insights gained from workshops or summaries of key takeaways from lectures on social media platforms like LinkedIn or Twitter.

Finally, stay adaptable as technology evolves; being involved in professional societies requires ongoing engagement—not just attending events but actively contributing ideas and feedback that reflect current trends and challenges facing industries today.

Engaging effectively with AI-related professional societies empowers individuals not only through skill acquisition but also by fostering meaningful connections that encourage collaboration across disciplines—an essential strategy for navigating the complexities of an increasingly automated job market.

Learning from Peers and Competitors

Learning from peers and competitors is essential for navigating the AI-driven job economy. This process extends beyond mere observation; it requires active engagement, collaboration, and a commitment to mutual growth. By adopting this mindset, professionals can leverage collective intelligence and effectively adapt to the rapid changes in the workplace.

To start, identify individuals or groups whose work resonates with your own. These might be colleagues within your organization, professionals from other companies, or thought leaders in the AI sector. Spend time exploring their projects, innovations, and approaches to challenges. Take this example, if you admire how a competitor has implemented AI tools to streamline operations, consider reaching out for a conversation. A simple email or LinkedIn message expressing your interest can open doors to insightful discussions.

Another effective way to foster connections is by setting up informal meet-ups or coffee chats. These relaxed environments promote candid conversations about industry trends, challenges in implementation, and shared learning experiences. For example, a marketing professional might connect with a data scientist to explore how AI-driven analytics are reshaping customer engagement strategies. Such dialogues can offer fresh perspectives that enhance your own approach.

Participating in collaborative projects is another excellent strategy for learning from others. Seek opportunities within your network where you can contribute your expertise while gaining insights from others' skills and knowledge. If you are involved in a cross-departmental initiative focused on integrating AI solutions into business processes, you will not only share what you know but also absorb new techniques and viewpoints that could improve your work.

Additionally, don't overlook online forums and professional groups as valuable sources of knowledge. Platforms like GitHub, Stack Overflow, or industry-specific Slack channels facilitate real-time exchanges of ideas and solutions among professionals facing similar challenges. Actively engaging in these communities can provide valuable feedback on your own projects and offer diverse insights from around the globe.

Social media can also serve as a powerful tool for learning. By following industry experts on platforms such as Twitter or LinkedIn, you gain access to real-time updates about trends and innovations in AI. Engaging with their content—by asking questions or sharing your thoughts—can lead to deeper connections and meaningful exchanges of knowledge.

Taking cues from competitors can provide strategic advantages as well. Analyze how successful companies have adopted AI technologies: What methodologies did they employ? What pitfalls did they encounter? Take this example, a company that effectively integrated machine learning algorithms into its customer service process may offer valuable lessons on user experience design and implementation challenges.

As you learn from others, it's beneficial to keep track of insights gained and strategies observed using structured notes or digital tools like Notion or Evernote. Regularly reviewing this information reinforces your learning and enables you to implement these insights effectively within your context.

Finally, embrace the principle of continuous improvement by sharing what you've learned with others. Organizing small workshops or discussion groups within your workplace can stimulate dialogue around best practices and cultivate an environment of collective growth. When everyone contributes their knowledge—whether through successes or failures—the entire team stands to benefit.

Cultivating a mindset that values learning from peers and competitors not only enhances individual skill sets but also strengthens organizations in an evolving job landscape shaped by AI innovation. This approach transforms challenges into opportunities for collaboration and shared success—a fundamental component of thriving in today's interconnected economy.

CHAPTER 5: REMOTE WORK AND THE GIG ECONOMY

Trends in Remote Work and AI

T he rise of remote work, driven by advancements in AI technology, has significantly transformed the employment landscape. This shift reflects not just a response to global events but a fundamental rethinking of how we view work, collaboration, and productivity. As organizations increasingly incorporate AI to enhance efficiency, the ability to work remotely has become closely linked to these technological advancements, fostering new dynamics in team structures and workflows.

In this evolving environment, flexibility is key. Remote work empowers employees to operate from anywhere, breaking down geographical barriers and cultivating a diverse workforce that enriches problem-solving with varied perspectives. Companies now have access to a global talent pool, enabling collaboration across different cultures and time zones. For example, a software development team might include programmers in New York, designers in Berlin, and project managers in Singapore. This diversity not only sparks innovation but also enhances creativity as team members contribute unique insights drawn from their individual experiences.

However, remote work also introduces challenges that organizations must confront to fully leverage AI's potential. When team members are scattered across various locations, communication can become disjointed. To address this issue, many companies are turning to AI-driven communication tools that facilitate seamless interactions. Platforms like Slack and Microsoft Teams now incorporate AI features to prioritize messages based on urgency or relevance, ensuring critical information reaches the right people at the right time. Training teams to effectively utilize these tools is vital, as doing so can significantly improve collaboration.

As organizations adapt to remote work, they also need to rethink their approaches to performance evaluation. Traditional metrics may no longer accurately reflect employee productivity or contributions. The focus is shifting toward outcomes rather than hours logged. Take this example, a marketing team might assess success based on campaign engagement metrics instead of merely counting weekly meetings. This results-oriented approach is crucial for sustaining motivation and aligning with broader business goals.

Simultaneously, the gig economy has gained traction alongside remote work trends. Freelancers and independent contractors are increasingly becoming essential contributors to project teams, offering specialized skills without the constraints of traditional employment structures. AI technologies play a pivotal role here as well; platforms like Upwork and Fiverr use algorithms to connect clients with freelancers based on skill sets and project needs. This evolution fosters an agile workforce capable of quickly adapting to changing market demands.

Yet, these opportunities also bring significant challenges related to job security and stability. The gig economy often lacks the safety nets typically associated with full-time employment—benefits such as healthcare and retirement plans are frequently unavailable for freelancers. Organizations must navigate these issues thoughtfully while building partnerships with gig workers that encourage mutual trust and long-term collaboration.

Legal considerations further complicate this new landscape. Remote work arrangements can vary widely across jurisdictions, raising questions about labor rights and compliance with local regulations. Take this example, businesses operating globally must adhere to tax laws governing remote workers' income in different countries. Developing clear policies that outline expectations and responsibilities for both employees and contractors is essential for effectively navigating these complexities.

Looking ahead, exciting possibilities emerge as AI continues to evolve alongside remote work trends. Innovations such as virtual reality (VR) environments for meetings and advanced analytics for monitoring employee well-being could redefine our approach to remote collaboration. Integrating these technologies has the potential not only to enhance productivity but also to improve job satisfaction by fostering genuine connections among team members.

To wrap things up, understanding the intricate interplay between remote work trends and AI advancements is vital for professionals navigating this new landscape. By embracing flexibility, leveraging technology effectively, and fostering a culture of results-oriented performance evaluation, individuals and organizations can position themselves for success in an era marked by rapid change and opportunity.

Tools and Technologies for Remote Collaboration

The landscape of remote collaboration has been transformed

by a diverse array of tools and technologies designed to enhance communication and productivity. As teams spread across various locations, the reliance on digital platforms has increased significantly, facilitating seamless interactions and fostering a sense of connectedness that transcends physical boundaries. This evolution highlights the importance of choosing the right tools to promote effective teamwork, ensuring that all members can contribute meaningfully, regardless of their location.

At the forefront of these tools are collaborative project management platforms such as Asana, Trello, and Monday.com. These systems empower teams to organize tasks, set deadlines, and visualize progress through intuitive dashboards. For example, a marketing team can use Trello to create boards for different campaigns, enabling members to move tasks through various stages—from ideation to execution—while maintaining transparency about each project's status. The ability to comment directly on tasks encourages real-time feedback and collaboration, keeping everyone aligned.

Equally essential are communication tools in this remote landscape. Platforms like Zoom and Google Meet have become staples for virtual meetings, and features like breakout rooms enhance their effectiveness by allowing more focused discussions among smaller groups. This functionality is particularly valuable during brainstorming sessions or workshops where deeper exploration of ideas is necessary. Take this example, during a product development meeting, teams can split into breakout rooms to discuss specific features before regrouping to share insights with the larger group.

AI-enhanced tools further elevate collaborative efforts by automating routine tasks and providing intelligent suggestions based on user behavior. Take AI-driven scheduling assistants like Calendly, which simplify the often tedious process of finding mutually agreeable meeting times. By analyzing participants' availability and preferences, these tools allow for more strategic conversations and decision-making processes.

In addition to communication and project management tools, file-sharing platforms like Google Drive and Dropbox have become essential in remote work environments. They offer secure spaces for document storage and enable real-time editing capabilities that enhance collaboration on shared files. For example, a team working on a presentation can edit slides simultaneously while providing feedback in real-time—eliminating the need for back-and-forth email exchanges that can slow down progress.

However, as we embrace these advanced technologies for remote collaboration, it is crucial to remain aware of potential pitfalls related to information overload. With numerous communication channels—email threads, chat messages, video calls—it's easy for critical information to get lost or overlooked. Establishing clear guidelines around communication practices can help mitigate this issue; for instance, designating specific platforms for different types of interactions (e.g., using instant messaging for quick questions versus email for formal communications) can streamline workflows.

And, creating a robust onboarding process that familiarizes new hires with these tools is essential. Without adequate training on how to use these technologies effectively, employees may feel overwhelmed or disengaged from team initiatives. Regular workshops or training sessions not only build proficiency but also foster an environment where continuous learning is valued.

As organizations adapt their strategies in response to evolving work dynamics driven by AI advancements, focusing on user experience becomes paramount. The more intuitive the technology—whether through user-friendly interfaces or personalized features—the more likely employees are to engage fully with it.

Looking ahead, emerging technologies such as augmented reality (AR) applications present exciting possibilities for enhancing remote collaboration even further. Imagine virtual brainstorming sessions where team members wearing AR headsets can manipulate 3D models together in real-time from different locations—a concept that is quickly moving from science fiction to practical application.

Navigating this new terrain requires both agility and foresight as professionals incorporate advanced collaborative tools into their workflows while remaining vigilant against potential challenges related to communication clarity and employee engagement. By fostering an environment that embraces innovation alongside human connection—regardless of geographical constraints—organizations can position themselves at the forefront of this transformative era in work culture.

successful remote collaboration hinges not just on selecting the right technologies but also on cultivating relationships built on trust and mutual respect among team members. This foundation ensures that every voice is heard and valued within an increasingly digital workspace—a critical factor in maintaining morale and driving long-term success in today's AI-infused job economy.

Benefits and Challenges of the Gig Economy

The gig economy has transformed the professional landscape, offering a unique mix of benefits and challenges that individuals must navigate. As more people turn to freelance work, contract positions, or project-based roles, they find that the flexibility and independence these options provide can often be countered by the uncertainties that accompany non-traditional employment.

One of the most notable advantages of the gig economy is the ability to customize one's work schedule. Freelancers and gig workers often have the freedom to choose when and where they work, which allows them to better balance personal commitments with professional responsibilities. Take this example, a graphic designer might select projects that fit seamlessly into their life, enabling them to dedicate time to family or personal pursuits. This flexibility can significantly enhance job satisfaction, as individuals are able to align their work with their lifestyles instead of conforming to rigid office hours.

Financial potential is another attractive aspect of gig work. Many freelance roles offer competitive pay rates, particularly for specialized skills in fields such as technology and creative services. A software developer who freelances may command higher hourly rates than their salaried counterparts due to the unique expertise they bring to each project. Additionally, the opportunity to take on multiple projects at once allows skilled workers to diversify their income streams, a particularly beneficial strategy during economic uncertainty.

However, these financial advantages come with their own set of challenges. Unlike traditional employment arrangements that typically provide health benefits, retirement plans, and paid leave, gig workers often have to shoulder these responsibilities on their own. This lack of stability means many freelancers must not only seek new clients but also manage taxes and healthcare costs without employer support. For example, a freelance writer may struggle to cover medical expenses during slow months without the safety net of a steady paycheck.

Job security is another significant concern for gig workers. How X works contract work offers little guarantee of continued employment once a project concludes. This uncertainty can lead to anxiety and complicate long-term financial planning. A marketing consultant who relies on short-term contracts may face income gaps during lean periods, making proactive budgeting essential and potentially increasing stress as they search for new opportunities.

Navigating client relationships also presents its own set of challenges. Communication styles vary widely across industries and individual clients; some may provide clear expectations while others leave freelancers guessing about their needs. Establishing strong relationships while setting appropriate boundaries is vital for long-term success in this environment. Developing effective communication strategies —such as creating detailed contracts that outline project scopes, deadlines, and payment terms—can help mitigate misunderstandings and ensure both parties remain aligned throughout the engagement.

Also, the digital nature of many gig opportunities requires self-promotion through online platforms or social media. Crafting an appealing portfolio or establishing an engaging presence on professional networks like LinkedIn is crucial for attracting clients in a crowded market. While this task can feel daunting for those lacking marketing experience, it is essential for distinguishing oneself from the competition.

The reliance on technology presents both opportunities and challenges for gig workers. Tools like video conferencing software facilitate seamless communication with clients across distances; however, technical glitches can disrupt critical meetings or collaborations. A web developer waiting for feedback during a virtual call might find themselves frustrated by connectivity issues at pivotal moments, highlighting the importance of having backup systems or alternative communication methods available.

As we explore the landscape shaped by the gig economy—rich with enticing prospects yet fraught with hidden pitfalls—it becomes essential to develop strategies that enhance resilience in the face of unpredictability. Building a diverse network can help mitigate periods of downtime; connecting with other professionals opens doors not only for job opportunities but also for mentorship and collaboration.

success within this dynamic workforce demands adaptability and resourcefulness alongside a keen understanding of market trends. By embracing both the opportunities afforded by flexibility and innovation while remaining vigilant against potential setbacks related to job security and client management, individuals can carve out fulfilling careers in an ever-evolving economic landscape—a landscape enriched by technological advancements yet deeply rooted in human connection and collaboration.

Finding Opportunities in Freelance Platforms

Freelance platforms have become essential tools for individuals looking to capitalize on their skills in a rapidly evolving job market. These platforms provide professionals with the opportunity to showcase their talents and connect with clients worldwide. However, successfully navigating this landscape requires strategic thinking and practical know-how.

The first step is to identify the right freelance platform for your skills. With a wide array of options available, each catering to different industries and expertise, it's important to choose wisely. For example, writers may find Upwork or Fiverr to be ideal due to their expansive user bases, while tech professionals might thrive on specialized sites like Toptal or GitHub Jobs, which prioritize quality and skill matching. Conducting thorough research can help you determine which platform aligns best with your abilities and career goals.

Once you've chosen a platform, creating a standout profile becomes essential. A well-crafted profile not only highlights your skills but also conveys your personality and professionalism. Include a professional headshot, an engaging bio that tells your story, and samples of your previous work that demonstrate your expertise. Take this example, graphic designers should showcase a diverse portfolio to capture the attention of potential clients. Tailoring your profile to meet the platform's audience expectations will significantly increase your chances of being noticed.

Effective communication is key when engaging with clients on these platforms. Clarity from the beginning can help prevent misunderstandings later on. When responding to inquiries or project briefs, take the time to clarify any uncertainties before agreeing to deadlines or deliverables. Providing detailed proposals that outline your approach not only showcases professionalism but also ensures both parties are aligned on project expectations.

Mastering the bidding process is another critical component of freelancing on these platforms. This unique feature allows professionals to propose prices for projects, so understanding market rates while valuing your own skills is essential. Avoid underselling yourself; instead, focus on articulating the value you bring to each project based on your experience and expertise.

Building strong client relationships is vital for long-term success in freelancing. A positive experience can lead to repeat business and valuable referrals. Maintaining open lines of communication throughout a project can reassure clients that progress is being made and any issues are being addressed proactively.

As you gain experience on these platforms, paying attention to feedback becomes increasingly important. Client reviews play a significant role in shaping future opportunities; high ratings enhance credibility while constructive criticism provides avenues for improvement. For example, if multiple clients mention missed deadlines in their reviews, it may be time to reassess your time management strategies or adjust your workload expectations.

Additionally, cultivating a robust network within freelance communities can yield significant benefits over time.

Engaging in forums or groups associated with specific platforms allows you to share experiences, tips, and resources with other freelancers who may have faced similar challenges. Collaborating with peers or seeking advice can expand your knowledge base while fostering camaraderie among those navigating similar paths.

Consider diversifying your income streams beyond reliance on a single platform as well; joining multiple freelance sites increases exposure to potential projects and safeguards against slow periods experienced on any one platform.

To wrap things up, finding opportunities within freelance platforms involves strategic positioning along with proactive communication and relationship-building efforts— key elements for thriving in an increasingly competitive environment marked by flexibility yet fraught with uncertainty. By embracing adaptability and leveraging available resources wisely, individuals can cultivate successful careers rooted in innovation while remaining connected in an ever-evolving workforce shaped by technology and collaboration.

Managing Remote Teams Effectively

The landscape of remote work is continually evolving, shaped by technological advancements and shifting workplace dynamics. In this new environment, effectively managing remote teams is crucial as traditional office boundaries dissolve and collaboration takes on new forms. Success in this realm hinges on a thoughtful approach that emphasizes communication, trust, and engagement.

Effective leadership starts with setting clear expectations. Team members must understand not only their individual responsibilities but also how their roles contribute to the organization's broader objectives. By articulating goals clearly, leaders can eliminate ambiguity and foster a sense of purpose. For example, when a marketing team is preparing for a campaign launch, outlining specific deliverables, deadlines, and key performance indicators creates a roadmap for success. Regular check-ins help maintain focus while providing opportunities for adjustments in response to unforeseen challenges.

Communication tools are vital in managing remote teams. Relying solely on emails can lead to misunderstandings or delays; therefore, integrating platforms like Slack or Microsoft Teams enables real-time conversations that enhance collaboration. Video conferencing tools such as Zoom or Google Meet further bridge the gap created by distance, allowing for face-to-face interactions that strengthen team bonds. Utilizing these technologies not only streamlines workflows but also humanizes the remote experience—an essential factor in maintaining morale and camaraderie.

Building trust within a remote team is paramount. Leaders should cultivate an environment where team members feel comfortable voicing concerns and sharing ideas. This openness encourages innovation and can lead to creative solutions for challenges that arise during projects. Take this example, during a brainstorming session, inviting input from all team members—even those who are less vocal—can reveal valuable insights that might otherwise remain hidden.

Recognizing individual contributions is equally important in fostering a motivated team culture. Celebrating achievements through virtual shout-outs or acknowledgments creates an inclusive atmosphere where team members feel valued. A simple message recognizing hard work can significantly boost morale, leading to higher engagement levels across the board.

Flexibility is another cornerstone of effective remote team management. Understanding that each member has different working styles and personal circumstances allows leaders to tailor their approaches accordingly. Some may thrive with early morning meetings, while others prefer to work late into the evening. Offering flexible schedules accommodates personal needs and enhances productivity by allowing employees to work when they are most effective.

In remote settings, conflict resolution becomes essential, as misunderstandings can escalate without immediate intervention. Establishing protocols for addressing disputes ensures conflicts are managed professionally and swiftly. Leaders should encourage open dialogue among team members to express grievances constructively, rather than letting tensions fester.

Monitoring performance in a remote environment requires metrics that differ from those used in traditional workplaces. Instead of focusing solely on hours logged or visible activity, evaluating outcomes becomes more relevant. Tools like Asana or Trello can help track project progress visually, providing insights into productivity without resorting to micromanagement—a practice that often leads to employee dissatisfaction.

Lastly, investing in professional development opportunities for remote teams fosters an atmosphere of continuous growth and engagement. Workshops, online courses, and mentorship programs can enhance skill sets while demonstrating an organization's commitment to its employees' futures—thus increasing loyalty and retention rates.

Navigating the complexities of managing remote teams involves blending strategic leadership with empathy and innovation. By prioritizing clear communication, building trust, recognizing contributions, maintaining flexibility, resolving conflicts effectively, focusing on outcomes rather than mere activity, and investing in development opportunities, organizations can position themselves not just to survive but to thrive in this new paradigm of work. As remote collaboration continues to shape our professional landscapes, embracing these strategies will be critical for building resilient teams ready to tackle future challenges together.

Building a Sustainable Remote Career

Remote work is not just a response to changing circumstances; it signifies a profound shift in how we approach our careers. To build a sustainable remote career, it's essential to understand this new paradigm and adapt to its demands. Embracing principles of flexibility, adaptability, and continuous learning will guide you as you navigate this evolving landscape.

A strong foundation is key to establishing a lasting remote career. Start by creating a dedicated workspace that minimizes distractions and boosts productivity. This area should reflect your professional identity while also offering comfort. A well-organized desk equipped with essential tools—such as high-speed internet, ergonomic furniture, and effective lighting—can greatly enhance your focus and output. Take this example, consider using dual monitors to facilitate multitasking or investing in noise-canceling headphones to maintain concentration despite household distractions.

Self-discipline is another critical aspect of remote work. In contrast to traditional office environments where external accountability is prevalent, remote work demands self-motivation. Setting clear daily goals can help create structure in your day. Begin each morning by outlining specific tasks you wish to complete, and consider employing productivity techniques like the Pomodoro Technique to break your work into manageable intervals with short breaks in between.

Networking remains essential, even in virtual spaces. Building professional relationships online opens doors for collaboration and growth. Engage in industry-specific forums or attend virtual conferences where you can connect with like-minded professionals. Platforms such as LinkedIn are excellent for showcasing your expertise through articles and discussions, helping you position yourself as an informed voice within your field.

As you cultivate these connections, actively seek out mentors who can provide tailored guidance for your career aspirations. A mentor's insights can reveal pathways that may not be immediately visible and offer valuable advice on navigating the challenges of remote work. Regular check-ins with mentors foster accountability and encourage personal growth.

Continuous learning is indispensable in the fast-paced realm of remote work. With a wealth of online courses and webinars available, there are numerous opportunities for skill enhancement—ranging from technical abilities like coding and data analysis to soft skills such as emotional intelligence and communication strategies. Websites like Coursera and Udemy offer accessible resources tailored to diverse interests and professional needs.

Remaining adaptable in the face of change is equally important. The remote work landscape evolves rapidly, influenced by technological advancements and shifting employer expectations. Staying informed about industry trends will empower you to pivot when necessary, whether that involves acquiring new skills or exploring emerging fields relevant to your expertise.

Striking a balance between work and life is another critical element of building a sustainable remote career. In remote settings, the lines between personal life and professional obligations often blur, leading to potential burnout if not managed effectively. Establishing boundaries —such as designated work hours or unplugging during non-work times—can help maintain mental health while ensuring productivity remains high.

Collaboration tools significantly enhance efficiency within remote teams but can also support individual projects. Familiarizing yourself with software such as Notion for project management or Google Workspace for document collaboration can streamline your processes. These tools facilitate seamless communication with colleagues while enabling you to manage your tasks independently.

Additionally, cultivating resilience is vital in navigating the inevitable ups and downs of any career path, especially one rooted in the uncertainties of remote work environments. Embrace challenges as learning opportunities rather than obstacles; maintaining a growth mindset will encourage perseverance amid setbacks.

Finally, seek out communities that align with your professional goals—whether they're industry-specific groups on social media or local meetups transitioning online due to global events. Engaging with these networks provides not only support but also avenues for collaboration that could lead to exciting new projects or job opportunities.

Building a sustainable remote career requires intentionality across various facets—from workspace setup to networking practices—and a steadfast commitment to personal growth amid changing circumstances. By prioritizing self-discipline, nurturing relationships, embracing continuous learning, maintaining adaptability, balancing personal boundaries, utilizing effective collaboration tools, fostering resilience, and engaging with communities aligned with your aspirations, you position yourself for enduring success in this new era of work. As the landscape continues to evolve, those who adapt will thrive not just professionally but personally as well.

Legal Considerations in the Gig Economy

The gig economy provides unparalleled flexibility, enabling individuals to select projects that resonate with their skills and interests. However, this independence also introduces a range of legal considerations that can profoundly affect gig workers. To thrive in this evolving landscape, it's essential to understand these legal intricacies, as missteps can lead to unexpected liabilities or loss of income.

One of the first things to grasp is the classification of workers in the gig economy: are you considered an independent contractor or an employee? This distinction is critical, influencing everything from tax obligations to eligibility for benefits. Independent contractors, for example, are responsible for their own taxes and typically do not receive employer-sponsored health insurance or retirement plans. In states like California, legislation such as Assembly Bill 5 (AB5) aims to classify many gig workers as employees, providing them with enhanced protections but also imposing additional costs on employers.

Navigating tax implications is another crucial aspect. Gig workers generally receive a Form 1099 from their clients rather than the standard W-2 form issued to traditional employees. So, you must calculate and pay your own taxes, including self-employment tax for Social Security and Medicare contributions. Maintaining meticulous records of income and expenses is vital in this context; using accounting software like QuickBooks or platforms like FreshBooks can simplify tracking your earnings and expenditures.

Intellectual property rights are also a significant consideration for freelancers and gig workers. When you create a product or service for a client, ownership questions can arise. Unless explicitly stated in a contract, you may retain rights to your work, while clients might seek exclusive ownership. Clear contracts that outline ownership can help prevent disputes later on. Take this example, consider including clauses that specify whether the client owns the final deliverable upon payment or if you retain rights for portfolio use.

Liability issues cannot be overlooked either. Depending on the nature of your work, you may face various legal risks. Many freelancers operate without liability insurance, which can leave them exposed to disputes or lawsuits over alleged negligence or unsatisfactory work. Investing in professional liability insurance can provide protection against claims that could otherwise threaten your financial stability.

Additionally, regulatory compliance is essential in industries that engage gig workers. For example, those working in healthcare or finance must adhere to specific regulations governing their fields, even as freelancers. Familiarizing yourself with these requirements ensures compliance and builds trust with clients who expect adherence to industry standards.

Creating robust contracts can mitigate many of the legal challenges associated with the gig economy. These contracts should clearly define the scope of work, payment terms, deadlines, and dispute resolution processes. Utilizing templates from legal resources like Rocket Lawyer or LegalZoom can streamline this process while ensuring all critical elements are included.

Engaging with local gig worker associations or unions can offer further support and resources. These organizations often advocate for better working conditions and fair compensation while providing educational workshops on legal rights and responsibilities. Networking within these communities can enhance your understanding of emerging regulations and connect you with others facing similar challenges.

In summary, navigating the legal landscape of the gig economy requires vigilance and proactive measures. From understanding worker classification to securing appropriate insurance coverage and crafting comprehensive contracts, each step plays a vital role in protecting your professional journey within this dynamic environment. While the complexities may seem daunting at first glance, equipping yourself with knowledge and resources empowers you to navigate potential pitfalls effectively while maximizing the opportunities this new economy has to offer.

Balancing Gig Work and Traditional Employment

The rise of the gig economy has fundamentally changed how many professionals engage with work, offering both remarkable flexibility and distinct challenges. For those navigating a blend of gig work and traditional employment, the stakes can be even higher. Successfully striking this balance requires a thoughtful approach that weighs the opportunities presented by gig roles against the stability provided by conventional jobs.

One of the primary advantages of gig work is the ability to diversify income streams. Freelancers can take on multiple clients and projects, creating a financial safety net in times of economic uncertainty. This strategy not only shields against potential downturns but also allows for a more personalized work experience. For example, a graphic designer might manage freelance projects while holding a part-time position at an agency. This arrangement enables them to pursue creative ventures aligned with their personal interests while still enjoying the security of regular paychecks.

However, effective time management becomes crucial when balancing these different types of employment. Competing deadlines and priorities can easily lead to overwhelm. To maintain productivity, it is essential to create a structured schedule that designates specific time blocks for both gig work and traditional responsibilities. Utilizing tools like Google Calendar or project management software such as Trello can help keep tasks organized and ensure that each obligation receives the attention it deserves.

Financial management also plays a pivotal role in successfully navigating dual employment pathways. Freelancers must handle their own taxes while potentially contributing to retirement savings through employer-sponsored plans in their traditional jobs. Financial tools such as Mint or YNAB (You Need A Budget) can assist in tracking income from various sources and forecasting expenses, promoting not just survival but thriving—allowing individuals to set aside funds for emergencies or future investments.

Effective communication is equally important when engaging in both arenas. Being transparent with employers about freelance commitments fosters trust and understanding regarding potential scheduling conflicts. Take this example, if you need to attend an important meeting at your primary job while also facing a tight deadline for a freelance project, discussing these conflicts openly can lead to more flexible arrangements that benefit both parties.

Networking is critical in this multifaceted career landscape as well. Professionals who successfully balance gig and traditional work often discover that connections made through one avenue can lead to opportunities in another. Attending industry events or participating in online communities related to your freelance work can result in referrals and collaborations that enhance both streams of income.

And, it's important not to underestimate the psychological impact of juggling different roles. While flexibility is appealing, it can sometimes lead to feelings of instability or burnout due to constant pressure to perform across various settings. Prioritizing self-care and establishing boundaries around work hours are vital for maintaining mental well-being. Techniques such as mindfulness meditation or regular physical exercise can help mitigate stress levels, fostering resilience amidst competing demands.

Finally, understanding the implications of benefits is crucial for those engaged in both gig work and traditional employment. Traditional jobs typically come with health insurance, retirement contributions, and other perks that are often absent in gig roles. Workers should seek alternative options for health coverage—whether through state exchanges or private insurance plans—to ensure comprehensive protection without the backing of an employer.

By integrating these considerations into your strategy for balancing gig work and traditional employment, you enhance your resilience and adaptability in an ever-changing job landscape. Focusing on organization, effective communication, networking, self-care, and sound financial planning creates a sustainable model that not only secures your current professional standing but also positions you for future success as market demands evolve.

CHAPTER 6:
INNOVATIONS
IN EDUCATION
AND TRAINING

The Role of AI in Education

T he integration of artificial intelligence (AI) into education signifies a transformative shift in how knowledge is imparted, absorbed, and applied. From elementary classrooms to university lecture halls, AI technologies are reshaping traditional pedagogical methods, tailoring educational experiences to accommodate diverse learning needs. This evolution offers immense potential for enhancing learning outcomes and fostering lifelong skills among students.

Essentially of this transformation is personalized learning. AI can analyze individual student performance data to adapt educational content accordingly. For example, platforms like DreamBox Learning and Knewton utilize algorithms that assess student progress in real time, adjusting difficulty levels and recommending resources based on specific learning styles and paces. A high school student struggling with algebra might receive tailored practice problems that address their weak points, while an advanced learner could tackle more complex equations. This customized approach not only keeps students engaged but also encourages mastery of subjects at their own pace.

The benefits of AI in education extend beyond personalized content delivery; they also enhance administrative efficiencies. Educators often spend significant time grading assignments and managing classroom logistics. Tools like Gradescope use AI to streamline grading processes, freeing teachers to focus on teaching rather than administrative tasks. By automating repetitive functions, educators can devote more energy to developing lesson plans that stimulate critical thinking and creativity among students.

And, AI-powered tools promote interactive learning experiences that encourage collaboration among peers. Platforms such as Socratic allow students to pose questions and receive instant explanations or resources from a vast database of information. This engagement fosters independent inquiry and cultivates a collaborative environment where students learn from one another, deepening their understanding through dialogue and shared perspectives.

Despite these substantial benefits, the implementation of AI in education presents challenges. One major concern is ensuring equitable access to technology. Students in underfunded schools may lack the necessary devices or high-speed internet connections, exacerbating existing educational disparities. As schools increasingly adopt AI-driven tools, it is crucial for policymakers to address these gaps by providing funding and resources that ensure all students can fully participate in this new educational landscape.

Additionally, the ethical implications of utilizing AI in

educational settings require careful consideration. Data privacy issues are paramount as schools collect and analyze student information for performance insights. Robust policies must be established to protect sensitive data while maintaining transparency about how AI technologies are utilized in the classroom. Engaging parents and guardians in these discussions fosters trust and ensures families understand the role of technology in their children's education.

Ongoing professional development for educators is essential to navigate this evolving landscape effectively. Training programs focused on integrating AI tools into curricula equip teachers with the necessary skills to leverage technology successfully. Workshops offering hands-on experience with AI-based platforms empower educators to enhance their teaching methods while fostering an innovative classroom culture.

Looking ahead, the role of AI in education is likely to expand further, driven by advancements in machine learning and data analytics. The combination of virtual reality (VR) with AI holds particular promise; envision immersive simulations where students can explore historical events or conduct scientific experiments within environments designed by intelligent systems tailored specifically for their educational needs.

embracing AI's role in education presents opportunities for individualized learning experiences as well as a holistic shift toward more effective teaching methodologies. By blending traditional approaches with cutting-edge technology, educators can prepare students not only to excel academically but also to become adaptable problem-solvers ready for the demands of an ever-changing world. To harness these transformative changes effectively, it is vital that all stakeholders—educators, administrators, and policymakers—collaborate toward establishing inclusive practices that benefit every learner in our society.

Personalized Learning Experiences

Personalized learning experiences are transforming the educational landscape, enabling opportunities that were once considered unattainable. With artificial intelligence as a driving force behind this shift, both educators and students are beginning to appreciate the significant benefits of tailored educational approaches. Unlike the traditional one-size-fits-all model, personalized learning recognizes the individuality of each student's abilities, interests, and pace of learning.

AI technologies play a crucial role by analyzing the vast amounts of data generated from students' interactions with learning materials. For example, platforms like Smart Sparrow employ adaptive learning technology that responds to individual performance in real time. When a student struggles with a specific concept, the platform provides immediate support through supplementary resources or alternative explanations. This feedback loop not only aids in comprehension but also alleviates feelings of confusion and frustration. By prioritizing personalized instruction, AI creates an environment where learners can flourish according to their unique needs.

The importance of data extends beyond academic performance; it also encompasses socio-emotional factors that influence how students learn. Tools like Classcraft gamify education by integrating social-emotional learning into their platforms, allowing educators to tailor interventions based on students' emotional states observed during interactions. Take this example, if a student shows signs of disengagement, teachers can implement strategies such as collaborative group work or interactive projects, fostering a sense of belonging and community within the classroom.

Personalized learning is not limited to K-12 education; it also extends into vocational and higher education, where adult learners seek specific skills relevant to their careers. Online platforms like Coursera and edX offer courses designed for skill acquisition aligned with industry demands rather than just general knowledge. By using algorithms to assess users' career aspirations and current competencies, these platforms can recommend tailored courses that enhance employability in real time. This adaptive approach empowers adult learners to engage in continuous education tailored specifically to their professional growth.

Despite these advantages, challenges persist in ensuring equitable access to personalized learning experiences powered by AI. Disparities in technology access can create significant barriers for students in under-resourced areas who may lack reliable internet connections or modern devices necessary for engaging with advanced educational tools. Addressing these inequalities is crucial; strategies such as government-funded initiatives or partnerships between tech companies and schools can help bridge this gap, ensuring all students benefit from AI-enhanced learning environments.

Additionally, ethical considerations surrounding data usage in personalized learning systems must be addressed. As educational institutions collect sensitive information about students' behaviors and performance metrics, protecting this data from breaches becomes essential. Establishing transparent policies regarding data privacy not only safeguards students but also builds trust among parents and guardians concerned about how their children's information is utilized.

Training educators to effectively integrate AI-driven personalized learning tools into their teaching practices is vital for maximizing their potential benefits. Professional development programs focused on technology literacy can empower teachers to adopt new pedagogical methods confidently while fostering an innovative atmosphere in classrooms. Take this example, workshops that provide hands-on experience with AI-based instructional tools enable educators to leverage technology creatively and enhance student engagement.

Looking ahead, as machine learning continues to advance, so too will the possibilities for personalized learning experiences. The integration of AI with immersive technologies like virtual reality (VR) presents exciting opportunities for experiential learning scenarios where students can engage deeply with complex subjects through tailored simulated environments.

The embrace of personalized learning experiences represents a significant shift in education—one that prepares students for not only academic success but also lifelong adaptability in a rapidly changing world. Engaging all stakeholders—educators, administrators, and policymakers—in collaborative efforts will be essential to ensure that these advancements serve every learner equitably and ethically as we progress toward an inclusive future powered by AI innovation.

Learning Platforms and Online Courses

Online learning platforms have become crucial in democratizing education and bridging gaps in skill acquisition, particularly in an era increasingly influenced by artificial intelligence. These platforms cater to a diverse range of learners, from those seeking foundational knowledge to professionals pursuing advanced skills tailored to industry needs. Platforms like Coursera, edX, and Udacity offer extensive course offerings, spanning subjects from computer science to creative arts, all while leveraging AI to enhance the learning experience.

For example, Coursera employs machine learning algorithms to analyze user behavior and engagement patterns. This data-driven approach allows the platform to recommend courses that align with individual interests and career aspirations. If a user demonstrates an interest in data science, the platform can suggest foundational courses in statistics or programming languages like Python, paving the way for more specialized topics such as machine learning or data visualization. This personalized strategy not only streamlines the educational journey but also keeps learners engaged and motivated.

In addition to traditional coursework, many online learning platforms are embracing micro-credentialing and certification programs. These bite-sized educational offerings enable learners to quickly acquire specific skills and showcase them through digital badges or certificates. Take this example, Google's Data Analytics Professional Certificate on Coursera provides practical training in data analysis using tools like Excel and SQL, all achievable within a few months. These programs are designed specifically for the fast-paced job market, offering flexible options for individuals who may lack the time or resources for a full degree.

A key feature of these platforms is their ability to provide feedback and assessment. By utilizing AI technologies such as natural language processing and automated grading systems, the evaluation process becomes more efficient. For example, edX incorporates formative assessments that deliver real-time feedback on quizzes and assignments. This immediate response allows learners to identify areas needing improvement without waiting for traditional grading cycles. If a student struggles with Python syntax in an introductory programming course, they receive instant suggestions for supplementary resources or practice exercises tailored to their specific challenges.

Despite these advancements, not all learners engage equally with online education due to various barriers, including financial constraints and limited access to technology. To address these disparities, many organizations are working towards enhancing accessibility through scholarships or subsidized courses aimed at underrepresented communities. Initiatives like Google's Grow with Google program strive to provide free resources and training specifically targeted at underserved populations, fostering equitable participation in digital economies.

Additionally, it is essential to consider the diversity of learners by integrating culturally relevant content into course offerings. Platforms can benefit from collaborating with local educators or industry experts who understand the unique challenges faced by different demographics. Such partnerships can lead to tailored content that resonates more deeply with learners from diverse backgrounds.

Looking ahead at the future of online learning platforms amidst AI advancements, fostering a sense of community among users is vital. Features such as forums, study groups, and live Q&A sessions create opportunities for peer interaction —an essential element often missing in online education that can boost motivation and accountability.

As AI technologies continue to evolve, they will further personalize educational experiences. Imagine future courses incorporating augmented reality (AR) components that allow students to visualize complex biological processes or historical events directly within their environment through smart devices. Such immersive experiences could transform traditional concept comprehension into engaging explorations.

Overall, online learning has shifted from merely providing access to information into sophisticated ecosystems designed for personalized growth—an evolution driven by technology yet heavily reliant on human connections and insights. As educators adapt their strategies and fully engage with these new tools, there is tremendous potential not only for individual success but also for cultivating inclusive educational environments that empower every learner to thrive amid rapid change.

Adapting Curricula to New Demands

Adapting curricula to meet the demands of an evolving job

market, particularly in the age of artificial intelligence, is essential for both educational institutions and learners. The rapid pace of technological change calls for a shift from traditional teaching methods to more dynamic and responsive educational frameworks. This adaptability not only helps students acquire foundational knowledge but also equips them with the skills necessary to navigate a workforce increasingly influenced by AI technologies.

A key element of curriculum adaptation is the incorporation of interdisciplinary approaches. As AI continues to permeate various sectors, it becomes crucial for learners to understand how their field interacts with technology. Take this example, a marketing student should not only grasp traditional principles but also become familiar with data analytics and machine learning applications in consumer behavior analysis. By integrating courses that focus on digital marketing strategies alongside data interpretation, educational institutions can create a more robust learning experience that prepares students for the multifaceted nature of modern careers.

Collaboration between educators and industry leaders is another vital aspect of shaping relevant curricula. By partnering with companies, educational institutions can identify specific skill gaps and emerging trends within their fields. These partnerships often lead to co-designing efforts where real-world challenges inform course content. For example, an engineering program might collaborate with tech firms to develop modules on AI ethics or robotics design, ensuring that graduates are not only technically proficient but also aware of the broader implications of their work.

In addition to collaboration, feedback mechanisms play a critical role in refining educational offerings. Continuous assessment and adjustment based on learner outcomes allow institutions to remain agile in their teaching strategies. If data reveals that students struggle with certain concepts in coding classes, instructors can adapt by introducing supplementary workshops or revising the material's complexity. Tools like Learning Management Systems (LMS) enable educators to track progress effectively and make informed decisions about necessary curriculum changes.

Project-based learning further enhances adaptability by immersing students in real-world scenarios where they can apply their skills practically. Students can collaborate on projects addressing current industry challenges influenced by AI—such as developing an app that utilizes machine learning algorithms to optimize supply chain management. These hands-on experiences bridge the gap between theoretical knowledge and practical application, fostering deeper engagement and understanding.

Embracing technology-enhanced learning environments is another strategy that allows for flexible and personalized education pathways. Adaptive learning technologies can tailor content delivery based on individual performance and preferences. Platforms like Smart Sparrow provide insights into how students interact with course materials, enabling educators to adjust instructional methods dynamically. If a student excels in certain topics but struggles in others, the system can recommend targeted resources or alternative explanations suited to their learning style.

And, prioritizing the development of soft skills is paramount, as these competencies are increasingly sought alongside technical expertise. Curricula must include training in communication, teamwork, problem-solving, and emotional intelligence—skills that machines cannot easily replicate but are essential for successful human collaboration in AI-enhanced environments.

Inclusivity should also guide curriculum adaptation. Recognizing the diverse backgrounds and needs of learners fosters an environment where all students feel valued and engaged. Culturally relevant pedagogy ensures that course materials reflect various perspectives and experiences while addressing historical inequities in educational access.

Looking ahead, the landscape of education will likely continue evolving, driven by technological advancements like AI's capacity for data analysis and predictive modeling. So, curricula must undergo regular updates—not only reacting to changes but also anticipating future needs based on workforce trends and societal shifts.

In summary, adapting curricula requires an innovative mindset that embraces collaboration between educators and industry experts while leveraging technology to create personalized learning experiences tailored to individual needs. By focusing on both the technical skills pertinent to specific fields and nurturing critical soft skills within inclusive frameworks, educational institutions can prepare learners for success amid the ongoing changes brought about by artificial intelligence—ensuring they thrive rather than merely survive in tomorrow's job economy.

Bootcamps and Coding Schools

The emergence of bootcamps and coding schools marks a significant transformation in how people approach learning in today's fast-paced job market. Unlike traditional educational pathways, which often require lengthy degree programs, these alternatives provide focused, intensive training that equips participants with the specific skills needed for immediate employment. As technology evolves—particularly in the realm of artificial intelligence—the need for quick and applicable knowledge becomes increasingly urgent.

Bootcamps aim to address gaps in the job market by offering practical training in high-demand fields such as software development, data science, and cybersecurity. Take this example, a coding bootcamp might specialize in full-stack web development, where students master both front-end and back-end programming languages within just a few months. This intensive curriculum typically includes real-world projects that replicate workplace scenarios, allowing participants to gain hands-on experience while enhancing their portfolios— an essential asset for attracting potential employers.

The flexible structure of bootcamps further broadens their appeal. Many programs offer part-time schedules or online formats that cater to working professionals or those managing multiple commitments. This adaptability enables individuals from various backgrounds to reskill or upskill without major disruptions to their lives. Consider Sarah, who spent several years in marketing before deciding to pivot into tech. By enrolling in an online data analytics bootcamp, she was able to learn at her own pace while still fulfilling her job responsibilities.

A key strength of bootcamps is their focus on community and networking opportunities. Many programs create environments where students can collaborate on projects and share insights with peers who share similar career goals. These interactions often lead to valuable industry connections— relationships that can be crucial when entering the job market. Additionally, many bootcamps maintain partnerships with tech companies and actively assist in job placements for their graduates.

However, selecting the right bootcamp requires careful consideration. Prospective students should assess factors such as the relevance of the curriculum and the expertise of instructors. Researching alumni outcomes can also shed light on how effective a program is at helping graduates secure jobs. Websites like Course Report and SwitchUp offer reviews and success stories from former students, empowering learners to make informed decisions based on real experiences.

Another noteworthy trend is the growing recognition of bootcamp certifications by employers. As these programs gain popularity and credibility within the tech industry, companies increasingly prioritize practical skills over traditional degrees alone. Hiring managers are starting to recognize that candidates with rigorous bootcamp training often possess not only technical abilities but also critical soft skills like problem-solving and adaptability—traits essential for thriving in fast-paced environments shaped by AI technologies.

And, coding schools extend beyond programming; they encompass various disciplines related to technology integration, such as user experience (UX) design and digital marketing focused on AI applications. Students interested in UX design might explore coursework that covers human-computer interaction principles alongside hands-on projects aimed at enhancing usability through AI-driven solutions.

Looking ahead, it's clear that ongoing support for graduates is vital for long-term success. Many bootcamps provide post-program resources like mentorship opportunities or career coaching sessions designed to help alumni navigate their next steps effectively. Accessing these resources can be invaluable for recent graduates who may feel overwhelmed as they transition into new roles within unfamiliar fields.

In summary, bootcamps and coding schools represent an innovative response to current workforce demands by offering targeted skill development through immersive learning experiences while fostering community connections among participants. These elements are crucial for adapting to an economy increasingly influenced by artificial intelligence technologies. By wisely leveraging these educational avenues —whether seeking immediate employment or pursuing career advancement—individuals can position themselves advantageously within this evolving landscape rich with opportunities waiting to be explored.

Corporate Training Programs

As technology advances at an unprecedented pace, corporate training programs have become essential in equipping the workforce with the skills needed to thrive in an increasingly AI-driven job market. Unlike traditional educational models, which often emphasize theoretical knowledge over long periods, corporate training prioritizes practical and relevant learning tailored to meet specific organizational needs. This shift reflects the growing demand for agility and adaptability in professional skill sets as automation and AI redefine roles across various industries.

One of the most notable aspects of corporate training programs is their ability to seamlessly integrate emerging technologies into the curriculum. Many organizations now offer courses that delve into machine learning applications pertinent to their fields. Take this example, a financial institution might introduce a module on predictive analytics using AI tools, enabling employees to leverage data for improved decision-making. These initiatives not only enhance individual competencies but also drive organizational efficiency by fostering a culture of continuous improvement.

Take, for example, a global manufacturing firm that has recognized the need for its workforce to adapt to automated processes. By investing in comprehensive training focused on robotics and AI system management, this company empowers its employees to operate effectively alongside advanced machinery. The outcome is a skilled workforce that navigates technology-enhanced environments with confidence, ultimately reducing resistance to change.

Additionally, collaboration between companies and educational institutions has become increasingly prevalent. Organizations partner with universities and training centers to co-create programs designed to address specific skill gaps identified within their operations. This collaborative approach ensures that training content remains relevant and practical. Take this example, a healthcare provider might team up with a local university to develop a program centered on AI-driven patient care solutions, enhancing staff capabilities while improving overall service delivery.

A hallmark of effective corporate training programs is their emphasis on soft skills alongside technical expertise. Employers recognize that success in an AI-enhanced workplace requires more than just hard skills; it demands adaptability, critical thinking, and emotional intelligence. Workshops focused on leadership development and team collaboration have become integral components of many corporate curricula, helping employees cultivate the interpersonal skills necessary for effective teamwork in diverse and technologically sophisticated environments.

The accessibility of corporate training has also transformed significantly. Online platforms and hybrid models enable employees to engage with learning materials flexibly while balancing work commitments. Companies like Coursera and LinkedIn Learning have established partnerships with organizations to deliver tailored courses that align closely with business objectives. This flexibility not only boosts participation rates but also fosters a culture of lifelong learning—an essential component for thriving in an unpredictable job market.

Evaluating the effectiveness of corporate training programs goes beyond assessing immediate outcomes; it necessitates ongoing feedback mechanisms and adjustments based on real-world performance metrics. Many organizations conduct regular assessments to measure skill acquisition and improvements in job performance following training initiatives. For example, after implementing a new program on data analysis using AI tools, a company might track how well participants apply these skills by analyzing project outcomes over several months.

And, companies are increasingly recognizing the importance of aligning their training strategies with employee career aspirations. By offering personalized development paths that connect training opportunities with potential career advancements within the organization, businesses can enhance employee engagement and retention rates. An employee who perceives clear connections between their growth opportunities and the organization's goals is more likely to invest fully in their professional development.

As we look ahead to the future of work shaped by AI advancements, corporate training will play an indispensable role in preparing employees for evolving job landscapes. Organizations that prioritize ongoing education—whether through internal programs or external partnerships—will be better positioned to adapt swiftly as industry demands shift under technological pressures.

In summary, corporate training programs serve as vital conduits for bridging skill gaps within today's workforce while promoting adaptability amid rapid changes brought about by artificial intelligence integration. By continuously evolving these educational initiatives, companies can cultivate an empowered workforce ready not just to face change but to thrive within it—ultimately enhancing both individual careers and organizational success in an ever-evolving job economy.

The Rise of Certifications

In today's fast-paced work environment, certifications have become essential credentials that validate skills and competencies in a competitive job market. As artificial intelligence (AI) continues to transform industries, the demand for formal recognition of expertise is growing rapidly. These certifications not only attest to individual capabilities but also provide a strategic edge in a job economy that increasingly values demonstrable skills over traditional degrees.

Several factors contribute to the rise of certifications. One significant aspect is the swift pace of technological change, which often leaves traditional educational pathways lagging behind current industry demands. Degree programs typically take years to develop and implement, whereas certification courses can be created and updated in response to emerging trends and technologies within months. This agility ensures that professionals acquire relevant knowledge and skills without unnecessary delays.

Take cloud computing as an example; its prominence has surged with the ongoing digital transformation across various sectors. Certifications from providers like Amazon Web Services (AWS) or Microsoft Azure have become highly desirable for employers seeking candidates who can effectively manage cloud-based systems. Those who earn these certifications demonstrate their readiness to engage with vital technologies—an attribute that employers increasingly prioritize when evaluating potential hires.

Also, certifications offer a practical way for individuals to distinguish themselves in a crowded job market. With many professionals possessing similar educational backgrounds, specialized credentials provide a means to stand out. Take this example, a marketing professional who earns certification in AI-driven analytics not only highlights their commitment to continuous learning but also signals their ability to leverage AI tools effectively in marketing strategies. This differentiation can lead to improved job prospects and career advancement opportunities.

The rise of online learning platforms has made obtaining certifications more accessible than ever. Websites like Coursera, edX, and Udacity offer a diverse range of courses tailored to various industries and skill levels. Many of these platforms collaborate with leading universities and industry experts, delivering high-quality content that culminates in recognized certifications upon completion. This democratization of education enables individuals from diverse backgrounds to gain valuable knowledge without the barriers often associated with traditional learning environments.

In addition to technical skills, soft skills are increasingly integrated into certification programs. Recognizing that success in modern workplaces requires more than just technical expertise, many programs now include modules on communication, leadership, and teamwork. For example, a project management certification may emphasize agile methodologies alongside interpersonal communication techniques crucial for leading cross-functional teams effectively.

Real-world application is another key factor driving the appeal of certifications. Many programs now feature hands-on projects or case studies that require learners to apply their knowledge in practical scenarios. This experiential learning approach not only solidifies understanding but also builds confidence in applying new skills directly within workplace settings—an aspect highly valued by employers looking for candidates who can hit the ground running.

The impact of certifications extends beyond individual achievement; organizations also benefit from having certified employees who bring enhanced capabilities to their teams. Companies often invest in employee certification programs because they recognize the return on investment associated with increased productivity and efficiency stemming from well-trained staff members.

As professionals navigate this evolving landscape dominated by AI-driven transformations, staying informed about which certifications will be most valuable in their fields is essential. Researching industry trends can illuminate the skills most sought after by employers and guide decisions about where to invest time and resources for certification training.

The significance of ongoing education through certifications cannot be overstated in adapting to a job economy reshaped by technological advancements. Professionals committed to lifelong learning will not only enhance their own career trajectories but also contribute positively to their organizations' adaptability and resilience against disruption.

As we move forward into this new era defined by rapid innovation, embracing certification opportunities offers a tangible pathway to not just survive but thrive amid change. It equips individuals with the knowledge and credentials necessary for success in an AI-driven world while addressing the evolving demands of the workforce.

Collaborative Learning Environments

The modern job market is increasingly complex, making it essential to prioritize collaborative learning environments that encourage innovation and adaptability. In this rapidly evolving landscape, collaboration is no longer optional; it is a crucial element of professional development. As organizations integrate AI into their operations, they are reimagining traditional learning models to create spaces where knowledge sharing and teamwork drive collective progress.

These collaborative environments empower individuals to learn from one another, leveraging diverse perspectives and skills. Take this example, a tech company may form cross-functional teams comprised of software developers, data scientists, and marketing specialists to tackle AI projects. Each team member brings unique insights to the table, resulting in more comprehensive solutions than any one individual could achieve alone. This blending of expertise not only accelerates problem-solving but also nurtures a culture of continuous improvement.

A notable example of effective collaboration is Google's Project Aristotle, which explored the dynamics of high-performing teams. The study found that psychological safety —where individuals feel they won't be penalized or humiliated for voicing their thoughts—was critical for enhancing team performance. When employees feel secure enough to share their ideas or concerns, creativity flourishes, leading to innovative solutions that are vital in an AI-driven economy. Cultivating such openness in collaborative learning environments can significantly boost both team effectiveness and morale.

Technology plays a vital role in facilitating collaborative learning. Digital platforms like Slack and Microsoft Teams have transformed professional interactions and knowledge sharing. These tools enable real-time communication and provide organized spaces for storing resources and maintaining discussions on projects. For example, a finance team can collaboratively develop machine learning models to predict market trends by effectively sharing data sets, insights from analytics, and feedback.

Additionally, organizations are increasingly utilizing virtual reality (VR) and augmented reality (AR) technologies to create immersive learning experiences. Take a manufacturing company training its employees on AI-driven robotic systems; VR can simulate the operational environment, allowing employees to practice troubleshooting without real-world risks. Such immersive experiences not only enhance retention but also help learners build confidence before applying new skills in their roles.

Collaborative learning opportunities are further enriched through partnerships with educational institutions. Companies can collaborate with universities to design curricula that reflect current industry demands, incorporating projects that challenge students to solve real business problems using AI tools. This collaboration not only prepares students for the workforce but also provides companies with fresh insights from the next generation of professionals.

Mentorship programs within these environments further amplify the benefits of collaboration. By pairing experienced employees with newer team members, organizations facilitate knowledge transfer and foster relationships that support career growth. Take this example, a senior data analyst mentoring a junior analyst on AI project methodologies not only solidifies best practices but also empowers the junior analyst to contribute meaningfully.

To create effective collaborative learning environments, leadership must be intentional in their approach. Companies should invest in training managers to cultivate teamwork and encourage participation at all levels of the organization. This could involve workshops on facilitating discussions or strategies for recognizing individual contributions within group settings.

And, leaders should prioritize diversity when forming teams for collaborative projects. Diverse teams bring varied perspectives that challenge assumptions and lead to more comprehensive problem-solving strategies. For example, including individuals from different cultural backgrounds can enrich discussions around the ethical implications of AI applications—an increasingly critical consideration as technology permeates every aspect of society.

fostering a culture of collaboration enhances organizational agility as companies adapt to technological advancements like AI. Professionals who actively engage in these environments not only enhance their skills but also build resilience against disruption by learning how to navigate challenges together.

By embracing collaborative learning environments, individuals position themselves at the forefront of innovation while building supportive networks rich in shared knowledge. As we move into an era where artificial intelligence influences every sector, those who thrive will be those who harness the power of collective intelligence—transforming challenges into opportunities through collaboration and mutual understanding.

Measuring and Validating Skills

In today's fast-evolving landscape of skill development, effectively measuring and validating competencies is crucial for individuals and organizations alike. As artificial intelligence becomes increasingly integrated into various sectors, traditional assessment methods are proving inadequate. This shift prompts a move toward more dynamic approaches that align with real-world applications and the changing nature of work.

Measuring skills transcends mere knowledge evaluation; it requires an assessment of how individuals apply that knowledge in practical scenarios. Take this example, a software developer's proficiency in a programming language should be evaluated not just through standardized tests but also by their ability to tackle complex problems in real coding projects. This transition from rote memorization to practical application fosters deeper learning and equips professionals to navigate challenges in an AI-driven environment.

Project-based assessments are one effective method for validating skills. These assessments enable individuals to demonstrate their capabilities in relevant contexts, rather than relying solely on theoretical questions. For example, an aspiring data analyst might engage in a capstone project where they analyze actual data sets and present their findings to stakeholders. Such experiences not only showcase technical skills but also highlight essential soft skills like communication and teamwork—qualities that are increasingly vital in collaborative environments.

Peer assessments also serve as a powerful tool for skill validation. In these scenarios, colleagues evaluate each other's work using predefined criteria, offering constructive feedback that reveals areas for improvement. This reciprocal learning process enhances team dynamics and fosters a comprehensive understanding of each member's strengths and weaknesses. In projects involving AI technologies, peer evaluations can identify individuals who excel in specific tasks, such as coding, data analysis, or user experience design, thereby facilitating more effective allocation of responsibilities.

And, organizations are harnessing technology to streamline the measurement and validation processes. Platforms like Coursera and LinkedIn Learning provide courses with integrated assessments that offer immediate feedback on progress. For example, after completing a module on machine learning, participants can take a quiz designed to assess their grasp of key concepts while reinforcing their learning. Digital badges or certificates upon completion act as tangible indicators of skill acquisition, adding credibility to professional profiles.

However, validation must also consider the relevance of skills in relation to industry demands. Collaborating with industry leaders can help educational institutions refine curricula to incorporate current technologies and methodologies used by organizations today. By aligning education with real-world needs, graduates emerge not only knowledgeable but also equipped with the skills that employers actively seek.

The importance of ongoing assessment cannot be overstated; continuous feedback loops are essential for tracking skill progression over time. Companies should adopt performance metrics tied to individual growth objectives instead of relying solely on annual reviews. Regular check-ins allow managers to discuss employees' successes and challenges throughout the year, enabling timely support when needed.

In addition to internal measures, external benchmarks such as industry certifications offer valuable insights into skill levels compared to peers within a field. These certifications signal proficiency recognized by employers globally, validating an individual's capabilities without ambiguity.

As we look toward a future shaped by AI advancements, adopting multifaceted approaches to measuring and validating skills will empower professionals at all levels. Individuals can chart their own learning paths while organizations ensure they cultivate talent capable of adapting swiftly as job requirements evolve.

embracing rigorous skill validation processes enhances workforce capability and fosters resilience against market fluctuations driven by technological change—preparing both employees and companies for sustained success amid uncertainty.

CHAPTER 7:
ENTREPRENEURSHIP
IN THE AI ERA

Identifying AI-Driven
Business Opportunities

I dentifying AI-driven business opportunities requires a nuanced understanding of emerging technologies and market dynamics. The success of any venture often hinges on recognizing gaps in the market where AI can add value, streamline operations, or create new revenue streams. This endeavor is both an art and a science, demanding a blend of analytical thinking and creative problem-solving.

To begin, examine existing processes within industries that are primed for disruption. Take the retail sector, for example; it has undergone significant transformations through AI applications, including personalized shopping experiences powered by machine learning algorithms. Companies like Amazon analyze customer behavior to tailor recommendations, enhancing user satisfaction while effectively driving sales. Entrepreneurs should reflect on the question: Which processes within my industry could benefit from similar insights?

Next, leverage data analytics to uncover hidden trends and opportunities. Data is an invaluable asset in the AI landscape, and businesses that harness its power can gain a competitive edge. Take this example, predictive analytics enables companies to forecast demand accurately, leading to better inventory management and targeted marketing strategies. Tools like Google Analytics or Tableau can help visualize data patterns, allowing entrepreneurs to pinpoint which products are gaining traction and which demographics remain underserved.

Networking with industry experts can also be a powerful way to uncover potential opportunities. Engaging with thought leaders may reveal insights not immediately apparent through research alone. Attending conferences or webinars focused on AI developments fosters knowledge exchange and collaboration. For example, participating in events centered around AI in healthcare might inspire innovations in patient management systems that enhance operational efficiency and improve care quality.

Additionally, aligning identified opportunities with ethical considerations surrounding AI deployment is crucial. In sectors such as finance and hiring, improper use of AI can lead to bias or privacy concerns that could damage a brand's reputation. Establishing ethical practices not only builds customer trust but also distinguishes a business from competitors who may overlook these important principles.

Prototyping and testing ideas rapidly can yield immediate feedback on their market viability. The lean startup methodology emphasizes creating minimum viable products (MVPs) to assess interest without substantial upfront investment. Take this example, a startup developing an AI tool for remote team collaboration might initially release a basic version that allows teams to communicate via voice commands. Gathering user feedback during this phase facilitates iterative improvements based on real-world usage.

Incorporating cross-disciplinary insights further enriches the opportunity identification process by blending knowledge from diverse fields. A tech entrepreneur collaborating with healthcare professionals could generate innovative solutions that address both operational efficiencies and patient engagement strategies—this approach fosters creativity by breaking traditional silos.

Finally, staying informed about technological advancements is essential for remaining relevant in an ever-evolving landscape. Subscribing to industry publications or following influential thought leaders on platforms like LinkedIn provides access to ongoing developments in AI technology and its applications across various sectors.

In summary, identifying AI-driven business opportunities involves a comprehensive approach: analyzing industry processes for inefficiencies, leveraging data analytics to identify trends, engaging with experts for innovative ideas, ensuring ethical practices guide implementation, utilizing rapid prototyping techniques for hypothesis testing, fostering cross-disciplinary collaborations for broader perspectives, and keeping abreast of evolving technologies. Each of these strategies equips entrepreneurs to navigate the complexities of an AI-driven economy while maximizing their potential for success in this dynamic environment.

Lean Startup Methodologies

Exploring Lean Startup methodologies offers entrepreneurs a powerful framework for rapidly testing and validating their business ideas within the dynamic AI landscape. This approach emphasizes flexibility and responsiveness, enabling entrepreneurs to take a proactive stance amidst uncertainty and rapid technological advancements. By embracing Lean principles, they can iteratively refine their concepts, reducing waste while maximizing learning—an essential strategy for successfully navigating the complexities of AI-driven ventures.

At the heart of the Lean Startup model lies the concept of the Minimum Viable Product (MVP). Rather than merely being a product with basic features, an MVP serves as a strategic tool aimed at extracting maximum validated learning from early users with minimal effort. For example, consider a startup developing an AI-based fitness app. Instead of pouring significant resources into full-scale development, they could first launch a simple prototype that tracks user workouts through basic data inputs. Feedback collected during this testing phase informs subsequent iterations, ensuring that feature development aligns closely with user needs.

The Build-Measure-Learn loop is integral to the iterative process that Lean methodologies promote. Startups should prioritize creating small increments of their product, measuring market performance, and learning from those results to guide future decisions. Each cycle yields critical data that facilitates adjustments in both product design and strategy. A prime example of this is Dropbox, which initially introduced a basic file-sharing capability but adapted significantly based on user feedback and behavior analysis over time.

In addition to refining product features, harnessing customer feedback plays a crucial role in validating assumptions and identifying areas for improvement. Tools such as surveys and A/B testing enable entrepreneurs to adjust their offerings based on real-time data. Take this example, if an entrepreneur rolls out an AI-driven customer service chatbot for a retail business, they might conduct A/B tests on different chatbot responses to determine which version yields higher customer satisfaction. This kind of real-world data is invaluable for shaping the final product.

Networking also holds significant importance within Lean methodologies. Engaging potential customers or industry stakeholders early helps establish trust and ensures alignment with market demands. Conducting interviews or focus groups can uncover customer pain points that theoretical market analyses might overlook. For example, a startup working on AI solutions for supply chain management could gain valuable insights by conversing with logistics managers facing everyday challenges—these discussions can reveal practical applications and essential features to prioritize.

Collaboration within interdisciplinary teams further enriches the ideation process. Diverse perspectives foster creativity and innovation by integrating various skill sets and viewpoints. In an AI startup focused on healthcare solutions, for instance, partnering with medical professionals ensures that technological implementations resonate with clinical realities, ultimately leading to more effective outcomes.

As businesses iterate through their MVPs, it's vital to establish clear success metrics during each testing phase. Key Performance Indicators (KPIs) related to user engagement, conversion rates, or operational efficiencies provide tangible measures of progress. If an AI application designed for remote collaboration experiences low engagement despite positive initial feedback, it becomes imperative to reassess user experience or functionality.

Finally, cultivating a culture of adaptability is crucial within any startup embracing Lean principles. Founders should create an environment where team members feel empowered to voice concerns or propose innovative ideas without fear of failure. This psychological safety fosters risk-taking and experimentation—qualities essential for thriving in an evolving technological landscape like AI.

By adopting Lean Startup methodologies, entrepreneurs arm themselves with practical strategies crucial for success in today's volatile markets shaped by rapid technological change. Through iterative design processes focused on real-time learning from users, fostering collaborative environments, and setting clear performance metrics, startups can not only navigate complexity but also position themselves advantageously against competitors rooted in traditional practices. In this era defined by innovation and adaptability, embracing these principles enables businesses to grow sustainably while maximizing value creation in an AI-driven economy.

Navigating AI Regulation and Compliance

Navigating the complex landscape of AI regulation and compliance is a significant challenge for both entrepreneurs and established businesses. As the AI sector continues to grow, the regulatory framework surrounding it is constantly evolving, requiring organizations to adopt a proactive approach. This means not only understanding current laws but also anticipating future developments to align business practices with regulatory expectations.

A solid foundation for effective navigation in this space begins with awareness of national and international regulations. Organizations must familiarize themselves with key frameworks, such as the General Data Protection Regulation (GDPR) in Europe, which governs data protection and privacy. Take this example, an AI company that uses consumer data to train its models must adhere to GDPR's stringent consent requirements. Noncompliance can lead to hefty fines and serious reputational damage. To facilitate adherence, businesses can implement data governance frameworks that promote transparent data handling while protecting user privacy.

Understanding industry-specific regulations is equally important, as they can vary significantly depending on the AI application. For example, healthcare AI solutions must comply with standards set by the Food and Drug Administration (FDA) in the U.S., which regulates medical devices, including software algorithms used in diagnostics and treatment plans. A relevant case study involves an AI system designed to assist radiologists; prior to deployment, developers had to undergo rigorous testing and validation processes mandated by the FDA to prove its safety and efficacy.

To enhance their adaptability, organizations should establish dedicated compliance teams responsible for monitoring regulatory changes. These teams should include legal experts well-versed in technology laws and compliance specialists who understand operational implications. Take this example, if new legislation emerges regarding algorithmic bias in hiring practices, this team would be essential in evaluating existing systems and ensuring they meet updated standards.

Collaboration with external stakeholders also plays a crucial role in navigating the shifting regulatory landscape. Engaging with industry associations or consortiums focused on AI can provide valuable insights into best practices and common challenges faced by peers. Participation in these networks allows organizations not only to stay informed about potential legislative changes but also to influence policymaking through collective advocacy efforts.

Implementing compliance measures practically involves structuring processes around AI development cycles. Organizations can integrate compliance checkpoints into their project management frameworks to assess adherence at various stages—from ideation through deployment—thereby identifying potential risks early on. For example, when developing an algorithm for predictive policing, conducting ethical assessments alongside technical evaluations ensures alignment with human rights considerations before launch.

Employee training is another essential component; staff must be equipped with knowledge about regulatory requirements relevant to their roles. Regular training sessions on topics such as data ethics and intellectual property rights foster a culture of responsibility, ensuring that every employee understands their role in maintaining compliance.

Finally, establishing robust feedback mechanisms allows companies to refine their compliance strategies continually based on real-world experiences. Insights gathered from audits or user reports can illuminate practical challenges encountered during regulation adherence and reveal opportunities for improvement.

By strategically approaching AI regulation and compliance —remaining vigilant about legislative changes, collaborating across industry sectors, structuring internal processes effectively, educating employees thoroughly, and creating responsive feedback mechanisms—businesses can position themselves not only as compliant entities but also as leaders in ethical innovation within the rapidly evolving world of artificial intelligence. In doing so, they contribute to an ecosystem where technology thrives under responsible stewardship while addressing societal concerns related to safety and fairness.

Financing AI Ventures

Securing financing for AI ventures is a complex process that demands a deep understanding of both the technological landscape and the financial mechanisms at play. Entrepreneurs often face the challenge of attracting investors who not only appreciate the innovative potential of their ideas but also grasp the unique risks associated with AI development. To navigate this landscape effectively, a comprehensive approach to financing is essential. This includes exploring various funding sources, understanding investor expectations, and crafting a compelling narrative that resonates with stakeholders.

Startups can access multiple funding avenues, each offering

distinct advantages. Bootstrapping remains a viable option for many entrepreneurs, particularly those with existing resources or robust personal networks. This self-funding approach enables founders to maintain full control over their vision without diluting equity prematurely. However, relying solely on personal funds can constrain growth potential. So, many entrepreneurs choose to blend bootstrapping with external financing options.

Angel investors and venture capitalists play crucial roles in the AI funding ecosystem. These individuals and firms actively seek high-growth potential in emerging technologies, often providing not only capital but also strategic guidance. For example, a tech startup developing an AI-powered analytics platform can attract venture capital by demonstrating how its unique algorithm outperforms traditional methods in deriving insights from vast datasets. Clearly articulating a market need, robust business model, and scalability potential is vital when pitching to these investors.

Understanding what investors prioritize in an AI venture can significantly enhance fundraising efforts. Investors typically look for teams with deep domain expertise, a clear go-to-market strategy, and a well-defined path toward profitability. A compelling business case includes detailed projections that illustrate how the technology will evolve alongside market trends. Take this example, an AI startup focused on healthcare solutions should present data showcasing how AI can reduce costs while improving patient outcomes, as this information resonates strongly with potential backers.

In addition to private investments, government grants and public funding initiatives offer another pathway for financing AI ventures. Many governments recognize the transformative potential of artificial intelligence for economic growth and societal benefits, leading to dedicated funding programs aimed at fostering innovation. Entrepreneurs should explore local and national initiatives designed to support research and development within technology sectors. Unlike private investments, this type of funding often comes with fewer strings attached, allowing greater flexibility in executing long-term projects.

Crowdfunding has also gained traction as a popular method for financing AI ventures. Platforms like Kickstarter and Indiegogo enable startups to present their ideas directly to potential consumers, generating interest and securing funds from those who believe in their mission. Successful crowdfunding campaigns typically convey a strong narrative around the product's benefits while showcasing prototypes or beta versions that demonstrate feasibility.

Equity crowdfunding further democratizes access to investment by allowing small contributions from numerous backers instead of relying solely on large institutional investors. This approach not only provides financial backing but also cultivates an engaged community around the product —creating potential customers who feel invested in its success.

Once funding is secured, effective financial management becomes crucial for sustaining growth in an AI venture. Startups should establish robust financial planning processes that incorporate projections based on various scenarios —ranging from optimistic growth trajectories to more conservative estimates—enabling them to pivot as necessary while maintaining financial health.

Monitoring cash flow is essential; understanding when expenses may outpace income allows for informed planning. Implementing sound budgeting practices helps allocate resources efficiently while avoiding common pitfalls such as overspending on development before validating market demand.

Networking within entrepreneurial ecosystems can unlock valuable mentorship opportunities as well as additional funding channels, such as incubators or accelerators focused specifically on AI startups. These organizations often provide access to industry experts who can offer guidance on refining business models and scaling operations effectively.

Finally, cultivating relationships with businesses in complementary sectors opens up partnership opportunities that enhance credibility while potentially attracting additional investments. Collaborations can lead to shared resources or co-development initiatives that leverage both parties' strengths—a particularly appealing proposition for investors seeking risk reduction through diversified portfolios.

In summary, navigating the financing landscape for AI ventures requires strategic exploration of diverse funding sources along with careful consideration of investor expectations and effective post-funding financial management practices. By blending innovative ideas with sound business strategies and nurturing relationships across ecosystems, entrepreneurs position themselves not only for securing initial investments but also for sustainable growth within this dynamic industry landscape.

Building a Technologically-Savvy Team

Building a technologically-savvy team is not just a strategic choice; it's essential for thriving in today's AI-driven economy. To foster a workforce that adapts to change and drives innovation, leaders should prioritize cultivating a culture of continuous learning, collaboration, and technological fluency. This journey begins by recognizing the diverse skill sets that each team member contributes.

Start with an assessment of your current team's capabilities by conducting a skills inventory to pinpoint strengths and gaps. Take this example, if you operate in the healthcare sector and aim to integrate AI into patient care, evaluate your team's familiarity with data analytics and machine learning tools specific to that field. Identify employees who may have experience with electronic health records but lack knowledge in AI. Recognizing these gaps is crucial for tailoring targeted training.

Once you've established your team's baseline capabilities, implement a structured upskilling program. This can take various forms, including formal training sessions led by external experts or internal workshops where team members share their insights. For example, if someone has completed a certification in data science or machine learning, encourage them to lead a workshop that explains key concepts and practical applications using real-world examples from your organization. This approach reinforces their learning while empowering others.

In addition, consider adopting technology-based learning platforms that offer personalized training paths tailored to individual needs and career goals. Platforms like Coursera or Udacity enable employees to learn at their own pace while tracking their progress through data analytics. This flexibility enhances engagement, allowing employees to focus on topics most relevant to their roles—whether it's deepening their understanding of Python for data analysis or exploring the ethical implications of AI in business.

Encouraging cross-functional collaboration within your team is also vital. Creating interdisciplinary project groups fosters an environment where diverse perspectives lead to innovative solutions. Take this example, when developing an AI tool for customer relationship management (CRM), involve not only data scientists but also marketing professionals and customer service representatives. Their insights can refine the tool's functionalities, ensuring it meets real user needs.

Effective communication plays a pivotal role in this process. As you build your technologically-savvy team, promote an open dialogue about the potential impacts of technology—both positive and negative. Schedule regular meetings for team members to discuss emerging technologies they've encountered or challenges they face while integrating new tools into their workflows. Facilitating these discussions cultivates an atmosphere of trust where everyone feels empowered to express concerns and share insights.

And, extend your efforts beyond immediate team members by engaging with external networks and resources. Attend industry conferences together or invite thought leaders to share fresh perspectives on technology trends and best practices in your field. Such interactions expose your team to broader ideas and innovations that can inspire creativity back at work.

Finally, leadership must demonstrate a commitment to technological advancement through both actions and words. Leaders should advocate for training initiatives while also participating actively—whether by enrolling in courses themselves or sharing experiences from their personal learning journeys related to new technologies. This commitment signals that continuous improvement is a shared value across the organization.

By following these steps—assessing current capabilities, implementing targeted training programs, promoting collaboration, facilitating open communication, leveraging external resources, and leading by example—you will cultivate a technologically-savvy team equipped not only to tackle today's challenges but also ready for tomorrow's opportunities. Investing time in building this type of workforce positions your organization at the forefront of innovation while ensuring resilience in the face of ongoing technological changes.

The Role of AI in Product Development

In the world of product development, AI is a transformative force, fundamentally altering the journey from initial concept to market-ready solutions. Companies are increasingly utilizing AI to streamline their processes, enhance creativity, and improve product offerings. To effectively harness AI, it's essential to understand its role throughout each stage of the product development lifecycle.

The ideation phase, in particular, greatly benefits from AI-driven insights. By employing data analytics tools, teams can rapidly analyze market trends and consumer preferences with remarkable speed and precision. For example, a fashion retailer might use AI algorithms to sift through social media data and sales patterns to spot emerging trends before they gain mainstream traction. This proactive approach not only sparks innovative product concepts but also ensures that they align with consumer demand right from the start.

As teams transition from ideation to design, AI tools facilitate rapid prototyping and design iterations. Generative design software allows engineers to input parameters such as materials and weight constraints, enabling the software to propose various design alternatives. This approach accelerates the design process while uncovering solutions that might not have emerged through traditional methods. Take this example, a furniture manufacturer can quickly generate multiple ergonomic chair variations that optimize comfort while minimizing material usage.

Once in the development and testing phases, AI continues to play a crucial role in enhancing efficiency and accuracy. Automated testing frameworks powered by machine learning algorithms can identify bugs or inefficiencies much faster than manual processes ever could. In software development, for instance, tools like Selenium allow teams to run tests across various devices simultaneously without human intervention. This automation not only speeds up release cycles but also helps maintain high quality.

AI's influence extends beyond technical aspects; it significantly enhances user experience as well. Personalization algorithms analyze user behavior and preferences in real time, allowing teams to tailor products dynamically based on individual needs. For example, a streaming service can use an AI model to suggest content uniquely suited to each user's tastes by analyzing their viewing habits. This level of personalization significantly boosts engagement and customer satisfaction.

However, effectively leveraging AI in product development requires collaboration across disciplines within an organization. Designers need insights from data scientists just as marketers must grasp the technical constraints set by engineering teams. Regular cross-functional meetings foster knowledge sharing that leads to cohesive product strategies— ensuring that all perspectives are considered during decision-making processes.

An illustrative example can be found in automotive manufacturing, where diverse teams collaborate during vehicle design discussions—engineers provide insights on technical feasibility while designers advocate for aesthetic appeal informed by consumer research supported by AI analysis. This collaborative environment nurtures innovation that aligns both technical possibilities and market expectations.

While embracing AI enhances capabilities across product development stages, ethical considerations are paramount throughout this process. Teams must address issues like data privacy and algorithmic bias as they build their products. Establishing ethical guidelines for using customer data during personalization efforts is crucial; transparency about data utilization fosters trust among consumers—a vital factor for long-term success.

Investing in training programs that educate employees about both the potential benefits and risks of AI applications empowers them to navigate these complexities with confidence. Workshops led by experts can demystify how algorithms work while addressing concerns about their implications—making this educational aspect integral when developing responsible products.

Finally, staying informed about industry advancements is essential for organizations aiming to remain competitive in their approach to incorporating AI into product development strategies. Regular attendance at conferences or engagement with thought leaders provides valuable insights into innovative practices being adopted elsewhere—igniting ideas that can be adapted back into one's own workflows.

Integrating AI into product development involves much more than simply adopting new technologies; it requires a fundamental rethinking of processes alongside fostering a culture of collaboration and ethical responsibility within your organization. By embracing these principles now—and committing to continuous learning—you position your team not only as participants but as leaders in the unfolding narrative of technological advancement shaping our future landscapes.

Market Validation in a Rapidly Changing Economy

In today's fast-paced marketplace, the importance of market validation has evolved significantly, particularly with the integration of AI into product strategies. To ensure a product idea thrives, it must be rigorously tested against real-world conditions and consumer demands. Market validation serves not only to assess the viability of a concept but also to provide essential insights that inform further development, effectively shaping the product's trajectory long before it reaches consumers.

The journey toward successful market validation begins with data-driven research. While traditional methods such as focus groups and surveys remain valuable, they often lack the rapid feedback loop that modern businesses need. This is where AI comes into play, offering near-instant access to vast datasets that unveil trends crucial for decision-making. For example, companies can utilize natural language processing tools to analyze customer reviews across various platforms. A startup in the beauty industry might discover through sentiment analysis that consumers prioritize clean ingredients over brand prestige. This insight could shift their product development focus from high-cost branding to a more transparent, ingredient-centered approach.

After gathering initial insights, iterative testing becomes vital. Agile methodologies combined with AI tools allow teams to efficiently cycle through prototypes and gather real-time feedback. Take this example, companies can implement A/B testing powered by AI algorithms to compare different variations of their product offerings instantly. Imagine a tech startup testing two versions of an app interface; machine learning models can predict which design will likely enhance user engagement based on interaction data collected during early beta tests. This predictive capability empowers teams to make informed decisions rather than relying on mere hope for success.

As organizations transition from prototypes to market-ready products, continuous validation against evolving customer needs is essential. Incorporating feedback loops throughout the product lifecycle facilitates this ongoing process effectively. By leveraging AI chatbots or community forums where users can share experiences and suggestions, companies can stay attuned to customer satisfaction and expectations even after launch. Take this example, a home appliance company might deploy smart devices that gather user data on functionality preferences, using this information to inform future iterations or new models.

And, market validation is intricately linked to branding and positioning strategies. The narrative surrounding a product is crucial for its acceptance in the marketplace. Brands must clearly communicate how they respond to consumer feedback—not only through messaging but also through tangible changes driven by data insights. A footwear company launching an eco-friendly sneaker line could use consumer feedback gathered from social media to refine marketing campaigns that highlight sustainability features, ensuring alignment with what resonates most with potential buyers.

Ethical considerations are paramount when leveraging consumer data for market validation. Transparency regarding how customer insights are collected and utilized fosters trust—an essential asset in today's informed marketplace. Establishing clear guidelines on data privacy safeguards both the organization and its users while enhancing the overall brand image. Thus, proactive communication about data usage not only complies with regulations but also strengthens consumer relationships.

To navigate these complexities successfully, organizations should invest in cross-training employees across departments —particularly in marketing, product development, and legal compliance—to ensure cohesion throughout the validation process. Take this example, equipping marketing personnel with knowledge of AI tools allows them to effectively harness analytics while being mindful of ethical considerations surrounding data collection.

Engaging with industry thought leaders through seminars or webinars also provides invaluable insights into best practices for market validation strategies. Staying attuned to emerging trends ensures organizations remain agile and enhances their capacity for innovative thinking based on validated consumer demands.

In this rapidly changing economy—characterized by technological advancements and shifting consumer expectations—market validation emerges as both an art and a science, driven by data yet reliant on human insight and understanding. By embracing AI-powered methodologies alongside ethical practices and interdisciplinary collaboration, companies position themselves not just for survival but for robust growth in an increasingly competitive landscape. Understanding this dynamic enables organizations to create compelling products that resonate with consumers long before they hit the market, ensuring both relevance and appeal in an ever-evolving marketplace.

Scaling AI-Driven Businesses

Scaling AI-driven businesses demands a comprehensive strategy that harmonizes technology with strategic growth. As organizations harness the power of artificial intelligence to improve their operations, establishing a solid framework for scaling becomes essential. This framework should not only focus on technological integration but also consider organizational culture, market dynamics, and customer engagement.

Central to successful scaling is a strong technological foundation. AI has the potential to streamline operations through automation, predictive analytics, and real-time decision-making. However, merely deploying AI tools is not enough. Companies must prioritize robust data management and infrastructure to ensure these tools function effectively. For example, a logistics company aiming to optimize its supply chain can employ machine learning algorithms to forecast demand fluctuations. By integrating AI with a cloud-based data infrastructure, they can analyze extensive historical data, adjust inventory levels accordingly, and significantly reduce overhead costs.

In addition to technology, organizational culture plays a pivotal role in successful scaling. Cultivating an innovation-driven mindset encourages employees at all levels to creatively explore AI applications. Consider a financial services firm that promotes a culture of experimentation—employees are empowered to test new AI models for fraud detection without fear of failure. This supportive environment not only accelerates innovation but also facilitates rapid iterations based on real-world performance. As teams witness their ideas come to fruition through AI, motivation soars, and a sense of collective ownership of results develops.

Equally important is a nuanced understanding of the market for effectively scaling AI initiatives. Organizations must continuously monitor market trends and customer behaviors to adapt their offerings accordingly. Take this example, a retail company can leverage AI-driven analytics to identify shopping patterns during holiday seasons. By dynamically tailoring marketing campaigns based on these insights—such as targeting specific customer segments with personalized promotions—they can enhance sales while minimizing wasted expenditure on ineffective strategies.

As businesses scale their operations using AI technologies, customer engagement becomes increasingly vital. Building relationships that go beyond mere transactions fosters loyalty and advocacy among consumers. Implementing AI-powered chatbots on e-commerce platforms enhances customer service capabilities by providing instant responses to inquiries. For example, an online clothing retailer can utilize these chatbots not only for answering questions but also for offering personalized styling advice based on previous purchases or browsing history. This tailored experience encourages repeat business and deepens customer trust.

As companies expand globally, they must also navigate the complexities of diverse regulatory environments regarding data usage and privacy laws. Establishing compliance frameworks that integrate legal considerations into AI strategies is crucial for maintaining credibility across various markets. A health tech startup, for instance, may face different patient data regulations in multiple countries; by developing adaptable compliance protocols early on, they can mitigate risks associated with international scaling.

Collaboration across functions within an organization further enhances scalability efforts in the age of AI. When marketing teams partner closely with data scientists, they can craft campaigns informed by deep analytical insights rather than relying solely on intuition. An automotive manufacturer exemplifies this approach by leveraging machine learning algorithms alongside marketing strategies to analyze consumer feedback on electric vehicle features—leading them to prioritize product development on aspects most valued by potential buyers.

Strategic partnerships can also significantly accelerate scaling initiatives. Collaborating with technology providers allows businesses to access cutting-edge tools without incurring heavy upfront investments in infrastructure or expertise. Take this example, a small startup partnering with an established cloud provider gains access to advanced machine learning platforms that empower rapid innovation while minimizing technical hurdles.

Investing in talent development is essential as companies scale AI-driven businesses. Upskilling existing employees ensures they possess the necessary competencies to effectively leverage emerging technologies—whether through formal training programs or mentorship opportunities within the organization. For example, tech firms that offer workshops on machine learning applications help bridge skill gaps while cultivating an agile workforce prepared for evolving challenges.

scaling AI-driven businesses requires embracing complexity while remaining focused on core objectives: enhancing operational efficiency and delivering exceptional value to customers. By intertwining advanced technologies with strategic frameworks rooted in culture, market insight, and collaboration, organizations position themselves not just for survival but as formidable players in competitive landscapes.

In this journey fueled by innovation and adaptability lies the promise of transformative success—where scaling transcends mere numbers; it becomes about forging meaningful connections with customers and reshaping industries through intelligent solutions that endure over time.

Case Studies of Successful AI Entrepreneurs

Successful AI entrepreneurs illustrate that innovation extends beyond technology; it encompasses vision, strategy, and execution. These leaders have skillfully navigated the intricate landscape of artificial intelligence by blending creativity with business acumen and a steadfast commitment to addressing real-world challenges. By examining their journeys, aspiring AI leaders can uncover valuable insights to apply in their own ventures.

Consider Andrew Ng, co-founder of Google Brain and Coursera. Ng's entrance into AI was inspired by his deep belief in the transformative power of education. His innovative approach to integrating AI into online learning platforms has not only democratized access to quality education but has also highlighted how AI can enhance personalized learning experiences. Coursera adapts its offerings based on user data and feedback, continuously improving engagement and completion rates. This is a good example of the importance of aligning technological capabilities with a mission that resonates on a human level.

Another compelling example is UiPath, a leader in robotic process automation (RPA). Founded by Daniel Dines and his team, UiPath started with a straightforward concept: automating repetitive tasks to allow human workers to focus on more valuable contributions. Their emphasis on user-friendliness enabled organizations, regardless of technical expertise, to quickly implement RPA solutions. This case underscores how prioritizing usability can accelerate adoption across diverse industries, making it essential for businesses seeking to scale AI solutions to understand user needs and create intuitive products.

In contrast, the story of OpenAI's GPT models reveals a different perspective on responsible innovation. The founders recognized the vast potential of natural language processing while also grappling with the ethical implications of deploying such powerful technologies. Their dedication to responsible AI development is evident through established guidelines that prioritize safety and societal benefit. Here, successful scaling hinges not only on technological prowess but also on maintaining transparency and ethical standards throughout the product development process.

Similarly, Tempus, a healthcare startup founded by Eric Lefkofsky, employs AI to personalize cancer treatment plans based on genetic data. By collaborating closely with healthcare providers and regulatory bodies from the beginning, Tempus navigated complex regulatory landscapes effectively. Their focus on building trust within these partnerships allowed for rapid scaling while addressing critical compliance issues, highlighting the importance of collaboration and stakeholder engagement in heavily regulated industries.

A different perspective comes from Kabbage, an online lending platform that uses AI to assess creditworthiness more accurately than traditional methods. By leveraging machine learning algorithms to analyze real-time data from various sources, Kabbage enables faster loan decision-making—an essential capability in the rapidly shifting financial services market. Their success illustrates how advanced data analytics can provide competitive advantages in both speed and customer satisfaction.

The startup Grammarly further exemplifies the intersection of AI and user experience design. By offering real-time feedback on writing through natural language processing technology, Grammarly empowers users—from students to professionals

—to communicate more effectively. The entrepreneurial spirit here lies in recognizing everyday challenges faced by users and creating seamless solutions that integrate into their workflows.

NVIDIA's commitment to community engagement also serves as a catalyst for innovation in AI development. The company's GPUs have become foundational for machine learning applications across various sectors due to its dedication to providing comprehensive resources for developers— ranging from tutorials to forums and cloud platforms for experimentation. This ecosystem not only cultivates talent but also fosters collaboration among innovators pushing the boundaries of what's possible with AI.

Lastly, Shopify demonstrates how adapting AI-driven tools can empower small businesses seeking e-commerce solutions amid rapid market shifts caused by global events like pandemics. By providing entrepreneurs with access to advanced analytics without requiring deep technical knowledge or significant capital investment, Shopify exemplifies how democratizing technology fosters broader innovation within ecosystems often overshadowed by larger players.

Collectively, these case studies illuminate several critical strategies employed by successful AI entrepreneurs: aligning purpose with technology; fostering user-centric design; prioritizing ethical considerations; navigating compliance through collaboration; leveraging data analytics for competitive advantage; supporting community growth; and empowering smaller entities within larger frameworks.

For those entering the realm of AI entrepreneurship or seeking inspiration in their current endeavors, these narratives serve as powerful reminders that success lies at the intersection of technological opportunities and human connections. Navigating this duality will be essential for thriving in an ever-evolving landscape shaped by artificial intelligence.

CHAPTER 8: ETHICAL CONSIDERATIONS AND AI

*Understanding Ethical
Dilemmas in AI*

U nderstanding the ethical dilemmas surrounding artificial intelligence requires a deep exploration of the complexities involved in decision-making processes, societal impacts, and technological advancements. AI systems are designed to optimize efficiency and boost productivity; however, they can unintentionally reinforce biases or prioritize profit over ethical considerations. The real challenge lies in ensuring that these powerful tools align with societal values and uphold human dignity.

At the heart of the ethical discourse on AI is the issue of accountability. When an AI system makes an error— such as misclassifying a job application or producing biased recommendations—who is held responsible? This question becomes even more pressing in cases where algorithms function autonomously, making decisions without human oversight. The ambiguity surrounding accountability highlights the need for frameworks that clarify responsibility and promote transparency in AI operations. Such frameworks encourage developers to create systems that are interpretable and understandable to both users and those affected by their decisions.

The deployment of facial recognition technology serves as a pertinent example. While many organizations advocate for its potential to enhance security, numerous studies indicate that these systems often exhibit significant bias against marginalized groups. Algorithms trained primarily on data from one demographic may perform poorly when applied to others, resulting in unjust outcomes. The ethical imperative is clear: AI systems must undergo rigorous evaluations for fairness and bias before they are implemented. This emphasizes the importance of utilizing diverse datasets and adopting inclusive practices during both development and testing phases.

Privacy concerns also play a critical role in the ethical landscape of AI. The vast amounts of data needed to train AI models raise important questions about user consent and data protection. In an era where personal information is a valuable asset, it is crucial to find a balance between the benefits derived from data analysis and individuals' rights to privacy. Implementing robust data governance policies can help outline how information is collected, stored, used, and shared, thereby mitigating risks associated with privacy violations.

And, ethical dilemmas extend into employment as AI continues to reshape traditional job markets. While automation offers efficiency gains, it also poses significant threats to job security for many workers. As organizations increasingly adopt AI technologies, they must weigh economic benefits against broader societal implications—especially for vulnerable populations who may be disproportionately affected by automation-driven job displacement.

This intersection of technology and humanity emphasizes the need for inclusivity in developing AI strategies. Engaging a wide range of stakeholders—from technologists to ethicists and community representatives—ensures that diverse perspectives are integrated throughout the design process. This collaborative approach can yield more equitable solutions that genuinely reflect societal values while leveraging technological advancements.

Navigating these ethical challenges also requires ongoing dialogue among industry leaders, policymakers, and society at large. Establishing multidisciplinary committees or ethics boards within organizations can facilitate continuous reflection on ethical issues while guiding best practices in AI usage.

Real-world examples illustrate how organizations are beginning to address these concerns proactively. Take this example, companies like Microsoft have created internal ethics boards tasked with evaluating new AI projects for potential risks before they reach deployment stages. By adopting such measures, businesses can foster a culture that prioritizes responsible innovation over unchecked expansion.

understanding the ethical dilemmas inherent in artificial intelligence demands commitment not just from technologists but from society as a whole. By fostering early conversations about ethics during development processes and actively engaging diverse stakeholders throughout implementation phases, we can collectively shape a future where technology enhances rather than undermines the principles we cherish as a society.

These discussions serve as a reminder that technology should serve humanity's greater good rather than becoming an abstract force detached from our values. Emphasizing ethics in AI development is not merely about compliance; it's about aligning our innovations with our aspirations for justice, fairness, and equity across all dimensions of society as we navigate this transformative era.

The Importance of Transparency

The growing integration of artificial intelligence into various facets of society highlights the urgent need for transparency. As organizations increasingly adopt AI technologies, it is crucial to clarify how these systems operate, what data they use, and the reasoning behind their decisions. Transparency not only fosters trust among users and stakeholders but also helps them comprehend both the capabilities and limitations of AI.

When an AI system functions without clear visibility into its processes, it breeds skepticism. For example, consider hiring algorithms that automatically screen applicants. If candidates are unaware of how their resumes are evaluated or what criteria the algorithm prioritizes, they may perceive the selection process as arbitrary or biased. By promoting transparency, companies can demystify these operations; disclosing evaluation criteria and offering insights into data usage can create an environment where users feel respected and valued.

Another important aspect of transparency involves data usage. Organizations frequently collect extensive personal data to train AI models, raising questions about ownership and consent. It is essential for companies to communicate how data is sourced, processed, and protected. Clear privacy policies can reassure users that their information is being managed responsibly and ethically. Take this example, Google's detailed user agreements specify what data is collected and how it is utilized across its services, instilling a sense of security among users.

And, transparency plays a critical role in addressing biases embedded within algorithms that can impact societal norms. Hidden biases may lead to discriminatory practices in areas such as lending or law enforcement. Organizations must be open about the potential limitations of their models and the datasets used for training. This willingness to disclose invites scrutiny from independent auditors or watchdogs who can evaluate fairness and accountability. IBM, for example, has established a framework for auditing AI algorithms to assess fairness across multiple dimensions before deployment.

Incorporating real-time transparency tools can further enhance understanding and oversight of AI systems in practice. Imagine a financial institution using an algorithm to assess loan applications; integrating a dashboard that provides insights into decision-making processes could empower customers by allowing them to track their application status and understand the factors influencing approval or denial.

Transparent communication also extends beyond internal practices; it involves actively engaging with external stakeholders—such as regulators, community leaders, and civil rights organizations—to ensure that diverse perspectives shape AI implementations. Initiatives like the Partnership on AI exemplify this approach by bringing together organizations from various sectors to discuss best practices for responsible AI deployment while addressing concerns about bias and accountability.

The connection between transparency and accountability is paramount. Establishing clear guidelines for who is responsible when AI systems make erroneous decisions ensures that mechanisms are in place for redress. When an automated system misclassifies an applicant or produces inaccurate predictions, organizations should have protocols that allow affected individuals to seek clarification or appeal algorithmic decisions.

embracing transparency in AI development and deployment not only mitigates risks associated with misinformation but also paves the way for innovation aligned with ethical standards. By championing open dialogue around AI's capabilities and limitations—among both users and developers—organizations foster a culture committed to integrity and ethical responsibility.

As we navigate the evolving landscape of artificial intelligence, it is essential to recognize that transparency goes beyond mere compliance; it serves as a foundation for building trust. When people understand how technology works and observe ethical considerations in action, they are more likely to support its adoption in both personal and professional contexts. Prioritizing transparent practices in AI development helps us fulfill our ethical obligations while better positioning us to harness technology's power while safeguarding our shared values as a society.

Bias and Fairness in AI Systems

The integration of artificial intelligence (AI) into various sectors has introduced intricate challenges related to bias and fairness. Decisions made by algorithms can have significant consequences, leading to discriminatory outcomes that affect individuals' lives and reinforce societal inequities. Therefore, it is essential to understand how bias infiltrates AI systems in order to develop fair and just technological solutions.

At the heart of bias in AI is the data used to train these systems. If the input data reflects existing prejudices or lacks diversity, the algorithms are likely to replicate those biases. For example, consider a hiring algorithm trained primarily on resumes from a specific demographic. This narrow dataset may cause the model to favor candidates who fit that profile while disadvantaging others. A study from the MIT Media Lab illustrates this concern, revealing that facial recognition systems demonstrate higher error rates for women and individuals with darker skin tones. Such disparities emphasize the critical need to scrutinize training data, ensuring it encompasses a wide range of perspectives.

To address bias, organizations must implement rigorous testing protocols before deploying AI systems. Conducting fairness audits can help identify potential discriminatory outcomes early in the development process. Take this example, tech companies like Microsoft have begun utilizing diverse teams to review algorithms for bias, conducting assessments that evaluate how different demographic groups are impacted by their technologies. This proactive approach not only enhances fairness but also fosters accountability within the organization.

In addition to testing, algorithmic transparency can serve as a powerful tool against bias. By documenting how algorithms operate and sharing insights into their decision-making processes, companies can build trust and enable stakeholders to understand potential pitfalls. Publicly available reports detailing algorithm performance across various demographics facilitate third-party evaluations and encourage community engagement in discussions about fairness. The Gender Shades project at MIT, for example, underscores the importance of transparency by analyzing commercial facial recognition systems and their differential accuracy based on gender and skin color.

The ethical implications of AI decision-making extend beyond mere compliance; they compel us to rethink our values regarding technology's role in society. Embracing an ethical framework involves not only correcting biases but also actively preventing future occurrences. This commitment requires creating spaces for stakeholder dialogue where marginalized voices are heard and considered during the design and implementation phases. Organizations like the Algorithmic Justice League advocate for these practices by promoting more inclusive representation in AI development.

And, continuous monitoring of deployed AI systems is vital for ensuring ongoing fairness and accountability. As societal norms evolve, so too must our understanding of what constitutes bias in AI. Systems deemed fair at launch may exhibit biased behavior over time due to shifts in cultural context or changes in underlying data inputs. Regular reassessments can provide valuable insights into these dynamics, allowing organizations to adjust their strategies accordingly.

Education plays a crucial role in combating bias within AI as well. Training programs focused on diversity and ethics empower developers to recognize their own biases while fostering a culture of inclusivity within tech teams. Companies like Facebook have invested significantly in workshops designed to educate employees about implicit biases and how they might manifest in algorithmic decision-making processes.

addressing bias in AI necessitates a multifaceted approach that combines robust data management practices with a commitment to ethical principles. This endeavor requires collaboration among technologists, ethicists, policymakers, and community stakeholders to create equitable technology use. Such collective efforts not only enhance the integrity of AI systems but also reinforce our shared responsibility for building a just society where technology uplifts rather than undermines human dignity.

As we navigate these challenges, it is crucial to cultivate an environment where vigilance against bias becomes integral to every phase of AI development—from initial design through deployment and beyond. By actively engaging with these issues, we can aspire to a future where artificial intelligence acts as an ally in promoting fairness rather than exacerbating existing inequalities.

The Role of AI in Decision-Making

Artificial intelligence has fundamentally transformed decision-making across a wide range of sectors, offering tools that significantly enhance efficiency and accuracy. However, the integration of AI into these processes raises important questions about its impact on human judgment and societal norms. By understanding how AI influences decision-making, individuals and organizations can harness its potential responsibly while remaining aware of its limitations.

AI systems excel at processing large volumes of data quickly, making them invaluable in fields such as healthcare and finance. For example, machine learning algorithms analyze patient data to predict health outcomes, allowing doctors to personalize treatments based on predictive analytics. Similarly, financial institutions utilize AI to assess creditworthiness by evaluating a borrower's history alongside numerous other factors. Yet, this ability for rapid analysis can lead to an over-reliance on algorithms, diminishing the critical role of human oversight in favor of automated processes.

This dynamic is particularly evident in the criminal justice system, where AI tools like risk assessment algorithms are used to predict recidivism rates. While these tools can offer insights that inform judicial decisions, they also risk reinforcing existing biases if not managed carefully. A 2016 investigation by ProPublica revealed that certain algorithms disproportionately flagged Black defendants as high-risk compared to their white counterparts. This case underscores how AI can inadvertently perpetuate systemic biases rather than alleviate them, highlighting the urgent need for careful scrutiny and accountability in algorithmic decision-making.

To navigate these complexities effectively, organizations should establish a comprehensive framework for integrating AI into their decision-making processes. This framework must prioritize transparency and explainability in AI models. Stakeholders should have a clear understanding of how decisions are made—what data is used and how algorithms reach conclusions—ensuring that each outcome has a well-defined rationale. Companies like Google are exploring strategies such as Explainable AI (XAI) to clarify how AI systems arrive at specific decisions through interpretable models.

Also, fostering interdisciplinary collaboration is crucial in addressing the multifaceted challenges associated with AI-driven decision-making. By engaging ethicists alongside technologists, organizations can better anticipate ethical dilemmas and develop guidelines that promote responsible technology use. Incorporating diverse perspectives ensures that the voices of various stakeholders—including those who may be adversely affected by automated decisions—are considered throughout the design process.

It is equally important for organizations to establish ongoing protocols for evaluating the effectiveness and fairness of AI-driven decisions. Regular audits assessing performance across demographic groups can help identify unintended consequences early on. Take this example, auditing hiring algorithms can uncover patterns indicating bias against specific demographics before they manifest as real-world disparities in employment opportunities.

Education is pivotal in this context; equipping employees with knowledge about both the capabilities and limitations of AI enhances their ability to critically evaluate algorithmic outputs. Training programs focused on data ethics and algorithmic accountability cultivate a workforce that values nuanced decision-making—an essential trait when human lives or livelihoods are at stake.

Despite the advanced technologies at our disposal, the role of human intuition remains indispensable in our decision frameworks. While algorithms aid in data analysis and pattern recognition, human judgment provides essential context and moral reasoning that machines currently lack. The best outcomes often arise from a collaborative relationship where human expertise complements AI's analytical capabilities rather than replacing them entirely.

By embracing this collaborative approach, organizations can optimize performance while upholding ethical standards within their operations. Valuing transparency, fostering interdisciplinary dialogue, conducting regular evaluations, and prioritizing education will help build a robust foundation for effective decision-making amid the complexities introduced by artificial intelligence.

navigating the intersection between human judgment and AI-driven insights requires ongoing reflection on our values regarding technology's role in society. As we strive toward informed decisions grounded in data-driven evidence while maintaining ethical integrity at every step, we lay the groundwork for a future where artificial intelligence serves as an ally rather than an adversary in our collective pursuit of progress and justice.

Privacy and Data Protection

Artificial intelligence (AI) is a powerful ally in decision-making, but it also poses significant challenges related to privacy and data protection. As organizations increasingly depend on AI to process vast amounts of personal and sensitive information, the ethical implications of these technologies become more pronounced. Protecting individuals' privacy is not merely a regulatory obligation; it is essential for maintaining trust and accountability in AI systems.

To navigate these complexities, organizations must address the intricacies of data collection, storage, and usage directly. Implementing robust data governance frameworks is crucial to establish guidelines for how data is acquired and utilized. For example, the General Data Protection Regulation (GDPR) in Europe sets a high bar for data protection, mandating that organizations obtain explicit consent from individuals before processing their personal information. Companies like

Apple have built their reputations on prioritizing user privacy and ensuring transparency in their data handling practices. This commitment aligns with legal requirements and fosters customer loyalty.

A key challenge for organizations is designing AI systems with privacy as a foundational element. This approach means that privacy considerations should influence decisions at every stage—from data collection to processing. Take this example, when developing predictive models in healthcare, organizations can utilize techniques such as differential privacy. This method adds noise to datasets to protect individual identities while still enabling meaningful insights. By adopting such strategies, businesses can harness the power of AI without compromising user privacy.

Beyond technical measures, fostering a culture of privacy awareness within organizations is essential. Employees at all levels should receive training on the importance of data protection and the ethical implications of their actions. Establishing clear policies on data handling empowers staff to make informed decisions when working with sensitive information. Regular workshops discussing case studies on data breaches or misuse can create an environment where employees feel accountable for upholding privacy standards.

The relationship between AI and data protection extends to third-party partnerships as well. Many organizations rely on external vendors to manage user data. In these situations, due diligence becomes paramount. Companies must ensure that their partners adhere to stringent data protection standards that match their own. This includes conducting audits and requiring contracts that specify compliance with relevant regulations.

As algorithms grow more complex and capable of learning from diverse datasets, the risk of inadvertently exposing sensitive information increases. A notable example is facial recognition technology, which has faced criticism for potential invasions of privacy and issues with misidentification. The backlash against such technologies underscores the need for clear policies governing their use, including establishing consent protocols before deploying them in public spaces.

The ethical landscape surrounding AI is further complicated by concerns about bias and discrimination in algorithmic outcomes—areas where privacy intersects with fairness. If training datasets are not carefully curated or if they reflect societal inequalities, the resulting AI models may reinforce these biases in decisions affecting individuals' lives—such as hiring or lending practices. Organizations must actively work to mitigate these biases by diversifying their training datasets and implementing fairness checks throughout the development process.

As technology evolves, so too must our understanding of privacy risks associated with AI applications. Engaging stakeholders—including users, ethicists, technologists, and regulators—in discussions around emerging technologies can foster a collaborative approach to addressing these challenges. Public consultations can provide valuable feedback on potential uses of AI in sensitive areas like surveillance or healthcare.

Transparency serves as a guiding principle in navigating the complexities of privacy and data protection in the context of AI. Organizations should strive to communicate clearly about what data is collected and how it is used, empowering individuals with choices regarding their personal information. Initiatives like open-data platforms can help demystify AI processes while offering users insights into how their data contributes to broader analyses without compromising confidentiality.

integrating AI into decision-making processes must not

overshadow the fundamental need to respect individuals' rights to privacy and protect them from misuse of their data. Striking a balance between leveraging advanced technologies for efficiency and safeguarding personal information requires careful consideration at every organizational level.

By prioritizing ethical practices around privacy alongside innovation in AI technologies, businesses can build trust within communities and establish an industry standard that others will aspire to emulate—creating an environment where technological advancement coexists harmoniously with individual rights and societal norms.

Developing and Implementing Ethical Guidelines

As organizations increasingly adopt artificial intelligence, the need for ethical guidelines becomes critical. These guidelines are not merely about compliance; they are essential for cultivating a culture of responsibility that permeates the entire organization. While many envision AI as complex algorithms analyzing vast datasets, the ethical use of AI fundamentally relies on human values and societal norms.

To develop effective ethical guidelines, it is crucial to start with a clear understanding of the organization's mission and core values. For example, if transparency is a priority for a company, its AI practices should mirror that commitment. This entails openly communicating how AI systems function and the data they utilize. A practical first step could be drafting an ethics charter that articulates the principles guiding AI use, encompassing fairness, accountability, and privacy from the outset. Such a charter serves as a reference point for decision-making, ensuring that every AI initiative aligns with the organization's ethical framework.

Engaging diverse stakeholders in the creation of these guidelines is equally important. Involving voices from various departments—such as legal, HR, IT, and customer service—ensures a comprehensive range of perspectives is considered.

Take this example, when discussing facial recognition technology, legal experts can shed light on potential regulatory challenges, while customer service representatives can raise user concerns. This collaborative approach not only enriches the guideline development process but also fosters a sense of ownership among employees.

Training is vital in embedding ethical practices into daily operations. Organizations might implement mandatory training sessions on ethical AI usage for all employees, from executives to interns. These sessions can explore real-world scenarios that highlight the importance of ethical considerations in AI development and deployment. Take this example, discussing a case where a company faced backlash due to biased algorithms can illustrate the consequences of overlooking ethical standards and spark meaningful conversations about preventive measures.

And, implementation should be accompanied by continuous evaluation and feedback mechanisms. Organizations should establish review boards or ethics committees responsible for monitoring AI initiatives after deployment. These committees can assess whether projects adhere to established ethical guidelines and recommend adjustments in response to emerging challenges or societal shifts. For example, if a new privacy regulation is introduced, the committee should analyze existing AI systems and make necessary changes to ensure compliance while upholding ethical integrity.

Transparency in algorithmic decision-making processes is also key to building public trust. Providing users with clear information about how their data is used and the algorithms driving specific decisions enhances accountability. For example, an online lending platform could publish details about how its credit scoring algorithm operates, including which factors influence decisions and how user data is safeguarded. Such transparency demystifies AI operations and reassures users that their interests are protected.

Incorporating external feedback further enriches the ethical framework. Engaging community representatives or consumer advocacy groups can yield valuable insights into public perceptions of AI technologies. Hosting forums or town hall meetings allows organizations to hear directly from those impacted by their technologies, fostering dialogue that can inform ethical practices.

The challenge extends beyond creating guidelines; organizations must navigate the complexities of evolving technological landscapes and societal expectations. Continuous research into emerging trends—such as advancements in machine learning or shifts in public sentiment—ensures that ethical guidelines remain relevant and effective. Staying informed about new developments enables organizations to proactively address potential risks rather than merely reacting to crises.

Looking toward the future, it is increasingly clear that ethical considerations will shape the trajectory of AI technologies. Organizations that prioritize ethics alongside innovation will not only protect their reputations but also contribute positively to society as a whole. The relationship between technological advancement and human values highlights the necessity for robust ethical frameworks that guide responsible AI use.

developing and implementing ethical guidelines is an ongoing journey rather than a final destination. It requires commitment at every level—from executive leadership driving initiatives to front-line employees embodying these principles in their daily tasks. By embedding ethics into the very fabric of AI projects, organizations can create a sustainable model that respects individual rights while harnessing technology's transformative power for the greater good.

Corporate Social Responsibility and AI

Corporate Social Responsibility (CSR) has become a fundamental element for organizations operating within the AI landscape. As companies leverage the capabilities of artificial intelligence, they must also recognize the societal ramifications of their innovations. CSR transcends mere compliance; it is a strategic framework that harmonizes business objectives with broader social goals, enhancing brand reputation and fostering trust among stakeholders.

In this dynamic environment, organizations stand to gain significantly by integrating AI into their CSR initiatives. Take this example, machine learning algorithms can be employed to analyze community needs with greater precision. By sifting through extensive datasets from diverse sources, companies can pinpoint urgent local challenges—such as access to education or healthcare—and tailor their CSR efforts accordingly. A notable example is a leading beverage company that utilized AI to refine its water conservation strategies, resulting in substantial reductions in water usage and strengthened community relations. This synergy between corporate strategy and social responsibility illustrates how the thoughtful application of AI can lead to meaningful change.

Engaging stakeholders is vital for developing effective CSR initiatives. Organizations should actively involve communities, employees, and customers in conversations about their needs and concerns related to AI deployment. For example, a tech company might facilitate focus groups where community members voice their perspectives on data privacy and algorithmic fairness. Such dialogues not only enrich CSR strategies but also provide organizations with insights into the societal context in which they operate. By listening to diverse voices, companies can foster transparency and build trust—essential elements in an era increasingly skeptical of technology.

And, measuring the impact of CSR initiatives enhances

accountability and signals a genuine commitment to societal welfare. Companies can implement metrics to track the effectiveness of their programs, utilizing data analytics to assess outcomes over time. An example of this is a nonprofit organization that partnered with a financial institution to analyze data on economic mobility within underserved communities. By evaluating how its initiatives influenced job placements and income growth, the organization refined its strategies based on concrete evidence rather than assumptions.

Sustainability also plays a crucial role in the CSR framework surrounding AI development. Organizations must account for the environmental implications of their technological advancements. A prominent automotive manufacturer adopted an AI-driven approach to minimize waste in its production processes. By employing real-time monitoring and predictive analytics, it successfully cut material waste by 30%, demonstrating how responsible innovation can yield significant ecological benefits while improving operational efficiency.

Also, ethical marketing practices should guide any outreach related to AI technologies. Organizations must communicate clearly about the capabilities and limitations of their AI solutions to avoid fostering unrealistic expectations or fear among consumers. A leading e-commerce platform provides a case in point; it launched transparent advertising campaigns regarding its AI-powered recommendation systems. By explaining how these algorithms function and the real benefits they offer without exaggeration, the company cultivated consumer confidence while adhering to ethical marketing standards.

As businesses pursue competitive advantages through technology, it is essential that they keep ethical considerations at the forefront of their strategies. Regular audits and assessments of AI applications can help ensure compliance with both internal ethical guidelines and external regulations. Take this example, a healthcare provider engaged independent ethics boards to regularly review its AI diagnostic tools. This proactive approach not only mitigated risks associated with biased algorithms but also bolstered public trust in its services.

Where X meets Y corporate social responsibility and artificial intelligence signifies a profound shift in how organizations view their societal role. Rather than solely focusing on profit maximization, companies are beginning to recognize their potential as catalysts for positive change through responsible technology use. By adopting this philosophy, businesses can contribute to social good while advancing innovation.

The path toward meaningful corporate social responsibility in an AI-driven world requires ongoing reflection and adaptation. As technology continues to evolve rapidly, organizational strategies must also adapt to address emerging ethical dilemmas and societal expectations. Establishing robust frameworks for accountability ensures that companies not only thrive in their business endeavors but also uplift communities and uphold human dignity.

In summary, aligning corporate objectives with social responsibility reframes the narrative around technology from one of fear to one of hope. By embedding ethical considerations into every layer of decision-making, organizations can navigate the complexities of the AI landscape while remaining dedicated to fostering a better future for all stakeholders involved.

Engaging with Stakeholders on Ethical Issues

Engaging stakeholders in discussions about the ethical implications of AI is essential for creating a resilient and responsible organization. By actively including diverse perspectives in decision-making, companies can better navigate the complexities of AI deployment. This engagement can take various forms, from formal town hall meetings to informal conversations with community members. Take this example, a software company that develops AI tools for local governments might hold workshops to gather citizen feedback on privacy concerns and desired outcomes, ensuring that the technology aligns with community expectations.

Stakeholders often bring valuable insights that internal teams may overlook. Involving employees in discussions about ethical considerations fosters a culture of inclusivity and shared responsibility. Organizations can establish cross-functional ethics committees with representatives from departments such as engineering, legal, and marketing to collaboratively assess the implications of AI projects. A notable example is a multinational technology corporation that formed such a committee and successfully identified potential biases in its algorithms before launching new products, thus preventing public backlash and enhancing user trust.

Transparency is crucial in stakeholder engagement, especially when addressing the ethical implications of AI. Organizations must communicate openly about their methodologies, including data collection and usage practices. A retail giant exemplified this approach by releasing an annual transparency report detailing its data usage policies and measures taken to mitigate AI-related risks. By clarifying its practices, the company not only reinforced consumer confidence but also set a benchmark for accountability within the industry.

To further engage stakeholders, organizations can utilize collaborative platforms where community members can share experiences or raise concerns regarding AI applications. For example, an online forum dedicated to local AI initiatives could facilitate ongoing dialogue between tech developers and residents impacted by these technologies. Such platforms empower communities to be active participants rather than passive observers in the evolution of AI solutions affecting their lives.

Educational initiatives also serve as effective tools for fostering engagement on ethical issues. Companies can organize training sessions or informational webinars aimed at educating stakeholders about the benefits and potential risks associated with AI technologies. This proactive strategy demystifies complex topics while equipping individuals with the knowledge needed to engage meaningfully in discussions about ethical dilemmas.

Building alliances with external organizations focused on ethics in technology is another valuable strategy. Partnering with academic institutions or non-profits dedicated to promoting responsible AI use creates opportunities for shared learning and development of best practices. Take this example, a tech startup collaborating with an ethics-focused university program may gain insights into emerging ethical frameworks, enhancing its ability to navigate challenges as they arise.

Establishing mechanisms for ongoing feedback allows organizations to adapt their strategies based on stakeholder input continually. Regular surveys or feedback loops encourage open communication between companies and their communities, fostering an environment where concerns are addressed proactively rather than reactively.

Recognizing the importance of ethics goes beyond compliance; it is about building trust within communities affected by technological advancements. When stakeholders see that companies prioritize ethical considerations alongside innovation, they are more likely to support those initiatives—leading to stronger relationships grounded in mutual respect.

In addition to effective stakeholder engagement, organizations must be ready to respond swiftly when ethical dilemmas related to AI arise. Having crisis management plans that incorporate stakeholder input ensures responses reflect both organizational values and community standards.

engaging stakeholders on ethical issues shifts the

narrative around AI from one of fear or skepticism to one of collaboration and shared growth. By fostering connections among diverse groups and maintaining open lines of communication, companies position themselves as trustworthy partners in society's journey through technological advancement. Active engagement means embracing responsibility—not just for what technology can achieve—but for how it impacts human lives daily on multiple levels.

CHAPTER 9:
MANAGING CHANGE
AND RESILIENCE

Psychological Impacts
of AI Disruption

U nderstanding the psychological impacts of AI disruption is crucial for individuals and organizations navigating this transformative landscape. The integration of AI technologies across various sectors has brought about significant changes in job roles, workplace dynamics, and even self-perception among professionals. As employees adapt to an environment increasingly shaped by AI systems, many experience uncertainty, stress, and anxiety about their career trajectories.

Take, for instance, a customer service representative who discovers that a new AI system now handles a substantial portion of their daily tasks. Initially, this change may trigger feelings of insecurity regarding job stability. The psychological burden extends beyond the fear of replacement; it also encompasses the challenge of redefining one's role and identity in an evolving work environment. Adapting to collaborate with AI tools rather than compete against them can be daunting, requiring emotional resilience and cognitive flexibility.

Also, the collective psychological response to AI integration within a team can significantly influence organizational culture. In workplaces where employees feel threatened by automation, mistrust and resistance can permeate the atmosphere. A team that views AI as an adversary is less likely to collaborate effectively with emerging technologies or embrace innovation. Conversely, when organizations proactively address employee concerns through transparent communication and training programs, they can cultivate a supportive environment that alleviates anxiety and fosters adaptive mindsets.

One effective strategy for mitigating the psychological stress associated with AI disruption is through education and upskilling initiatives. By providing training focused on how to leverage AI tools, organizations empower employees, transforming fear into confidence. For example, if a marketing team receives instruction on using AI-driven analytics platforms for campaign optimization, they may begin to see these tools as allies rather than threats. Through hands-on workshops or online courses that reinforce their skills alongside technological advancements, employees enhance their capabilities and employability.

Mental health support systems also play a vital role in helping individuals cope with the stresses related to job changes brought about by AI disruptions. Organizations should prioritize resources such as counseling services or peer support groups, allowing employees to express their concerns openly. A tech company that implemented regular mental health check-ins alongside technology rollouts observed a marked improvement in employee morale and engagement. Providing space for dialogue around fears related to AI fosters resilience while reinforcing community among colleagues.

Exploring the idea of community-building further highlights its potential in creating psychologically safe environments where innovation can flourish. When teams feel secure enough to voice concerns or share ideas without fear of judgment, they are more likely to engage collaboratively with new technologies, ultimately driving successful outcomes in project initiatives. Encouraging open conversations about fear and uncertainty enables individuals to process their feelings while promoting group cohesion.

It's equally important for leaders within organizations to model adaptive behaviors when confronted with technological changes. Leadership sets the tone for organizational culture; when executives openly discuss their experiences with new tools or processes, they normalize struggle and reduce the stigma surrounding help-seeking or asking questions. This transparency encourages employees at all levels to embrace change rather than resist it.

The cumulative effect of addressing the psychological impacts stemming from AI disruption is profound: it transforms organizations from mere workplaces into thriving ecosystems where individuals feel valued and understood throughout their transformative journeys. Beyond survival in an evolving landscape lies an opportunity for growth—one where collaboration between humans and machines paves the way for innovative pathways forward.

By prioritizing both technical skills development and emotional well-being strategies, organizations equip their workforce with the resources necessary to navigate disruptions effectively while fostering resilience amidst uncertainty—an essential component for sustainable success in today's ever-changing economy. Embracing this holistic approach results in an empowered workforce ready not just for survival but also for thriving in the complexities of a digitally transformed world.

Building Personal and Organizational Resilience

Navigating the complexities of an AI-driven work environment demands not only technical skills but also a solid foundation of personal and organizational resilience. This resilience is built on a mindset that welcomes change and uncertainty, equipping both individuals and teams with the necessary tools to adapt effectively. As we explore this topic further, it becomes evident that resilience is not just an individual trait; it is a collective attribute that empowers organizations to thrive amid disruption.

To start, fostering personal resilience hinges on self-awareness. Individuals must acknowledge their emotional responses to the changes brought about by AI—be it anxiety over job security or excitement about new opportunities. Engaging in self-reflection practices, such as journaling or mindfulness meditation, can help professionals recognize their feelings and reactions. Take this example, someone transitioning from traditional marketing strategies to data-driven campaigns may feel overwhelmed by the new metrics they need to master. By understanding these emotions, they can take proactive steps to address them, like seeking mentorship or pursuing targeted learning opportunities.

Organizations also play a crucial role in nurturing an environment that fosters resilience. Cultivating a culture of psychological safety encourages employees to voice their concerns without fear of judgment. Establishing regular feedback loops, where leaders actively seek input from team members about their experiences with AI integration, helps identify pain points and areas where support is needed. For example, a financial services firm implemented monthly check-ins focused on technology adaptation; these discussions not only revealed employee challenges but also fostered camaraderie as teams worked through obstacles together.

Another vital component of resilience is flexibility—the ability to adapt swiftly in response to changing circumstances. Organizations that promote flexible work arrangements empower employees to manage their workloads more effectively amidst technological shifts. Take this example, offering remote work options can help employees adjust to new AI systems, whether at home or in the office. Flexibility also encompasses encouraging diverse thinking within teams. When team members are invited to explore innovative solutions rather than strictly adhering to established methods, they cultivate a culture of experimentation that bolsters resilience.

Implementing comprehensive training programs further enhances both personal and organizational resilience. Training should extend beyond technical skills to include emotional intelligence and adaptability. For example, workshops on leveraging AI tools can be paired with sessions on stress management and navigating workplace uncertainty. A healthcare organization that introduced integrated training modules for staff learning electronic health record systems combined technical skill development with coping strategies for managing workflow disruptions, resulting in increased confidence and improved patient care outcomes.

Leadership plays an equally important role in fostering a resilient organizational culture. Leaders who openly share their experiences with technological transitions demonstrate vulnerability and encourage others to do the same. This openness cultivates trust and reinforces the idea that adapting to change is a shared journey rather than a solitary endeavor. Take this example, during an AI rollout at a tech startup, executives participated in hands-on training alongside their teams, sharing insights from both successes and challenges encountered along the way.

Additionally, promoting peer support networks within organizations can further amplify efforts to build resilience. Employees who connect with colleagues facing similar challenges often find comfort and encouragement through shared experiences. Establishing mentorship programs or informal buddy systems enables individuals navigating AI disruptions to exchange tips and resources while strengthening interpersonal relationships across departments.

To wrap things up, building personal and organizational resilience involves more than just coping with AI-induced changes; it requires fostering an adaptive mindset rooted in self-awareness, community support, flexibility, and effective leadership engagement. By dedicating time to develop these aspects of resilience, both individuals and organizations enhance their capacity to navigate current disruptions and position themselves for long-term success in an increasingly automated future. This proactive approach ensures they are not merely surviving amidst change but thriving as innovative leaders capable of harnessing the full potential of AI advancements.

Strategies for Coping with Change

Change is an ever-present force in today's fast-paced work environment, particularly as AI technologies reshape industries and job roles. Navigating this change demands not only adaptability but also a proactive approach to personal and professional development. Embracing change involves understanding its nuances, preparing for its implications, and cultivating resilience to overcome its challenges.

One effective way to cope with change is by fostering a growth mindset. This concept, popularized by psychologist Carol Dweck, emphasizes that abilities and intelligence can be developed through dedication and hard work. By viewing challenges as opportunities for learning rather than insurmountable obstacles, you create a solid foundation for navigating uncertainty. For example, when confronted with new AI tools at work, instead of feeling intimidated or resistant, see it as an opportunity to enhance your skills. Engaging in online courses or workshops tailored to these tools—offered by platforms like Coursera or Udemy—can transform anxiety into competence.

Networking is another vital component during periods of transformation. Building relationships with peers who are also experiencing these changes can provide essential support and insights. Consider joining industry-specific groups or forums where professionals share their experiences with AI adoption. Participating in LinkedIn discussions about AI impacts in your field not only helps you connect with others but also broadens your understanding of how various professionals are adapting. Such community engagement fosters shared learning and emotional support—crucial elements when facing change.

Additionally, developing strong emotional resilience is key to managing change effectively. Emotional resilience involves maintaining a positive outlook amid uncertainty. Mindfulness techniques such as meditation or journaling can help center your thoughts and emotions during turbulent times. When you manage stress effectively, you position yourself to make clearer decisions about your career path amidst shifting landscapes.

Establishing flexible routines is equally important for accommodating sudden changes in work dynamics. Take this example, if you're transitioning from an office setting to remote work due to unforeseen circumstances, consider creating a home workspace that resembles your office environment. This could include setting regular hours and dressing professionally to signal a shift into 'work mode.' These practices help maintain productivity while allowing adaptability when new challenges arise.

Seeking mentorship from individuals who have successfully navigated significant changes can also provide valuable guidance. Mentors offer experience and wisdom that can illuminate pathways you might not see on your own. Their insights into how they handled transitions—and the lessons learned from their mistakes—can save you time and effort in finding solutions to your own challenges.

And, embracing technology as an ally rather than perceiving it as a threat is crucial in an AI-driven environment. Familiarizing yourself with productivity tools like Trello or Asana can streamline project management amid evolving workflows influenced by automation. By integrating these technologies into your daily processes, you'll not only enhance efficiency but also demonstrate adaptability—a highly valued trait in today's job market.

Finally, set realistic goals that focus on both short- and long-term outcomes related to the changes you're facing. Breaking larger objectives into manageable tasks helps alleviate feelings of overwhelm while providing clear benchmarks for assessing progress. Celebrate achievements along the way; even small victories significantly contribute to building confidence during periods of transformation.

By actively engaging with these strategies—cultivating a growth mindset, expanding your network, strengthening emotional resilience, establishing flexible routines, seeking mentorship, leveraging technology effectively, and setting attainable goals—you empower yourself to thrive amid the inevitable changes brought about by AI integration into the workforce. Successfully adapting positions you not only as a survivor but also as a leader ready to embrace future challenges head-on.

The Role of Leadership in Managing AI Transitions

Leadership is crucial in navigating organizations through the complexities of AI transitions. It extends beyond merely managing resources; it involves creating an environment that nurtures innovation and adaptability. As AI technologies transform industries, leaders must leverage their vision to cultivate a culture that embraces change while ensuring their teams feel supported and empowered.

At the heart of effective leadership is clear communication. Leaders need to articulate the rationale behind AI implementation, addressing concerns and highlighting potential benefits. For example, when a company opts to integrate AI into its customer service operations, it's essential for leaders to explain how this will enhance efficiency and allow employees to focus on more valuable tasks. Regular updates about the AI journey can help demystify the technology, reassuring employees that they are not being replaced but rather supported in their roles.

Another critical aspect of leading through transitions is fostering a sense of ownership among team members. Encouraging employees to actively participate in the integration process not only builds buy-in but also taps into diverse insights that can improve implementation outcomes. Forming cross-functional teams to explore how AI can optimize specific workflows empowers employees, giving them a stake in the transition and reinforcing their value within the organization.

Investing in training and development is also vital for effective leadership during AI transitions. By offering tailored educational resources—such as workshops, webinars, or online courses—leaders can help employees acquire the skills needed to work alongside new technologies. Take this example, training on data analysis tools can enable team members to leverage AI-generated insights more effectively, enhancing decision-making processes. When leaders prioritize skill development, they demonstrate their commitment to employee growth and adaptability.

And, recognizing and addressing the emotional landscape during transitions is essential for effective leadership. Change often brings anxiety and resistance; therefore, leaders should foster an open dialogue where employees feel safe expressing their concerns. Regular check-ins allow leaders to gauge team morale and promptly address any issues that arise. Incorporating team-building activities can further alleviate stress by promoting camaraderie and collaboration amidst uncertainty.

Leaders must also model resilience. Demonstrating a positive attitude toward change can inspire similar responses from team members. Sharing personal stories about overcoming challenges can humanize the leadership experience, forging authentic connections with employees who may be grappling with their own feelings about the transition. This approach fosters trust and encourages a collective mindset focused on solutions rather than obstacles.

In addition to soft skills like empathy and communication, embracing data-driven decision-making during AI transitions is crucial. Utilizing analytics tools helps leaders assess progress and effectiveness while identifying areas needing adjustment or support. For example, tracking employee engagement levels or productivity metrics before and after implementing AI solutions provides valuable insights into how well the transition is being received. Data-informed decisions empower leaders to make adjustments based on evidence rather than intuition alone.

Finally, fostering a culture of continuous improvement is essential for maintaining momentum throughout an AI transition. Encouraging feedback loops allows employees to share their experiences with new technologies, providing leadership with actionable insights for further enhancements. Implementing regular retrospectives—where teams reflect on successes and areas for improvement—can refine processes and ensure ongoing adaptation as new technologies evolve.

In summary, effective leadership during AI transitions

demands a multifaceted approach that encompasses clear communication, empowerment, emotional intelligence, resilience, data-driven strategies, and a commitment to continuous improvement. By embodying these principles, leaders not only guide their organizations through the challenges of change but also inspire their teams to thrive in an increasingly complex landscape shaped by artificial intelligence. This proactive approach lays the groundwork for long-term success while positioning organizations as adaptable players in the evolving job economy.

Creating Flexible Work Environments

Creating flexible work environments is essential in today's AI-driven landscape, where agility often determines success. How X works work is evolving; organizations are moving away from traditional office spaces and embracing hybrid models that integrate remote and in-office dynamics. This flexibility not only meets the diverse needs of employees but also aligns with the fast-paced changes in technology.

A key element of a flexible work environment is the design of the physical workspace itself. Offices that prioritize adaptability can foster collaboration while also allowing for individual focus. For example, using modular furniture enables teams to reconfigure their spaces according to project requirements. Open areas for brainstorming can coexist with quiet zones designated for deep work. A case study from a leading tech firm revealed that such adaptable setups increased team productivity by 20%, highlighting the tangible benefits of thoughtful design.

In addition to physical space, establishing clear communication channels is vital for supporting both remote and on-site employees. Tools like Slack or Microsoft Teams facilitate real-time collaboration, regardless of location. Regular virtual check-ins help ensure all team members stay aligned, fostering a sense of inclusion and cohesion.

Scheduling weekly meetings that accommodate various time zones can further enhance participation, allowing everyone to engage meaningfully with their peers.

Training programs tailored for flexible environments are equally important. Providing resources that help employees navigate new technologies empowers them to take ownership of their workspaces effectively. Take this example, implementing an onboarding program focused on digital collaboration tools equips new hires with essential skills from day one. A company that recently transitioned to a hybrid model found that new employees who completed this training felt more confident and integrated within their teams.

Encouraging a results-oriented culture also significantly boosts the effectiveness of flexible work arrangements. By shifting the focus from micromanaging processes to emphasizing outcomes and deliverables, leaders can motivate employees to take ownership of their projects and manage their schedules independently. Organizations that adopt this philosophy often see increased job satisfaction among employees, which leads to lower turnover rates.

Recognizing the diverse circumstances of employees is crucial when crafting flexibility policies. Family-friendly initiatives—such as flexible hours or remote work options—can support those with caregiving responsibilities or other commitments outside of work. Recent surveys indicate that organizations offering such benefits experience heightened employee loyalty and morale.

Feedback mechanisms are indispensable for refining strategies in flexible workplaces. Encouraging employees to share their experiences helps identify areas for improvement or innovation within the organization. Conducting regular pulse surveys can provide valuable insights into how employees are adapting to new systems and what additional support they may need. By actively responding to feedback, companies demonstrate their commitment to continuous improvement —a vital aspect of effective change management.

Establishing strong cultural foundations within flexible environments is equally important. A culture rooted in trust allows employees greater freedom in managing their time and responsibilities while maintaining accountability. Transparency about performance expectations helps alleviate uncertainties regarding productivity in remote settings.

Incorporating wellness initiatives further enhances flexibility within workplace structures, especially as mental health has gained prominence in discussions about employee well-being during transitions toward remote work. Organizations that provide resources such as mindfulness programs or access to counseling services show a commitment not only to productivity but also to the holistic health of their employees.

Finally, as technology continues to evolve rapidly, investing in upskilling becomes essential for maintaining a competitive edge within flexible environments. Continuous learning opportunities enable teams to adapt seamlessly alongside technological advancements and remain relevant amid disruptions caused by AI integration across sectors.

A comprehensive approach to cultivating flexibility is not only an immediate necessity but also a long-term strategy rooted in resilience against future changes. This helps organizations not just to survive but thrive amid ongoing transformations driven by advancements in artificial intelligence.

Identifying and Overcoming Barriers to Change

Navigating the complexities of an AI-driven landscape requires organizations to identify and overcome barriers to change. Each transformation presents unique challenges, often stemming from established practices, mindsets, or structural limitations. Recognizing these barriers is essential for creating an environment that embraces innovation and adaptability.

Resistance to change is frequently fueled by fear—fear of the unknown, fear of job displacement, or even fear of being overwhelmed by new technology. Employees accustomed to certain routines may feel threatened when their workflows are disrupted. Take this example, a manufacturing plant transitioning to automated systems may encounter pushback from workers worried about job security. Addressing these concerns through transparent communication is crucial. By engaging employees in discussions about the benefits of AI, organizations can alleviate fears and empower staff to see themselves as vital contributors to the transformation.

Inadequate training is another common barrier that can hinder the adoption of new technologies. If employees feel unprepared to navigate advanced systems, their reluctance can escalate into outright resistance. A healthcare organization that introduced an electronic health record (EHR) system experienced significant pushback from its staff due to insufficient training. However, by implementing comprehensive training sessions and providing ongoing support, they transformed resistance into enthusiasm. This shift underscores the importance of equipping employees with the necessary skills to thrive in a changing environment.

Organizational structure also plays a pivotal role in facilitating or obstructing change. Hierarchical models can stifle agility and slow decision-making processes, making it challenging for organizations to respond quickly to emerging technologies. A tech startup that moved from a traditional hierarchy to a flat organizational structure saw marked improvements in collaboration and innovation. Teams became empowered to make quicker decisions, experiment with new ideas, and adapt strategies without being bogged down by bureaucratic delays.

Cultural factors significantly influence how change is embraced within an organization. A culture that does not prioritize learning and growth will struggle with change initiatives. Encouraging a mindset of experimentation—where failures are viewed as learning opportunities—can foster resilience and adaptability among team members. For example, a finance firm implementing AI-driven analytics tools recognized that initial missteps were part of their journey toward success. By celebrating these experiences rather than stigmatizing them, they cultivated a culture that actively embraced change.

Leadership commitment is paramount in addressing barriers to change. Leaders must model the behaviors they wish to see throughout the organization, demonstrating flexibility and openly sharing their own learning journeys with new technologies. When leaders champion change by discussing their challenges and successes, it creates a ripple effect that inspires others to follow suit.

A lack of resources can also impede progress, particularly when organizations attempt changes without adequate financial backing or technological infrastructure. An automotive company exploring AI for predictive maintenance faced setbacks due to budget constraints that limited its ability to invest in essential tools and training programs. By reallocating funds and prioritizing innovation initiatives, they overcame this barrier and successfully integrated AI solutions.

Engaging with external partners can further mitigate barriers by introducing fresh perspectives and expertise. Collaborations with academic institutions or industry experts can offer valuable insights into best practices for navigating AI adoption challenges. Take this example, a retail chain partnered with local universities to research consumer behavior in AI-enhanced environments, which led to more informed decision-making about technology integration.

Monitoring progress during the transition process is vital for identifying ongoing challenges and adjusting strategies accordingly. Regular check-ins can help determine whether employees feel supported or if persistent issues arise. For example, an IT department conducting biweekly feedback sessions during its rollout of new software discovered that open dialogue enabled quick adjustments that significantly improved user satisfaction.

Finally, establishing structured pathways for feedback ensures employees have a voice in shaping change initiatives. Creating channels such as anonymous surveys or suggestion boxes empowers staff members to contribute ideas and express concerns regarding transitions they experience firsthand.

Addressing barriers to change requires a multifaceted approach rooted in understanding human behavior, fostering open communication, prioritizing training, and maintaining agility within organizational structures. By proactively tackling these obstacles, organizations build resilience against future disruptions and cultivate environments where innovation thrives amidst rapid technological advancements.

Developing a Change Management Framework

Creating a change management framework is vital for organizations aiming to succeed in an AI-driven economy. This structured approach ensures that changes are not only managed effectively but also embraced at all levels of the organization. The success of such a framework hinges on its adaptability and alignment with organizational goals, empowering teams to navigate transitions while minimizing disruption.

Essentially of an effective change management framework is a clear vision that outlines the desired outcomes of the transition. Establishing this vision involves explaining not just what changes will occur, but also why they are important. For example, an insurance company integrating AI into its customer service should communicate how these enhancements will lead to faster response times and personalized experiences, ultimately benefiting both employees and customers. This clarity fosters buy-in from stakeholders, who can recognize the tangible advantages of the proposed changes.

Once the vision is set, assessing current capabilities becomes essential for understanding the organization's strengths and weaknesses. A thorough analysis allows leaders to identify gaps that must be addressed for successful implementation. Consider a financial services firm that discovered its workforce lacked the digital skills necessary for AI integration. By identifying this gap early, the firm developed targeted training programs to enhance employee competencies in critical areas, facilitating a smoother transition.

Engaging employees throughout the change process is equally important. Involving team members in discussions about upcoming changes cultivates a sense of ownership and accountability. Take this example, a technology company adopted an inclusive approach by forming cross-functional teams to provide feedback on proposed changes and test new systems before full-scale implementation. This participatory model surfaced potential issues early on and generated enthusiasm among employees who felt their input was valued.

Training and support structures are crucial components of any change management framework. Organizations must prioritize equipping their workforce with the necessary skills to adapt effectively. A pharmaceutical company undertaking AI-driven drug discovery faced initial challenges due to employees' unfamiliarity with data analytics tools. By offering comprehensive workshops and ongoing mentorship from data specialists, the company transformed uncertainty into confidence, enabling scientists to effectively leverage AI technologies in their research.

Effective communication strategies also play a vital role in guiding organizations through change. Establishing clear communication channels ensures that everyone remains informed about progress, setbacks, and evolving expectations. A retail chain experienced notable success by implementing weekly updates through newsletters and town hall meetings during its transition to an automated inventory management system. These communications kept staff engaged and informed about milestones while providing opportunities for real-time feedback.

Feedback mechanisms are essential for continuously refining the change management process. Regularly soliciting input from employees helps identify emerging challenges that may not have been anticipated initially. An automotive manufacturer introduced monthly feedback loops during its deployment of AI solutions on production lines, allowing workers to voice concerns regarding system usability or functionality issues promptly. By addressing these points quickly, management demonstrated responsiveness and maintained employee morale.

Creating an environment that encourages learning is another critical aspect of successful change management. Organizations thrive when they cultivate a culture that embraces experimentation and iterative improvements rather than one that penalizes failure. A nonprofit organization integrating AI for fundraising initiatives encouraged team members to explore diverse approaches without fear of negative consequences, leading to innovative strategies that enhanced donor engagement.

Monitoring key performance indicators (KPIs) throughout the transformation journey offers valuable insights into how well changes are being received and implemented. Setting specific metrics—such as employee engagement levels, operational efficiency rates, or customer satisfaction scores —enables organizations to evaluate progress objectively. Take this example, a telecommunications provider tracked call resolution times before and after implementing an AI system, revealing substantial improvements that validated their change efforts.

Finally, sustaining momentum after initial implementation is crucial for long-term success. Changes should be viewed not as one-off events but as part of an ongoing evolution within the organization. Continuing education programs or refresher training sessions can reinforce skills learned during transitions while keeping employees engaged with new technologies as they develop.

A robust change management framework empowers organizations by fostering clarity, engagement, training, effective communication, feedback integration, a learning-oriented culture, performance tracking, and sustained momentum. Together, these elements create pathways toward innovation in an ever-evolving landscape driven by AI advancements. By embracing this comprehensive framework, companies can not only survive but thrive in an increasingly automated future where adaptability is essential.

Encouraging a Culture of Adaptability

Cultivating a culture of adaptability is essential in today's fast-paced environment, particularly as organizations face the transformative impact of AI. Adaptability transcends being just a buzzword; it is a crucial competency that enables organizations to navigate change with resilience and creativity. When employees feel empowered to embrace change, they become active contributors to the organization's evolution instead of mere observers.

A key factor in fostering this adaptability lies in effective leadership. Leaders set the organizational tone, and their behaviors significantly influence how teams respond to change. For example, leaders at a global tech firm initiated regular "innovation sprints," where employees were encouraged to share ideas for improving processes and products. This initiative not only generated valuable insights but also instilled a sense of ownership among employees, who felt their contributions were vital to shaping the company's future.

Continuous learning is another vital strategy for nurturing an adaptable culture. Organizations can implement training programs that are responsive to current needs while also anticipating future demands. A noteworthy instance comes from a healthcare organization that integrated AI into patient care management. To prepare staff, they established an ongoing educational series focusing on emerging technologies and trends in healthcare AI. This proactive approach allowed employees to adapt swiftly when new tools were introduced, boosting their confidence and competence.

Creating safe spaces for experimentation further supports adaptability. When employees are encouraged to test new ideas without fear of failure, innovation thrives. A startup specializing in app development adopted a policy allowing team members to propose projects outside their typical responsibilities during designated "hack days." These sessions led to groundbreaking applications that were later integrated into the company's offerings, illustrating how fostering a culture of experimentation can yield significant advancements.

Communication is also critical in cultivating an adaptable workforce. Transparent dialogue about organizational changes demystifies the process and alleviates employee anxiety. Take this example, during an internal restructuring at a large manufacturing firm, leaders held open forums to discuss upcoming changes and directly address concerns. This level of transparency built trust and ensured employees felt informed and involved throughout the transition.

Additionally, recognizing and rewarding adaptability among employees can reinforce desired behaviors within the organization. Recognition programs that celebrate individuals who demonstrate flexibility or innovative thinking encourage others to adopt similar mindsets. A financial services company launched a "Change Champion" initiative, spotlighting individuals who actively embraced new methodologies in monthly communications. This not only motivated those recognized but also inspired colleagues to cultivate a similar attitude toward change.

As organizations promote adaptability, they must also remain mindful of the potential for burnout associated with constant change. Balancing demands with support systems is crucial; providing resources such as mental health support or wellness programs alongside high performance expectations during transitions is essential. A multinational corporation introduced wellness initiatives during its digital transformation journey—offering yoga sessions and mindfulness workshops—to help employees manage stress while adapting to new technologies.

Finally, organizations should continuously evaluate their progress in fostering an adaptable culture. Gathering feedback through surveys or focus groups offers valuable insights into employee sentiments regarding change initiatives and highlights areas for improvement. For example, a retail chain utilized post-implementation surveys after launching new AI tools to collect feedback from staff on usability and overall satisfaction with the changes made. This feedback loop enabled them to refine processes based on employee experiences continuously.

By embedding these practices into everyday operations, organizations can create environments where adaptability thrives at all levels. Employees become more resilient and innovative as they engage positively with change instead of resisting it passively. The benefits are evident: organizations that nurture adaptable cultures not only navigate transitions effectively but also position themselves as leaders in their respective industries—ready to seize the opportunities presented by the ever-evolving landscape shaped by AI advancements.

CHAPTER 10: DIVERSE PERSPECTIVES ON AI IMPACT

*Understanding Global
Variations in AI Adoption*

Understanding global variations in AI adoption is essential, as different regions and cultures respond uniquely to technological advancements. In North America, for instance, there is a strong emphasis on integrating AI across various sectors. This drive is largely fueled by a tech-savvy population and significant investments in research and development. Companies like Google and Microsoft are leading the way in AI solutions, setting global benchmarks for innovation. The ready availability of venture capital further accelerates this trend, creating a competitive environment where businesses must embrace AI to remain relevant.

In contrast, Europe adopts a more cautious approach to AI integration, influenced by stringent regulations focused on data privacy and ethical considerations. The General Data Protection Regulation (GDPR) has instilled a sense of caution among businesses regarding their use of data-driven technologies. This regulatory landscape encourages companies to prioritize transparency and ethical practices when implementing AI solutions. For example, in Germany, substantial government support aims to establish standards guiding AI deployment, reflecting a preference for societal welfare over rapid technological advancement.

Asia presents a diverse landscape of AI adoption with varying degrees of enthusiasm. Countries like China are aggressively pursuing AI initiatives, viewing them as vital to their national strategy for economic growth. Chinese firms are at the forefront of implementing technologies such as facial recognition, smart city initiatives, and manufacturing automation, bolstered by government backing through funding and infrastructure investments. Conversely, nations like India are focusing on using AI to address socio-economic challenges—like improving agricultural productivity and healthcare access—rather than competing globally with cutting-edge innovations.

Cultural attitudes toward technology also play a significant role in AI adoption rates. Scandinavian countries tend to exhibit higher public trust in technology, thanks to long-standing welfare systems that prioritize social equity. So, these nations often embrace innovations like robotics in elder care and automated systems in public services with minimal resistance. In contrast, regions with historical skepticism toward technology may experience pushback against AI initiatives, which can slow down implementation due to concerns about job displacement or privacy violations.

In Africa, the landscape of AI adoption is marked by both promise and challenges. Countries like Kenya have made significant strides in mobile-based technologies that leverage AI to address local issues, such as enhancing health service delivery through mobile clinics powered by data analytics. However, infrastructural limitations and skill gaps hinder broader implementations across the continent. Initiatives aimed at education and capacity-building are crucial for cultivating local talent capable of harnessing the benefits of artificial intelligence.

Exploring regional disparities reveals how industries adapt differently based on their environments. In agriculture-heavy economies like those in parts of South America, AI applications targeting crop management and livestock monitoring are gaining traction but are often constrained by accessibility issues related to technology infrastructure. Additionally, language barriers can impede the effective deployment of natural language processing tools designed for customer service interactions across diverse populations.

There is much to learn from one another's experiences in adopting AI technologies effectively while avoiding common pitfalls associated with hasty implementations. Take this example, a successful pilot program by an Indian startup utilizing drone technology for precision farming could inspire similar initiatives elsewhere seeking to enhance agricultural efficiency through technological innovations.

Cross-border collaborations present promising opportunities to overcome the barriers posed by uneven adoption rates. Global partnerships can facilitate knowledge-sharing, allowing developed regions to exchange best practices with emerging markets striving to advance their capabilities without repeating past mistakes. Such relationships can deepen understanding not only of what works technologically but also ethically, emphasizing the importance of local contexts when considering widespread adoption strategies.

recognizing these global variations provides professionals with insights necessary for shaping strategies that honor local nuances while leveraging universal principles behind successful AI implementations. As organizations navigate increasingly complex landscapes influenced by artificial intelligence, understanding these dynamics will be crucial—not just for thriving within specific markets but also for contributing positively to global advancements that promote sustainable growth across economies worldwide.

Gender and AI: Opportunities and Challenges

Gender dynamics in the context of artificial intelligence (AI) present a complex landscape filled with both opportunities and challenges that warrant careful consideration. As AI technologies increasingly permeate various industries, the implications for gender equity and representation become more pronounced. Women, who have historically been underrepresented in tech fields, face unique obstacles as AI reshapes the job market. While the integration of AI can create pathways for greater participation, it also poses the risk of perpetuating existing inequalities unless proactive measures are implemented.

The underrepresentation of women in STEM (science, technology, engineering, and mathematics) fields remains a significant issue in many regions, particularly in roles directly associated with AI development and deployment. The World Economic Forum has repeatedly emphasized that the lack of female representation in technology limits diversity and can skew the design and functionality of AI systems. When women are excluded from decision-making processes, their perspectives and priorities may be overlooked, leading to biased algorithms that reinforce stereotypes instead of dismantling them.

Despite these challenges, there are encouraging signs of progress. Organizations such as Women Who Code and Girls Who Code are actively working to close the gender gap by creating communities that empower women to pursue careers in technology. Through mentorship programs and coding bootcamps, these initiatives help cultivate skills that enhance employability in the tech sector. Additionally, corporate diversity initiatives aimed at increasing the number of women in technical roles reflect a growing recognition of the importance of inclusivity.

The potential for AI to act as an equalizer is evident across various sectors. Take this example, in healthcare, AI can streamline processes and provide insights that improve patient outcomes, benefiting society while also creating new job opportunities for women in health tech roles. Similarly, advancements in remote work technologies driven by AI offer greater flexibility in employment, allowing more women to balance their careers with family responsibilities.

However, this optimistic outlook must be tempered with caution regarding the ethical implications of AI systems themselves. Gender bias present in training data can result in models that unfairly disadvantage women or reinforce societal biases. A notable example occurred when certain AI recruitment tools favored male candidates over equally qualified female applicants due to historical data patterns reflecting gender biases in previous hiring practices. Such instances highlight the critical need for diverse teams working on AI projects—not only to achieve equitable outcomes but also to ensure accountability during development.

Cultural variations also significantly influence how gender dynamics intersect with AI adoption. In some societies where traditional gender roles prevail, women's participation in tech may be further hindered by societal norms and insufficient support systems. Conversely, countries that prioritize educational equity often experience higher rates of female enrollment in STEM fields. In these environments, government policies promoting gender parity can catalyze significant advancements toward greater inclusion.

Real-world examples illustrate both the opportunities and

challenges faced by women navigating this evolving landscape. In India, initiatives like "Digital Sakhi" train rural women to become digital entrepreneurs using mobile technology—showcasing how AI-driven tools can uplift communities while economically empowering women. On the other hand, some sectors struggle with high turnover rates among female employees due to workplace cultures resistant to change or lacking adequate support structures.

Addressing these complexities requires more than mere awareness; it necessitates intentional actions from organizations and governments alike. Companies must invest not only in hiring practices that promote diversity but also in creating environments where women feel valued and empowered to contribute fully. Policies supporting family leave, flexible work arrangements, and professional development opportunities can foster a more inclusive atmosphere conducive to innovation.

Engaging men as allies in this endeavor is also crucial for dismantling systemic barriers that inhibit women's advancement in tech sectors typically dominated by male leadership. Conversations about gender equity should focus on collaboration rather than competition among genders, fostering a collective commitment to cultivating equitable workplaces where everyone can thrive.

The journey toward achieving gender equity amidst AI integration is multifaceted yet essential for unlocking innovation potential within organizations worldwide. By recognizing these challenges while championing opportunities, we can create pathways not only to bridge gaps but also to transform industries through diverse perspectives —ultimately reshaping narratives around both gender and technology for generations to come.

The Impact of AI on Different Demographics

The impact of AI on various demographics is both

profound and complex, affecting multiple facets of life, work, and societal structures. As AI technologies evolve and permeate numerous sectors, the implications for age, race, socioeconomic status, and education level become increasingly apparent. Each demographic group experiences these changes in unique ways, presenting distinct challenges and opportunities that must be addressed to ensure equitable progress.

Beginning with age demographics, the rise of AI highlights a generational divide that requires attention. Younger individuals often have a natural affinity for technology; growing up in a digital environment has made skills like coding and digital literacy commonplace for them. This positions them well to navigate AI-driven job markets. For example, in fields such as marketing or data analysis, younger professionals can effectively leverage AI tools to enhance their efficiency and creativity. Conversely, older workers may face significant challenges in adapting to rapid technological shifts. To mitigate this issue, companies should invest in reskilling initiatives tailored to older employees, creating training programs that address their specific needs and help bridge the generational gap.

Race is another crucial factor influencing experiences within the AI landscape. Underrepresented minorities often encounter systemic barriers that limit their access to tech education and career opportunities. A report from McKinsey indicates that companies with diverse workforces are 35% more likely to outperform their peers in profitability. This finding underscores that promoting diversity is not just a social responsibility but also a strategic business imperative. Initiatives aimed at increasing representation among racial minorities in tech can drive innovation through diverse perspectives. Programs like Code2040 specifically support Black and Latinx individuals by providing mentorships and internships that connect them with industry leaders.

Socioeconomic status further complicates the dynamics of AI adoption across demographics. Individuals from lower socioeconomic backgrounds frequently lack access to quality education and resources essential for thriving in an AI-driven economy. This situation perpetuates a cycle where talent goes unnoticed due to systemic inequities rather than a lack of capability or ambition. In response, community colleges have begun offering accessible training programs focused on developing AI skills, creating pathways for individuals who may not possess traditional four-year degrees but have significant potential.

Educational attainment is yet another critical factor shaping how different demographics engage with AI technologies. Those with higher levels of education generally find themselves better positioned within emerging industries driven by AI advancements. In contrast, individuals without post-secondary degrees may struggle as many entry-level jobs become automated or require specific technical skills not included in traditional curricula. Addressing this gap necessitates collaboration between educational institutions and tech companies to create curriculum standards aligned with industry needs—ensuring students acquire relevant skills before entering the workforce.

Regional disparities also significantly influence how various groups interact with AI technology. Urban areas typically enjoy better access to high-speed internet and advanced infrastructure compared to rural communities, resulting in residents of rural regions facing barriers such as limited job opportunities leveraging AI technologies or insufficient training resources nearby. Telecommunication companies have begun initiatives to expand internet access into underserved areas; these efforts not only enhance connectivity but also unlock remote work opportunities powered by AI tools.

As we delve deeper into these demographic influences, it becomes evident that one-size-fits-all solutions are inadequate when addressing the challenges posed by integrating artificial intelligence across diverse populations. Tailored approaches grounded in community engagement will be vital for developing strategies that accommodate unique demographic needs while fostering inclusivity.

Real-world examples demonstrate how targeted interventions can yield positive outcomes for demographics affected by the proliferation of AI. In South Africa, organizations like The Digital Skills Academy focus on equipping young people from disadvantaged backgrounds with essential digital skills necessary for successful careers in technology—helping them confidently navigate an increasingly automated world.

Recognizing these varied impacts enhances our understanding of artificial intelligence's role within society and highlights the necessity for collaborative efforts among governments, educational institutions, and private organizations committed to creating equitable pathways into tech-focused careers.

By actively engaging with demographic diversity when implementing AI solutions—from inclusive hiring practices to reskilling initiatives targeting underrepresented groups—we can cultivate environments conducive to innovation while ensuring equal opportunities for all amidst the transformative wave of technological advancement.

embracing this multifaceted perspective on demographic impacts not only helps us identify challenges but also uncovers promising avenues for growth—leading us toward an inclusive future where everyone benefits from the possibilities ushered in by artificial intelligence.

Regional Economies and AI Integration

Examining the integration of AI within regional economies

reveals that local contexts significantly shape the challenges and opportunities these technologies present. Factors such as geography, industry composition, and infrastructure play crucial roles in how regions adapt to and leverage AI advancements. These variations drive distinct approaches to AI adoption, which can either empower or hinder economic development.

Silicon Valley serves as a prime example of successful AI integration. Renowned for its concentration of venture capital, research institutions, and a highly skilled workforce, this region has made AI a core element of business strategies across various sectors. Companies like Google and Facebook are at the forefront of AI development, continuously pushing boundaries through extensive research initiatives and innovative products. This dynamic ecosystem fosters collaboration between startups and established firms, creating a fertile ground for experimentation and growth.

In contrast, rural areas face significant hurdles in adopting AI technologies. Limited access to high-speed internet restricts their ability to utilize cloud-based services or engage in remote work—an increasingly vital aspect of the modern economy. Take this example, farmers relying on smart agriculture tools encounter challenges in implementing AI-driven solutions without adequate connectivity or technological resources. To address these disparities, targeted investments in infrastructure development must be paired with training programs aimed at enhancing digital literacy within these communities.

Industrial composition also plays a pivotal role in how regions harness AI's potential. Regions with robust manufacturing bases may adopt automation solutions to boost productivity while retraining workers for emerging roles. A notable example is Germany's automotive sector; companies like BMW are integrating AI into production processes while simultaneously investing in upskilling initiatives that prepare their workforce for a future where human-machine collaboration is commonplace.

Conversely, regions heavily reliant on traditional industries —such as coal mining or textiles—may struggle more significantly with AI adoption due to entrenched economic structures resistant to change. As markets shift towards technologically advanced sectors, these areas risk becoming economically marginalized unless proactive measures are taken. Community-based initiatives offering retraining programs can help workers transition into fields with higher growth potential, thereby enhancing local resilience against technological disruptions.

Government policy plays an influential role in shaping regional differences in AI integration. Policies promoting research and innovation hubs often yield beneficial outcomes by fostering collaboration among academia, industry leaders, and startups—creating environments where groundbreaking ideas can thrive. The European Union's investment strategies aimed at enhancing regional digitalization exemplify this approach by directing funds into projects that improve digital skills across diverse populations while ensuring equitable access to technology.

Addressing each region's unique needs requires engagement from multiple stakeholders. Local governments must collaborate with educational institutions and private companies to align training programs effectively with market demands. For example, partnerships between community colleges and tech companies can facilitate tailored educational offerings focused on developing specific skills relevant to local industries impacted by AI advancements.

A case study illustrating effective regional integration is Atlanta's burgeoning tech ecosystem—a city not traditionally known for its technology sector but which has experienced rapid growth due to strategic investments in education and infrastructure. Local universities have partnered with businesses like Microsoft and AT&T to create coding boot camps designed to equip students from diverse backgrounds with the critical skills needed for the evolving job market.

The implications of these developments extend beyond immediate economic benefits; they highlight the importance of fostering inclusivity within the labor force while ensuring equitable access to technological advancements across all demographics. By tailoring approaches based on regional characteristics alongside demographic considerations, we can cultivate environments conducive to innovation—ultimately paving pathways for sustainable growth that embraces diversity.

Recognizing regional nuances enriches our understanding of the broader implications of AI integration and underscores the significance of collaborative efforts among stakeholders committed to creating balanced ecosystems where every community can thrive amidst this technological revolution. By fostering an adaptable mindset capable of navigating challenges unique to each locality, we enhance our collective resilience as we shape an inclusive future driven by artificial intelligence's transformative potential.

Cultural Differences in AI Acceptance

Cultural attitudes toward AI are as varied as the technologies themselves, influencing how societies either embrace or resist these innovations. Understanding these cultural differences is essential, particularly when considering their implications for workforce integration and the acceptance of AI technologies. While some cultures adopt AI as a natural progression of technology, others exhibit skepticism or outright resistance due to historical, social, or economic factors.

In Japan, for instance, the relationship with technology is deeply rooted in cultural values. The Japanese have a long-standing appreciation for technological advancements, viewing them as tools to enhance quality of life. This positive outlook has fostered widespread acceptance of AI across various sectors, including robotics and healthcare. Companies like SoftBank have pioneered AI-driven robots that assist the elderly, reflecting a societal inclination to integrate technology in ways that resonate with communal values. Such acceptance creates an environment conducive to AI solutions that not only boost productivity but also address pressing social challenges.

In contrast, many European countries approach AI integration with caution. Concerns regarding privacy, data security, and ethical implications dominate public discussions. The European Union has enacted stringent regulations governing data use and AI development, underscoring a cultural commitment to safeguarding individual rights over the rapid pace of technological advancement. While this regulatory framework may slow down the adoption of AI, it also encourages meaningful dialogue about ethical considerations and societal impacts—critical elements for sustainable technology integration.

Similarly, India's cultural landscape regarding AI is complex and varies significantly between urban and rural populations. Urban areas enthusiastically embrace digital innovation, fueled by a burgeoning tech startup culture in cities like Bangalore. Young professionals here often see AI as a gateway to growth and entrepreneurial success. In contrast, rural communities may view these advancements with skepticism or indifference due to limited exposure and understanding of technology's benefits. Bridging this gap requires initiatives focused on education and awareness; programs that illustrate practical applications of AI in agriculture or healthcare can demonstrate tangible benefits and foster acceptance.

Cultural narratives also shape how AI's potential is communicated across different societies. In the United States, discussions often revolve around individualism and innovation—positioning AI as a tool for personal empowerment and economic advantage. Silicon Valley exemplifies this ethos, where stories of startup success driven by AI inspire many to pursue careers in technology. On the other hand, cultures that prioritize collectivism may frame discussions around AI in terms of its potential impact on community welfare and shared resources rather than individual gain.

The generational divide adds another layer of complexity to cultural acceptance of AI. Younger generations tend to be more technologically savvy and open to integrating AI into their daily lives compared to older individuals who may feel overwhelmed by rapid change. Surveys conducted across various countries indicate that millennials and Gen Z are more inclined to trust AI-driven decision-making in areas such as healthcare than their older counterparts, who often prioritize human judgment.

To effectively navigate these cultural differences in AI acceptance, tailored strategies must resonate with local values and beliefs. Educational campaigns aimed at informing communities about the benefits and risks associated with AI can help alleviate fears while promoting understanding. For example, workshops featuring local leaders discussing how AI can enhance traditional practices might build trust among skeptical populations.

A successful case study emerges from Finland's educational system, which emphasizes digital literacy from an early age. By incorporating technology education into school curricula, Finland nurtures a culture of acceptance toward new technologies among children who grow up comfortable with digital tools—including AI applications—ultimately preparing them for future technological landscapes.

fostering acceptance of AI requires recognizing and respecting cultural differences while promoting inclusivity and collaboration among stakeholders. Engaging communities in meaningful discussions about the implications of AI tailored to their specific contexts—whether through local initiatives or national policies—can pave the way for broader acceptance across diverse cultural landscapes.

These efforts not only facilitate smoother transitions into an increasingly automated future but also ensure that the benefits of AI are equitably distributed across all segments of society—empowering individuals while preserving cultural identities amidst technological evolution.

Policy and AI Across Borders

The landscape of AI policy is continuously evolving, shaped by the diverse needs and perspectives of nations around the world. As governments navigate the complexities of AI technologies, they must balance innovation with regulation and consider the broader societal impacts. AI policies extend beyond mere technological management; they define the relationship between citizens and digital advancements, a dynamic that varies significantly from one country to another.

In Canada, for example, a proactive approach to AI policy emphasizes collaboration among government, academia, and industry. The Canadian government has made substantial investments in AI research while also prioritizing ethical guidelines for its development. This collaborative framework has positioned Canada as a leader in responsible AI implementation. Initiatives like the Pan-Canadian Artificial Intelligence Strategy illustrate how comprehensive policies can drive economic growth while addressing ethical concerns. By fostering public-private partnerships, Canada sets a standard for integrating technological progress with societal values.

In contrast, nations that have historically lagged in technological adoption often encounter challenges in developing effective AI policies. Many developing countries grapple with limited infrastructure and resources necessary for robust AI governance frameworks. Without adequate regulatory bodies or expertise, these nations risk missing out on the benefits of AI. However, this gap also creates opportunities for international collaboration. Global partnerships focused on knowledge sharing can equip these countries with the tools needed to address their unique challenges effectively. Programs aimed at skill development within local communities can empower individuals to engage with and benefit from technological advancements.

As different regions adopt varying approaches to AI regulation, it becomes clear that a one-size-fits-all strategy is inadequate. The European Union, for instance, enforces strict data protection laws like the General Data Protection Regulation (GDPR), reflecting a cultural emphasis on privacy and individual rights. While this regulatory framework fosters public trust in technology, it can also stifle innovation if compliance becomes overly burdensome for businesses. The challenge lies in finding a balance between protecting citizens and encouraging innovation—an ongoing dialogue among policymakers, businesses, and civil society is essential.

Where X meets Y international trade and AI policy further complicates this landscape. As countries negotiate trade agreements that include technology provisions, they must carefully consider how these agreements impact local economies and cultural attitudes towards technology use. Trade policies that favor certain technologies or companies can inadvertently marginalize local innovators who do not meet stringent international standards. Addressing these disparities is crucial for fostering an equitable global economy where all nations can participate meaningfully in the digital transformation.

Cross-border data flows also pose significant regulatory challenges that differ among countries. Data localization laws restrict how data can be transferred internationally, impacting both multinational corporations and startups alike. Take this example, India has implemented strict data localization policies with the aim of protecting citizen data; however, such regulations may hinder innovation by limiting access to global markets and resources. Conversely, countries with more lenient data policies may face heightened risks of privacy breaches without adequate safeguards in place.

Engaging in international discussions around AI governance is essential for creating coherent policies that respect individual nations' contexts while promoting collaboration on global standards. Initiatives like the Global Partnership on Artificial Intelligence (GPAI) represent efforts to unite stakeholders worldwide around shared principles of responsible AI development. By actively participating in these collaborations, countries can help shape standards that benefit their citizens while ensuring competitiveness in the global arena.

Public perception is also a critical factor in shaping AI policy across borders. Citizens' trust in their governments' ability to manage technology directly influences how policies are received and implemented. To foster public confidence, policymakers must communicate transparently about the potential risks and benefits associated with AI deployment. Engagement strategies that incorporate community outreach or public consultations can demystify complex technological concepts and ensure diverse voices contribute to regulatory development.

navigating the multifaceted terrain of AI policy requires an awareness of how each nation's context informs its approach to technology adoption and regulation. Developing adaptable frameworks grounded in local cultures promotes inclusivity and paves the way for innovations that resonate with societal values.

As we move towards an interconnected future defined

by artificial intelligence's capabilities, fostering international cooperation will be vital to address shared challenges without compromising national priorities or cultural identities.

Case Studies of Success and Failure

Understanding the factors that contribute to both success and failure in AI integration is essential for professionals navigating today's rapidly changing landscape. Analyzing real-world case studies not only highlights effective strategies but also uncovers pitfalls to avoid. By examining these examples, we can glean valuable insights that empower individuals and organizations to make informed decisions on their own AI journeys.

One notable success story comes from the healthcare sector, where AI has significantly transformed patient care. The implementation of IBM's Watson Health illustrates how advanced analytics can revolutionize diagnostics and treatment planning. Hospitals utilizing Watson have reported a marked reduction in misdiagnoses, resulting in improved patient outcomes. For example, through machine learning algorithms, Watson can swiftly analyze vast amounts of medical literature, providing physicians with data-backed treatment recommendations. This integration enhances clinical decision-making and streamlines workflows, ultimately leading to cost savings for healthcare providers.

In contrast, the automotive industry serves as a cautionary tale regarding AI adoption. The ambitious launch of autonomous vehicles by several companies has faced numerous setbacks due to regulatory challenges and safety concerns. A high-profile failure in this space was Uber's self-driving car program, which drew criticism after a pedestrian was fatally struck during testing. This incident highlighted the critical importance of robust safety measures and public trust when deploying transformative technologies. Companies venturing into autonomous systems must prioritize transparency and ethical considerations to foster acceptance and mitigate risks.

Meanwhile, in the financial sector, JPMorgan Chase exemplifies how AI can enhance operational efficiency while addressing compliance challenges. By employing machine learning algorithms for fraud detection, the bank has significantly reduced instances of fraudulent transactions. Their system analyzes patterns in real-time data, allowing for immediate intervention when suspicious activities arise. This proactive approach not only safeguards customer assets but also ensures regulatory compliance by minimizing risks associated with financial crimes.

However, a lack of strategic alignment can impede progress in AI initiatives, as demonstrated by a case study involving a large retail chain. Despite substantial investments in AI-driven inventory management systems, the company struggled due to insufficient integration with existing supply chain processes. That's why, their anticipated efficiency gains did not materialize; instead, they faced stock shortages and overstock issues that confused customers and resulted in lost sales opportunities. This situation underscores that technology alone cannot solve problems without aligning it with business objectives and operational realities.

The education sector provides further insights into both successful implementations and notable failures of AI technology. A positive example is Carnegie Learning's use of AI-driven platforms to personalize math education for students across various skill levels. Their software adapts to individual learning paces, ensuring tailored instruction that effectively meets each student's needs. Schools implementing this program have reported significant improvements in student engagement and performance metrics.

Conversely, some educational institutions have encountered obstacles when trying to integrate AI tools without adequate training for educators or necessary support structures in place. A university's attempt to deploy an AI-powered grading system led to teacher frustration due to inaccuracies that did not align with classroom expectations. The backlash prompted administrators to rethink their approach toward adopting technology, highlighting that effective change management is vital for successful integration.

These diverse examples underscore a central theme: success hinges on understanding the complexities surrounding AI implementation while remaining adaptable in response to challenges encountered along the way. Organizations must cultivate an environment where feedback is valued and lessons learned from failures lead to iterative improvements rather than punitive responses.

As professionals evaluate their strategies for integrating AI into existing frameworks or launching new initiatives, prioritizing thorough research alongside stakeholder engagement is crucial. Fostering open dialogues about potential impacts will ultimately drive more successful outcomes.

In summary, case studies from various sectors illuminate critical lessons regarding what determines an organization's success or failure in adapting to AI—whether it's emphasizing safety measures as seen with autonomous vehicles or ensuring technology aligns with business objectives as evidenced by retail challenges. While the path ahead may be fraught with uncertainties, taking cues from past experiences can empower individuals and organizations alike as they navigate this evolving landscape.

Learning from International Collaborations

Exploring the experiences of various countries and organizations offers valuable insights into the complexities of AI integration on a global scale. These collaborations showcase the different approaches and innovations that emerge when diverse cultures, regulatory environments, and technological landscapes intersect. By analyzing these global interactions, we can identify best practices that can be adapted to local contexts, ultimately fostering a more inclusive and effective AI job economy.

One notable example is the partnership between governments and tech companies in Singapore. The Smart Nation initiative highlights how public-private collaborations can lead to innovative AI solutions in urban planning and public services. Through AI-driven analytics, Singapore has enhanced citizen engagement by improving public transport efficiency and reducing traffic congestion. This collaboration illustrates the advantages of combining resources and expertise to tackle complex societal challenges.

In contrast, the European Union has adopted a different approach to AI governance, emphasizing ethical frameworks and regulatory compliance among member states. The General Data Protection Regulation (GDPR) serves as a prime example of how collective action can influence global data privacy standards. While implementing these regulations has presented challenges for businesses, it has also fostered consumer trust in AI technologies. This demonstrates that international cooperation can establish robust safeguards that promote responsible AI usage while encouraging innovation within ethical boundaries.

Further afield, partnerships between research institutions in Kenya and technology firms have led to significant advancements in agricultural AI applications. By combining local knowledge with cutting-edge technology, initiatives like Precision Agriculture aim to optimize crop yields through data-driven insights. Farmers now have access to mobile tools providing real-time weather forecasts and soil health assessments, significantly enhancing productivity. This grassroots approach underscores the importance of contextually relevant solutions tailored to specific regional needs.

However, not all international collaborations have achieved positive outcomes. The attempt at cross-border AI integration in healthcare systems between India and Western nations encountered obstacles due to differences in infrastructure readiness and cultural attitudes toward technology adoption. Although the goal was to improve patient care through shared data systems, varying levels of digital literacy among healthcare providers hampered implementation efforts. This experience serves as a cautionary tale about overestimating partners' readiness without thoroughly assessing local capabilities.

The implications for workforce development are also apparent when considering global perspectives on education initiatives in AI training programs. Countries like Canada have made substantial investments in reskilling their workforces by collaborating with industry leaders to create comprehensive curricula focused on emerging technologies. These initiatives not only equip individuals with essential skills but also align educational outcomes with labor market demands, thereby enhancing employability.

Conversely, some regions face challenges due to fragmented education systems that lack cohesion between academic institutions and industry requirements. For example, a consortium of universities in Brazil aimed to develop an AI curriculum but received criticism for failing to engage local businesses during its creation. So, graduates found themselves without viable pathways into employment—highlighting that successful educational initiatives depend on ongoing dialogue among stakeholders.

These international case studies collectively illustrate crucial lessons for professionals navigating the evolving AI landscape. Understanding the nuances of cross-cultural collaborations enhances strategic planning and fosters adaptability—an essential trait as new challenges arise.

learning from both successes and failures enables professionals to build resilient strategies grounded in global best practices while effectively tailoring approaches to local contexts. Each story provides valuable insights into how diverse responses shape our collective future in an increasingly interconnected world driven by artificial intelligence.

As professionals reflect on these examples from varied international collaborations, it becomes evident that success lies not only in technological capabilities but also in nurturing strong partnerships based on shared objectives and mutual understanding—qualities essential for thriving amid change.

The Role of Global Organizations

Exploring the role of global organizations in the AI landscape reveals a complex interplay of collaboration, innovation, and shared learning. These entities—ranging from multinational corporations to international regulatory bodies —are instrumental in shaping how artificial intelligence is integrated across borders. By pooling their expertise and resources, they create an environment that fosters AI advancements while tackling the multifaceted challenges that arise.

A notable example is the World Economic Forum (WEF), which actively engages a variety of stakeholders, including governments and academic institutions, in discussions about the future of work in an AI-driven economy. Their reports on reskilling initiatives and the ethical deployment of AI highlight the importance of global dialogue, illustrating how shared knowledge can lead to actionable strategies tailored to specific regional contexts. The WEF's initiatives go beyond theory; they offer collaborative frameworks that have inspired national policies and local programs aimed at preparing workforces for the disruptions brought about by technology.

In a similar vein, organizations like UNESCO are addressing the urgent need for equitable access to AI education around the world. Their commitment to fostering inclusive educational practices ensures that developing nations are not left behind as AI technologies advance. Initiatives such as the Global Education Coalition exemplify this effort by uniting partners from various sectors to equip youth with essential digital skills for navigating tomorrow's job market. The success of this coalition demonstrates how collaborative frameworks can democratize access to information and resources, contributing to a more equitable global job economy.

International research collaborations further emphasize the value of bringing together diverse talent and ideas. The European Union's Horizon 2020 program illustrates this approach by funding transnational research projects focused on AI applications across various domains, from healthcare innovations to environmental sustainability. By integrating insights from different cultural perspectives, this collaborative model amplifies research outcomes and fosters solutions that address global challenges more effectively.

Organizations also play a critical role as mediators between competing interests and differing regulatory environments. Take this example, the International Telecommunication Union (ITU) facilitates discussions on setting standards for emerging technologies, including AI. By creating platforms for dialogue among member states, the ITU helps align varying national policies on data privacy and security, enabling smoother cross-border cooperation and technology integration.

However, navigating these collaborations presents challenges. Diverse political landscapes can hinder efforts to standardize practices or implement shared strategies effectively. Recent trade tensions between major economies have underscored how geopolitical factors can impact technological collaboration, potentially stalling progress in areas crucial for AI development.

In light of these complexities, it is essential for professionals involved in international initiatives to cultivate cultural intelligence—a skill set that enhances understanding and effective communication within diverse teams. This awareness strengthens partnerships and increases project success rates when addressing complex issues that span multiple regions.

Reflecting on these dynamics within global organizations' roles in shaping the AI landscape yields several key insights: first, collaboration is vital; shared objectives bring together diverse stakeholders toward common goals. Second, adaptability is crucial; professionals must remain agile in response to changing political climates and emerging technologies. Lastly, prioritizing inclusivity ensures that all voices are heard and valued throughout this transformative journey.

As we deepen our understanding of how global organizations influence AI integration across borders, it becomes clear that they are not just catalysts for innovation but also essential facilitators of a more collaborative and equitable future—one where artificial intelligence serves humanity's best interests on a global scale. This perspective allows us to approach challenges with optimism while drawing on valuable lessons learned from experiences around the world.

CHAPTER 11:
THE FUTURE OF
WORKFORCE
PLANNING

*Strategic Workforce
Planning in the AI Age*

S trategic workforce planning in the age of AI goes beyond merely adapting to new technologies; it requires a fundamental reevaluation of how organizations approach talent acquisition, development, and retention. As AI tools evolve rapidly, businesses must not only grasp the capabilities these technologies offer but also align them with their workforce strategies to enhance productivity and foster innovation.

Organizations today face the pressing challenge of anticipating future skill needs, which calls for a proactive mindset. Traditional workforce planning often relied on historical data and trend analysis; however, AI offers real-time insights that enable companies to forecast skill requirements with greater accuracy. Take this example, machine learning algorithms can analyze job market trends to help organizations anticipate shifts in demand for specific skills. This foresight allows for more informed decisions regarding priority areas for training and development.

One effective strategy is to integrate AI tools into Human Resource Management (HRM) systems. These tools can sift through large datasets that include employee performance metrics, industry benchmarks, and emerging job roles. For example, predictive analytics might reveal a potential shortage of data science skills within a team as new analytics-driven projects arise. With this information, HR departments can take proactive steps—such as targeted recruitment or customized training programs—to address anticipated skill gaps.

Consider a manufacturing company that implements robotics in its production lines. To ensure smooth integration, it must assess its workforce's current skills against those needed to operate alongside AI-powered machines effectively. By mapping existing competencies and identifying gaps, management can develop tailored upskilling initiatives that empower employees to thrive in this evolving environment rather than risk displacement.

And, strategic workforce planning involves nurturing an organizational culture that embraces continuous learning. As technology advances rapidly, the workforce's skills must evolve alongside it. Establishing a framework for ongoing professional development ensures employees are prepared not only for their current roles but also for future opportunities. Collaborating with educational institutions or online platforms can provide access to essential resources for skill enhancement.

Companies like Google exemplify innovative workforce planning by fostering a culture of learning through initiatives such as their "20% time" policy, which allows employees to devote part of their workweek to pursuing projects outside their regular responsibilities. This approach empowers individuals and aligns with broader company objectives by nurturing creativity and adaptability in an ever-changing technological landscape.

In this context, the role of HR is transforming significantly. Rather than solely managing personnel issues, HR professionals now act as strategic partners who leverage data-driven insights to align talent strategies with organizational goals. Building an integrated HR ecosystem enables organizations to closely monitor employee engagement levels and assess how well teams adapt to technological changes. Engaged employees are more likely to embrace change positively and actively contribute to integrating AI solutions into daily operations.

As businesses increasingly incorporate AI into their functions, developing robust succession plans becomes essential for preserving institutional knowledge while preparing future leaders capable of thriving in a digital economy. Leadership development programs should focus on instilling both technical expertise and emotional intelligence—qualities crucial for navigating complex human-machine interactions effectively.

Additionally, fostering diverse teams creates a rich tapestry of perspectives vital for addressing the challenges presented by AI innovations. Teams composed of members from various backgrounds—whether gender, ethnicity, or career trajectories—are better positioned to challenge existing paradigms and conceive creative solutions that drive progress.

In summary, strategic workforce planning in the age of AI requires a comprehensive understanding of current capabilities alongside forward-looking foresight regarding emerging skill needs. It encourages organizations to adopt flexible training frameworks while cultivating cultures that value lifelong learning and innovation. This way, businesses can not only survive but thrive amid the complexities introduced by advanced technologies—ensuring they remain competitive in an evolving global landscape where talent is increasingly recognized as one of their most valuable assets.

Utilizing AI for Predictive HR Analytics

Integrating AI into human resources through predictive analytics enhances operational efficiency and empowers organizations to make data-driven decisions that shape their workforce strategies. This innovative approach equips HR professionals with powerful tools to analyze patterns and trends, enabling them to forecast talent needs and align workforce capabilities with business objectives.

One of the primary benefits of using AI in predictive HR analytics is its ability to process vast amounts of data rapidly. Traditional methods often relied on static reports generated from historical data, which can overlook dynamic shifts in the job market or evolving organizational needs. In contrast, AI algorithms analyze real-time data from diverse sources, including employee performance metrics, recruitment statistics, and industry trends. For example, organizations can employ predictive models to assess how economic changes affect job availability in specific sectors, allowing them to proactively adjust hiring strategies.

A clear illustration of this can be found in companies using AI-driven tools like IBM's Watson Talent Insights. This platform helps organizations identify which skills will be in demand based on market trends and internal shifts. By leveraging such tools, HR departments can pinpoint areas where additional training is needed or where talent acquisition efforts should be intensified. Take this example, if analytics reveal a surge in demand for machine learning experts, HR teams can launch targeted recruitment campaigns or develop upskilling programs before the need becomes critical.

As organizations implement these predictive strategies, fostering a culture of adaptability among employees becomes essential. Encouraging continuous learning ensures that team members remain engaged and ready for shifts in their roles brought about by technological advancements. Companies might offer workshops or online courses focused on emerging technologies relevant to their industry, facilitating skill enhancement without disrupting work-life balance.

Microsoft serves as an exemplary case of how integrating AI into HR systems can transform workforce planning. The company utilizes predictive analytics not only to identify skill gaps but also to monitor employee engagement and satisfaction levels. By regularly analyzing this data, Microsoft can intervene early when engagement dips—implementing targeted initiatives that boost morale while preparing staff for future challenges.

Refining recruitment processes through AI insights is another critical component of successful implementation. Advanced algorithms can identify the best-fit candidates based on specific criteria derived from successful hires in similar roles, streamlining hiring while attracting top talent suited for the evolving demands of the workplace.

Organizations should also focus on developing robust succession plans that leverage predictive analytics. By identifying high-potential employees early, businesses can nurture leadership skills through targeted mentorship and training programs. This proactive approach not only secures institutional knowledge but also cultivates future leaders who are well-equipped to navigate an increasingly complex digital landscape.

Building diverse teams is another vital aspect of leveraging AI insights. By recognizing patterns related to recruitment biases or gaps in representation during hiring processes, HR departments can actively work towards creating equitable opportunities for all candidates. This commitment enhances creativity within teams by bringing together varied perspectives—an essential factor when addressing challenges posed by technological advancements.

Through comprehensive application of predictive analytics in HR practices, organizations gain a clearer understanding of their current capabilities and future workforce requirements. Embracing flexibility while promoting continuous education fosters an agile environment where innovation flourishes amid rapid technological change.

this holistic integration leads not only to improved productivity but also drives employee satisfaction as team members feel empowered and prepared for future changes. By transforming potential threats into opportunities within the evolving business landscape fueled by AI advancements, organizations cultivate a resilient workforce capable of navigating uncertainties while remaining aligned with their goals and visions—a shared journey toward success.

Identifying Future Skill Gaps

To effectively identify future skill gaps in a rapidly changing job landscape, organizations must adopt a proactive and data-driven approach. This process begins with recognizing the key drivers of change in the market—such as technological advancements, shifts in consumer demand, and evolving business models. By analyzing these factors, companies can better anticipate the skills necessary to maintain their competitiveness.

A crucial step in this endeavor is conducting a comprehensive skills inventory within the organization. By assessing current employee capabilities against anticipated future needs, businesses can identify discrepancies. Take this example, if a company anticipates an increased reliance on artificial intelligence for data analysis, it should evaluate whether its workforce has the requisite expertise in programming languages or data interpretation methods. Tools like competency mapping or skill matrices can be invaluable for visualizing these gaps and aligning training resources accordingly.

Engaging with industry trends is equally vital for understanding where the market is headed. Resources such as industry reports, labor market analyses, and insights from professional networks provide valuable information about emerging skills. For example, consider a healthcare organization that recognizes the growing importance of telehealth services. By monitoring trends in patient care technology and regulatory changes, it can anticipate the need for staff skilled in virtual communication tools and remote patient management.

Leveraging AI itself plays an essential role in predicting skill gaps. Advanced analytics can process extensive datasets to reveal patterns indicating where skills are lacking or which competencies may soon be in demand. Organizations might utilize platforms like LinkedIn Learning Insights to track trending skills among competitors or within similar industries. These data-driven insights enable HR departments to effectively strategize around recruitment and training initiatives.

Collaboration with educational institutions also proves effective in bridging identified skill gaps. Establishing partnerships allows businesses to influence curricula based on real-world requirements while offering students practical experiences through internships or co-op programs. This alignment between educational outcomes and industry needs creates a pipeline of talent equipped with relevant skills upon graduation.

To ensure that these strategies yield results, regular reassessment of both workforce capabilities and market demands is essential. Creating feedback loops through employee performance reviews and satisfaction surveys can provide ongoing insights into areas requiring further development or adjustment. If employees express uncertainty about new technologies introduced at work, this signals an immediate need for targeted training sessions or mentorship programs.

Fostering an organizational culture that prioritizes continuous learning is another critical element in successfully identifying and addressing skill gaps. Encouraging employees to pursue professional development opportunities—not just within their current roles but across different functions— ensures adaptability as job requirements evolve. Organizations might implement initiatives such as lunch-and-learn sessions or online learning subscriptions to cultivate this culture.

And, leadership commitment plays an integral role in this process; when leaders actively advocate for upskilling efforts and allocate resources toward learning programs, employees are more likely to embrace opportunities for growth. A notable example is AT&T's investment in workforce development through "AT&T University," which provides resources for employees to continually enhance their digital skills.

Lastly, understanding demographic shifts within the workforce can inform strategic planning around skill development initiatives. As younger generations enter the job market with different expectations regarding career progression and work-life balance, organizations must adapt their approaches accordingly. Offering flexible learning paths that cater to diverse preferences fosters engagement while simultaneously addressing skill shortages.

By integrating these multifaceted strategies into workforce planning processes, organizations position themselves not just to survive but to thrive amid the transformation driven by technological advancements. The dynamic nature of today's economy necessitates agility—recognizing when specific skills become obsolete while preparing for those that will define tomorrow's landscape ensures continued relevance and success within competitive markets.

As businesses navigate these complexities, embracing collaboration among stakeholders—from HR professionals to frontline managers—will not only lead to effective identification of future skill gaps but also foster environments where innovation flourishes alongside skilled talent ready to tackle emerging challenges head-on.

The Role of HR in AI Strategy

The role of Human Resources (HR) in shaping and implementing AI strategies is becoming increasingly vital as organizations navigate the complexities of integrating advanced technologies into their workforce. HR professionals have evolved beyond traditional administrative functions to become strategic partners, aligning workforce capabilities with organizational goals in a rapidly changing landscape.

This shift begins with a new perspective on what HR can achieve. Once viewed primarily as gatekeepers of talent, HR is now at the forefront of cultivating a culture that embraces technological advancement. This involves recognizing how AI can enhance both operational efficiency and employee experience. Take this example, by leveraging AI-driven recruitment tools, HR can streamline hiring processes, enabling a greater focus on cultural fit and potential for growth rather than merely qualifications listed on resumes.

As organizations move further into AI integration, HR's responsibilities expand to include training and upskilling employees to work effectively alongside these new technologies. Continuous learning programs become essential, ensuring that staff remain competitive and adaptable to evolving job requirements. For example, in a retail company adopting AI for inventory management, HR would need to implement training sessions to help employees confidently interact with these systems instead of feeling intimidated.

Effective communication between departments is crucial for crafting a cohesive AI strategy. Collaboration among HR, IT, and operations can yield valuable insights into how AI can be tailored to meet specific departmental needs. If the marketing department utilizes predictive analytics powered by AI, it is essential for HR to ensure that team members possess the skills necessary to interpret and act upon the insights generated by these tools. Regular interdepartmental meetings can facilitate alignment, fostering a shared vision of how each team contributes to broader organizational objectives.

An equally important aspect of effective HR strategy in an AI context is maintaining an ethical framework for technology use. As companies increasingly adopt AI solutions across various functions—from recruitment to performance evaluation—they must carefully consider the ethical implications of algorithmic decision-making. HR must champion transparency and fairness in these processes by ensuring that the data used in AI models is representative and free from bias. For example, when developing an automated performance review system, it's crucial to incorporate diverse employee perspectives during the design process to prevent perpetuating existing disparities.

In addition to addressing the immediate impacts of AI integration, HR's role encompasses long-term workforce planning. Anticipating shifts in job roles due to automation requires foresight into future trends and potential skill shortages. Engaging with labor market analytics tools can provide valuable data on emerging skills within specific industries. If an organization identifies a trend toward remote collaboration tools becoming standard practice, it may choose to invest early in training programs focused on digital communication skills and project management methodologies tailored for virtual environments.

HR also plays a pivotal role in fostering employee engagement during periods of change. Addressing concerns about job security or shifts in responsibilities calls for open lines of communication between management and employees. Regular town hall meetings or Q&A sessions can alleviate uncertainties while reinforcing the message that employees will receive support throughout transitions— whether through training or other resources.

as organizations embrace an AI-driven future, it is imperative for HR to evolve alongside technological advancements. Building strong partnerships within and outside the organization—such as collaborating with educational institutions or industry groups—can further enhance workforce strategies aimed at maximizing human potential alongside machine capabilities.

By integrating these multifaceted approaches, HR positions itself not only as a facilitator of change but also as an architect of future-ready organizations equipped to harness the full potential of artificial intelligence while maintaining human-centric values at their core. This evolution highlights that successful navigation through technological advancements relies not only on adopting new technologies but also on nurturing a skilled workforce capable of leveraging these innovations effectively and ethically.

Succession Planning in the AI Context

Succession planning in the era of AI integration requires a thoughtful approach that acknowledges the evolving dynamics of the workforce. As organizations increasingly depend on technology, preparing for future leadership becomes vital—not just for ensuring operational continuity but also for fostering a culture that prioritizes adaptability and innovation. Here, strategic foresight aligns with actionable planning.

The initial step in effective succession planning involves

identifying key roles that will transform due to AI advancements. Traditional job functions are expected to evolve as automation and intelligent systems take over certain tasks. For example, in a manufacturing setting, production supervisors may transition into data analysts tasked with interpreting AI-generated insights to enhance operational efficiency. By recognizing this shift early, organizations can develop targeted training programs that equip potential successors with the skills needed for these new roles.

Next, it is essential to outline potential career paths within the organization. Aspiring leaders must not only acquire technical expertise but also embody emotional intelligence and adaptability—qualities crucial in an AI-driven landscape. Mentoring programs serve as a practical example of this dual focus, pairing emerging leaders with seasoned executives to promote knowledge sharing and collaboration. Such initiatives are vital for creating an environment that supports the integration of advanced technologies.

Assessment tools are another critical element in succession planning. Implementing performance evaluations and 360-degree feedback can offer valuable insights into candidates' readiness for promotion and their capacity to thrive amidst rapid change. Take this example, an employee who demonstrates exceptional adaptability and innovation during an AI project may be ideally suited for a leadership role overseeing future AI initiatives.

Incorporating AI into the succession planning process itself can significantly enhance decision-making. Predictive analytics can identify high-potential employees by analyzing their performance data, engagement levels, and career aspirations. By examining trends across various metrics—such as project success rates and peer feedback—organizations can make informed decisions about who should be positioned for advancement.

A comprehensive succession plan must also consider the ethical implications of leadership in the context of AI. Leaders play a pivotal role in shaping organizational culture and establishing guidelines for ethical technology implementation. Ensuring a diverse pipeline of future leaders brings varied perspectives to decision-making, fostering fairness and inclusivity as AI systems are adopted. Providing training on ethical considerations—such as bias mitigation and transparency—will prepare leaders to address the complex dilemmas arising from algorithmic decision-making.

Additionally, establishing continuous feedback mechanisms is essential for monitoring the effectiveness of succession plans. Regular check-ins with potential leaders regarding their progress and aspirations help align individual goals with organizational objectives while allowing for adjustments based on changing business needs or technological advancements.

A successful succession strategy must embrace flexibility as a core principle. As the landscape shifts—whether through technological breakthroughs or changes in market demands—the criteria for leadership must also adapt. Organizations need to remain agile, ready to modify their plans and invest in talent development as new challenges arise.

Finally, engaging employees at all levels in conversations about their career trajectories fosters a sense of ownership over their professional development. When organizations actively communicate their commitment to employee growth within an evolving context, they cultivate loyalty and motivation among staff who see clear pathways forward despite uncertainty.

By proactively addressing these elements of succession planning within an AI framework, organizations position themselves not only to fill key roles but also to drive transformational change effectively. This forward-thinking approach ensures that future leaders are equipped not only with essential skills but also with a mindset that embraces innovation, ethical responsibility, and collaboration—traits necessary for navigating the complexities of tomorrow's workforce landscape.

Adapting Hiring Processes for AI Integration

The integration of AI into hiring processes is fundamentally transforming how organizations identify, evaluate, and select talent. As businesses adapt to rapid technological advancements, traditional hiring methods must evolve to ensure they attract candidates who not only possess the necessary skills but also embody a mindset suited for a dynamic work environment.

A crucial first step in this evolution is redefining job descriptions to better align with the capabilities of AI. Roles that once prioritized routine tasks now require an emphasis on problem-solving, creativity, and collaboration. For example, a customer service position may evolve from merely handling inquiries to interpreting AI-driven analytics in order to enhance customer interactions. By clearly articulating these updated requirements, organizations can attract candidates who are not only skilled in their fields but also eager to embrace technology as an integral part of their daily responsibilities.

Incorporating AI tools into the recruitment process can further streamline candidate sourcing and screening. Platforms powered by machine learning algorithms can analyze resumes at scale, efficiently identifying individuals who meet specific criteria more effectively than traditional methods. Take this example, an AI tool might assess candidates' past experiences and educational backgrounds against revised job specifications, helping to reduce biases that often accompany manual reviews. While these tools significantly enhance efficiency, organizations must remain vigilant about maintaining transparency and fairness in AI-driven decision-making.

The interview process also stands to gain from innovative applications of AI. Virtual interviews supported by intelligent systems can assess not just verbal responses but also non-verbal cues like body language and tone of voice. Take this example, an AI system could analyze a candidate's facial expressions during a remote interview to gauge their confidence or engagement level. These insights provide interviewers with additional data points that enrich traditional assessments.

Another effective strategy for modernizing hiring processes is the incorporation of skill assessments. Rather than relying solely on interviews or resumes, organizations should consider practical evaluations that reflect real-world scenarios relevant to the role. For example, a tech company seeking software developers might ask candidates to complete coding challenges or solve complex problems using collaborative platforms like GitHub or CodePen. This hands-on approach not only showcases technical proficiency but also demonstrates how well candidates engage with technology—a crucial factor in an AI-integrated workplace.

And, establishing feedback loops is essential for refining the hiring process over time. Gathering input from new hires about their recruitment experiences provides valuable insights into what worked well and what could be improved. If multiple candidates indicate that the assessment process was confusing or did not accurately reflect daily tasks, it signals an opportunity for organizations to reassess their methods. Continuous improvement through feedback ensures that hiring practices evolve alongside technological advancements and shifting workforce expectations.

As companies increasingly prioritize diversity in their hiring strategies, leveraging AI can help minimize biases in candidate selection. Tools designed to screen applications while anonymizing personal information—such as names or demographic data—can promote inclusivity by focusing solely on qualifications and skills. This approach aligns with broader goals of creating diverse teams capable of fostering innovation through varied perspectives.

Additionally, investing in training for HR teams on how to effectively integrate AI tools while maintaining human oversight is critical. While automation enhances efficiency, there remains a vital need for human judgment when assessing cultural fit and growth potential within the organization.

Lastly, adapting hiring processes necessitates clear communication about organizational values concerning AI use. Candidates should understand how technology will impact their roles and what ethical considerations govern its implementation within the workplace. This transparency builds trust and attracts individuals committed to responsible innovation—an essential aspect for forward-thinking companies aiming to thrive amid ongoing transformation.

By embracing these adaptive strategies, organizations position themselves not only as employers but as leaders within their industries—dedicated to attracting top talent capable of navigating an increasingly complex technological landscape while fostering an inclusive environment where innovation flourishes organically. By thoughtfully blending traditional methods with cutting-edge technologies—and doing so ethically—businesses can remain competitive while cultivating a workforce ready for tomorrow's challenges.

Designing AI-Friendly Work Environments

The physical workspace often serves as a new employee's first glimpse into an organization. In today's AI-driven job economy, creating environments that are conducive to both technology and innovation is essential. These spaces should not only encourage collaboration and creativity but also seamlessly integrate advanced technologies, fostering an atmosphere where fresh ideas can flourish.

Designing an AI-friendly work environment begins with the workspace layout. Open floor plans, for instance, enhance collaboration and communication among teams— key elements when incorporating AI tools that thrive on collective input and expertise. However, it is equally important to maintain privacy and quiet areas; this can be achieved by integrating designated spaces for focused work. For example, a tech company might include "focus pods" where employees can engage in deep work without distractions while still feeling connected to an open, collaborative culture.

Equipping these environments with robust technological infrastructure is crucial. High-speed internet access, cutting-edge video conferencing tools, and smart boards for brainstorming are vital components that enhance connectivity. Utilizing platforms like Miro or Microsoft Teams allows remote team members to contribute in real time during brainstorming sessions or project planning meetings, promoting inclusivity regardless of physical location.

Flexibility within the workspace is another important consideration to accommodate diverse working styles and preferences. This may involve adjustable desks for both sitting and standing positions or informal meeting areas with couches or communal tables. Such versatility not only increases comfort but also aligns with the dynamic nature of AI-related tasks that often require quick pivots throughout the day.

Integrating AI tools into daily workflows fundamentally alters how tasks are completed in these environments. Implementing AI-driven project management systems like Asana or Trello can streamline processes by using algorithms to predict project timelines based on historical data. This approach allows teams to focus their energies on creative problem-solving rather than getting bogged down by administrative tasks.

Training employees on effectively utilizing these AI systems is equally important. Regular workshops and training sessions can empower staff to become proficient with new technologies, ensuring they feel confident navigating tools designed to enhance productivity. Take this example, a software development team might benefit from coding boot camps that teach them how to leverage machine learning libraries like TensorFlow or PyTorch in their projects.

Fostering a culture of experimentation further enhances an AI-friendly environment. Allowing employees time to explore innovative ideas without the fear of failure encourages creativity and can lead to breakthroughs in technology applications within their roles. A financial services firm might implement "innovation days" where teams brainstorm new uses for existing data analytics tools, resulting in fresh strategies for client engagement.

To ensure continuous improvement, organizations should establish feedback mechanisms that gauge employee sentiment regarding their workspace and available technology. Regular surveys can provide insights into what works well and what needs adjustment. If employees express frustration with outdated software or ineffective communication tools, it's crucial for organizations to address these issues promptly rather than allowing dissatisfaction to linger.

And, implementing ethical considerations when adopting AI technologies fosters trust and security among employees. Transparency about data collection and usage—especially concerning performance monitoring systems—is essential. For example, if a company uses an AI tool for performance tracking, clear communication about its purpose and functionality helps alleviate concerns about surveillance.

Creating inclusive environments where all voices are heard during discussions about technology adoption is also vital. Diverse teams bring unique perspectives that enhance problem-solving capabilities; actively seeking input from various demographics leads to more comprehensive strategies for responsible AI integration.

Finally, promoting wellness initiatives alongside technological advancements ensures a holistic approach to employee satisfaction. Providing mental health resources or encouraging regular breaks helps balance the demands of a tech-driven environment with personal well-being. A company might offer mindfulness sessions or provide access to wellness apps that assist employees in managing stress effectively while engaging with cutting-edge technologies.

Designing AI-friendly work environments extends beyond physical space; it involves cultivating a culture that embraces change while empowering employees through technology integration. By creating adaptable workplaces filled with supportive resources, organizations position themselves as innovators ready to lead in an ever-evolving landscape. This thoughtful approach ensures that individuals are equipped not only with the necessary tools but also with the inspiration to push boundaries—ultimately driving success in the age of artificial intelligence.

Strategies for Talent Retention

A strategic approach to talent retention in today's AI-driven job economy involves a deep understanding of employees' evolving needs and aligning these with organizational goals. Retention now extends beyond salary; it encompasses a wider range of factors, including employee engagement, satisfaction, and development. To foster loyalty, companies must cultivate an environment where individuals feel valued, supported, and empowered to grow alongside technological advancements.

Regular engagement through feedback is vital for this process. Establishing open lines of communication allows employees to voice their concerns and aspirations. Tools like anonymous surveys or suggestion boxes can offer valuable insights into workplace morale and highlight areas for improvement. Take this example, a tech firm might conduct quarterly pulse surveys to assess employee sentiment regarding workload, team dynamics, and available resources. This proactive approach not only demonstrates management's commitment to valuing employee input but also nurtures a sense of belonging within the organization.

Professional development opportunities are another essential element of talent retention. As employees increasingly seek workplaces that invest in their growth, offering personalized training programs tailored to individual career paths can enhance job satisfaction and loyalty. For example, a healthcare organization could provide staff with access to courses on AI applications in patient care, equipping them with relevant skills while keeping them engaged with the latest technological advancements.

Additionally, mentorship programs can significantly bolster retention by fostering relationships between seasoned employees and newer hires. A well-structured mentorship initiative facilitates knowledge transfer and cultivates a supportive culture where individuals feel guided in their professional journeys. An engineering firm might pair junior engineers with experienced mentors who share insights on navigating challenges related to emerging technologies. Such relationships encourage loyalty as mentees recognize the tangible investment in their growth.

Flexibility in work arrangements also plays a critical role in retention. With many employees prioritizing work-life balance more than ever, companies that offer remote or hybrid options often experience improved retention rates. Take this example, a marketing agency could implement flexible hours that allow staff to choose when they complete their tasks—whether early in the morning or late at night—based on their peak productivity times. This adaptability accommodates diverse working styles and enhances overall job satisfaction.

Recognition and rewards systems are pivotal for reinforcing positive behaviors and contributions within the workplace. Celebrating achievements—big or small—can significantly boost morale and encourage ongoing performance excellence. An organization might establish monthly recognition awards where teams highlight peers who have excelled in effectively leveraging AI tools for projects. Such acknowledgment not only fosters camaraderie but also motivates others to strive for excellence.

And, investing in health and wellness initiatives reflects an organization's commitment to its workforce's overall well-being. Programs focusing on mental health support and physical wellness activities—such as yoga sessions or gym memberships—can greatly enhance employee engagement levels. For example, a tech company might launch a wellness challenge that encourages employees to participate in physical activities while incorporating gamification elements for added motivation.

Creating clear pathways for career advancement is equally crucial. Employees who see defined trajectories within their organizations are more likely to remain committed long-term. Regular discussions about career goals during performance reviews can help align individual aspirations with organizational objectives. A financial institution might implement structured career development plans that outline potential growth opportunities based on performance metrics and targeted training sessions.

Additionally, fostering diversity within teams not only leads to innovative solutions but also contributes significantly to employee retention by creating an inclusive environment where everyone feels represented and valued. Companies should actively seek diverse perspectives when forming teams or making decisions about technology integration, recognizing that varied experiences enrich discussions and drive better outcomes.

Finally, cultivating an adaptable corporate culture that embraces change positions organizations favorably for retaining talent amidst the uncertainty brought about by rapid technological advancements. Encouraging continuous learning initiatives keeps employees motivated and prepares them for future challenges in the evolving landscape shaped by AI.

At its core, effective talent retention strategies hinge upon an organization's ability to prioritize employee engagement through transparent communication, professional development opportunities, recognition efforts, flexible work arrangements, health initiatives, clear advancement pathways, diversity promotion, and a culture of adaptability. By addressing these key areas holistically, organizations can create environments where talent not only remains but thrives—a fundamental aspect of success as we navigate the complexities of an AI-driven economy together.

CHAPTER 12:
THE ROLE OF
GOVERNMENTS
AND POLICY

Government Initiatives for AI
Workforce Development

G overnment initiatives aimed at AI workforce development are becoming increasingly important as countries recognize the need to prepare their citizens for a rapidly evolving job landscape. These initiatives serve as essential frameworks that bridge the skills gap, promote lifelong learning, and ensure equitable access to opportunities created by artificial intelligence. As AI technologies continue to advance, it is crucial for governments to implement strategies that equip individuals with the necessary skills and foster an environment conducive to innovation and economic growth.

A key approach for governments is to invest in education systems that incorporate AI literacy from an early age. By weaving AI concepts into curricula at various educational levels, students can build a foundational understanding of technology that will be vital in their future careers. Take this example, coding boot camps or workshops in schools could offer hands-on experiences with platforms like Scratch or Python, allowing students to engage with programming in an enjoyable yet educational way. These early introductions not only ignite interest but also prepare future generations for roles where AI will play a significant role.

In addition to educational reforms, governments can collaborate with industries to develop targeted training programs that address specific skill shortages in the job market. Partnerships with tech companies can lead to initiatives that provide apprenticeships or internships, offering individuals valuable real-world experience alongside professionals in the field. For example, a government-backed program might involve local businesses mentoring recent graduates on the latest machine learning applications, thus enhancing employability while directly supporting industry needs.

Public investment in reskilling and upskilling programs is another critical aspect of workforce development. With many workers facing displacement due to automation, it is essential to provide opportunities for them to acquire new skills and maintain economic stability. Governments could establish grants or subsidies for organizations offering training in high-demand areas such as data analytics or cybersecurity. Imagine a scenario where a city launches an initiative that allocates funding to local community colleges for developing specialized courses aimed at helping laid-off workers transition into emerging tech sectors.

And, fostering innovation through research and development grants is integral to government strategies for workforce development. Supporting tech startups and small businesses with financial assistance can spur creativity and entrepreneurial endeavors within communities. Take this example, a national fund designed specifically for startups focused on creating AI solutions for societal challenges could not only encourage innovative thinking but also generate employment opportunities.

Equitable access to technology and training resources is another responsibility that governments must uphold, ensuring that all citizens can benefit regardless of geographic location or socioeconomic status. Digital divide initiatives aim to improve internet connectivity and access to devices in underserved areas. Projects might include deploying public Wi-Fi networks in rural communities or providing subsidized technology kits for low-income families. Such efforts enhance educational prospects and promote inclusivity within the burgeoning digital economy.

Collaboration between public sector entities and private companies is crucial for crafting comprehensive workforce strategies tailored to the future job markets shaped by AI advancements. Regular forums where industry leaders share insights on evolving skill requirements can inform government policy decisions regarding workforce development programs.

Finally, cultivating a culture of continuous learning among citizens is vital for adapting to the ongoing technological changes driven by AI evolution. Governments can incentivize this mindset by offering tax breaks for lifelong learners who invest time in professional development courses or workshops throughout their careers.

To wrap things up, successful government initiatives surrounding AI workforce development must prioritize education reform, targeted training programs, innovation funding, equitable access policies, collaborative partnerships between sectors, and the promotion of lifelong learning. By proactively addressing these areas through well-planned strategies and sustained investment efforts, nations can better prepare their workforces—not only ensuring individual prosperity but also fostering economic resilience amid the shifting tides of technology-driven change.

Regulation and Legislation in AI

As governments navigate the complexities of artificial intelligence, regulation and legislation emerge as essential tools for fostering a responsible future. The rapid integration of AI technologies has often outstripped existing legal frameworks, underscoring the urgent need for regulatory bodies to establish guidelines that protect individuals and society while simultaneously encouraging innovation. This balancing act is intricate, encompassing ethical concerns, privacy issues, and the potential biases that may arise within AI systems.

A primary focus for legislators is the establishment of clear standards governing data usage and privacy. The European Union's General Data Protection Regulation (GDPR) stands as a pioneering model in this domain, imposing stringent rules on the collection, processing, and storage of personal data. Such regulations compel organizations to prioritize transparency and accountability, empowering individuals to maintain control over their own information. As other countries consider adopting similar frameworks, they must also explore effective compliance mechanisms that do not stifle the very innovations they aim to regulate.

Addressing algorithmic bias is another critical concern that requires attention. If left unchecked, biases inherent in AI can perpetuate existing inequalities. Take this example, facial recognition technologies have shown significant disparities in accuracy across different demographic groups, prompting calls for legislation that mandates fairness audits for AI systems prior to deployment. These audits would require developers to evaluate their algorithms against established fairness criteria, thus promoting equity in AI applications.

Regulatory measures like these should not only guide development but also encourage continuous improvement as new challenges emerge.

Also, intellectual property (IP) rights present unique dilemmas in the context of AI-generated content. Traditional IP laws may struggle to accommodate works created autonomously by AI systems. As courts grapple with cases involving AI-generated creations—ranging from artwork to music—legislators need to reassess existing frameworks to determine whether rights should be attributed to AI itself or remain with the creators of the technology. This discussion goes beyond ownership; it raises ethical questions about attributing human-like creativity to machines.

Collaboration between government entities and technology companies is vital for effective policy development. Engaging stakeholders through public consultations allows diverse perspectives to inform regulations that align with societal values while promoting innovation. Initiatives like "AI Roundtables" could serve as forums where industry experts, ethicists, and citizens convene to discuss regulatory needs and opportunities in AI development.

International cooperation is equally crucial given the borderless nature of technology. Establishing global standards can help harmonize regulations across jurisdictions, minimizing fragmentation that could otherwise stifle innovation or create exploitable loopholes. Organizations such as the OECD are already working toward formulating guiding principles for trustworthy AI that countries can adapt to their specific contexts.

Regulatory bodies face the ongoing challenge of keeping pace with technological advancements without becoming overly prescriptive. A flexible regulatory approach might involve frameworks that evolve alongside emerging technologies rather than relying on static laws that risk becoming obsolete within a short time frame. This could include sandbox models, allowing companies to test new products under regulated conditions without fear of punitive repercussions, while still adhering to essential ethical standards.

Effective enforcement mechanisms are also critical; they ensure compliance with regulations while deterring violations through penalties or sanctions. Transparency in enforcement processes fosters public trust in regulatory bodies and encourages businesses to strive for ethical practices.

As nations increasingly recognize these imperatives within their legislative agendas, they will undoubtedly encounter both challenges and opportunities ahead. Navigating this landscape requires vigilance from regulators who must balance the drive for innovation with the need for protection —creating an ecosystem where technology can flourish responsibly while safeguarding societal interests.

addressing these multifaceted regulatory considerations will shape not only the implementation of AI technologies but also their broader societal impact. Through thoughtful legislation that promotes ethical practices, protects individual rights, and fosters collaborative dialogue across sectors, governments can harness AI's potential while mitigating its risks—laying a foundational step toward a balanced relationship between humanity and technology in the future.

Incentives for AI Research and Development

The rapid advancement of artificial intelligence (AI) presents tremendous opportunities, but it also necessitates a thoughtful approach to its development. Governments play a pivotal role in this process by offering incentives for research and development that stimulate innovation while upholding ethical standards. These incentives come in various forms, such as grants, tax breaks, and collaborations with academic institutions.

One key way that governments encourage AI research is

through direct funding initiatives. Many countries have implemented national AI strategies that allocate significant financial resources to foster innovation. For example, the United States has introduced the National Artificial Intelligence Research Institutes program through the National Science Foundation (NSF), which funds collaborative projects aimed at advancing AI technologies. This funding not only supports cutting-edge research but also promotes collaboration between universities and industry, ensuring that academic discoveries are transformed into practical applications.

Tax incentives also play a crucial role in bolstering AI development. Countries like Canada have established programs that allow businesses to receive tax credits for their research and development expenditures. This model encourages companies to invest more heavily in innovative technologies without the immediate worry of financial loss. By reducing some of the financial pressures associated with R&D, these incentives foster an environment where experimentation and risk-taking are encouraged, ultimately leading to breakthrough AI solutions.

Also, partnerships with educational institutions significantly enhance the potential for innovation in AI. When governments collaborate with universities and research organizations, they can leverage a wealth of knowledge and expertise. Take this example, Finland's AI for People project exemplifies this collaborative approach by uniting government agencies, academia, and private sector stakeholders to create an inclusive ecosystem that nurtures talent and addresses societal challenges related to AI deployment.

In addition to these incentives, establishing regulatory frameworks is vital for promoting responsible AI development. Clear guidelines regarding data privacy and security help build trust between consumers and businesses involved in AI technologies. When users feel secure about how their data is managed, they are more likely to engage with AI systems, thereby driving growth in the sector. Countries that prioritize strong data protection laws will have a competitive edge as consumers increasingly seek assurances regarding their digital safety.

However, it is essential that regulatory measures do not hinder innovation or create unnecessary obstacles for startups entering the market. Striking a balance between regulation and support mechanisms enables emerging companies to thrive while adhering to ethical standards. For example, establishing "innovation hubs" can provide controlled environments where new AI applications can be developed and tested within existing legal frameworks before broader deployment.

Another important area for incentivization lies in diversity and inclusion initiatives within the tech workforce. By funding programs aimed at increasing representation among underrepresented groups in technology fields, governments can ensure a wider range of perspectives in AI development. Research indicates that diverse teams often produce more innovative solutions; therefore, investing in educational programs targeting women and minorities could yield substantial benefits for both society and technological advancement.

And, promoting interdisciplinary collaboration is essential for unlocking new avenues of innovation within AI research. Encouraging cross-disciplinary partnerships—such as those between psychology, sociology, and computer science —can lead to breakthroughs that traditional approaches might overlook. Collaborations between tech companies and social scientists can help design AI systems that better understand human behavior, improving user experiences while addressing ethical concerns about bias.

Finally, international cooperation should be a key consideration when discussing incentives for AI development. Global challenges require collective action; aligning policies across countries can facilitate shared learning and progress toward common goals such as environmental sustainability or public health. Joint funding initiatives or collaborative research efforts can enable countries to tackle pressing issues more effectively together than they could alone.

As governments continue to shape the landscape of AI through various incentives for research and development, it is crucial that they remain adaptable—responsive not only to technological advancements but also to societal needs. By fostering an environment where ethical considerations take precedence while still encouraging exploration and creativity, we can build a future where AI serves as a powerful ally in addressing some of humanity's most pressing challenges.

National AI Strategies Across the Globe

AI has emerged as a cornerstone of national strategies, profoundly influencing economies and societies worldwide. Countries have recognized that to remain competitive in this rapidly evolving technological landscape, they must develop coherent policies that foster AI innovation while addressing its ethical, social, and economic implications. The strategies adopted vary significantly, reflecting each nation's unique priorities and cultural contexts.

In the United States, the National AI Initiative Act was established to coordinate a comprehensive national strategy. This initiative seeks to accelerate AI research and development and enhance collaboration between federal agencies and the private sector. A key focus is promoting AI education at all levels, ensuring future generations are equipped with the skills needed for an AI-driven job market. Educational programs are being redesigned to integrate AI training into science, technology, engineering, and mathematics (STEM) curricula, fostering a skilled workforce ready to tackle the challenges posed by AI.

Conversely, China's national AI strategy aims for the country to become a global leader by 2030. The Chinese government emphasizes significant investment in AI research through state-owned enterprises and funding initiatives designed to attract private investment. By creating technology parks and incubators, China encourages startups to innovate while providing the necessary infrastructure for rapid growth. There is also a strong focus on practical applications of AI in public services such as healthcare and transportation, demonstrating how technology can enhance daily life.

Europe presents another compelling case with its emphasis on ethical considerations in technological advancement. The European Commission's White Paper on AI outlines a regulatory framework designed to ensure that AI systems are trustworthy and uphold fundamental rights. This includes initiatives aimed at privacy protection and transparency in algorithms. Countries like Germany have introduced their own strategic frameworks to promote AI while adhering to ethical guidelines, exemplifying a model for balancing innovation with societal values.

India's strategy highlights a different approach focused on inclusive growth through AI. The National Strategy for Artificial Intelligence acknowledges the importance of equitable access to technology across diverse populations. By targeting sectors such as agriculture and healthcare, India aims not only to boost productivity but also to uplift marginalized communities through enhanced access to resources and services powered by AI technologies.

These varied national strategies illustrate that there is no one-size-fits-all approach to integrating AI into societies. Each country's strategy reflects its distinct challenges, aspirations, and cultural narratives. However, a common thread is emerging: nations increasingly recognize the importance of international collaboration. As challenges like climate change and public health crises are universal, countries understand that sharing knowledge and resources can yield greater benefits than isolated efforts.

International partnerships allow nations to pool their expertise in addressing shared issues while navigating the complexities of technological regulation. Initiatives like the Global Partnership on Artificial Intelligence facilitate dialogue between countries aimed at fostering collaboration on best practices and policy development regarding ethical AI use.

As these national strategies evolve, it is crucial for policymakers to stay attuned to rapidly changing technologies while remaining committed to inclusivity and ethical standards. Creating an environment where innovation thrives alongside responsible practices can ensure that all members of society benefit from advances in artificial intelligence.

The interplay of national strategies for AI reflects broader societal goals; our engagement with technology today will shape our economic landscapes tomorrow. With foresight and collaboration at the forefront of these efforts, nations have an opportunity not only to adapt but also to lead in creating a future where artificial intelligence effectively and ethically serves humanity.

Bridging Public and Private Sector Efforts

To fully harness the potential of AI technologies, the public and private sectors must work together in a cohesive manner. This collaborative approach is vital for fostering an ecosystem that not only encourages innovation but also addresses the ethical and social implications associated with AI. By bridging these two sectors, we can ensure that advancements in artificial intelligence are equitable, sustainable, and beneficial for everyone.

The private sector often leads in AI research and development due to its agility, resources, and pursuit of competitive advantage. Companies are at the forefront of technological innovation, creating cutting-edge solutions with practical applications across various industries. Take this example, major tech companies like Google and Amazon utilize AI to enhance customer experiences, optimize operations, and improve efficiencies. Their initiatives continually push the boundaries of what is possible with AI, setting benchmarks for performance and capabilities.

However, this rapid pace of development can sometimes outstrip the regulatory frameworks established by governments. Without adequate oversight or ethical guidelines, the implementation of AI technologies may lead to unintended consequences, such as job displacement or increased inequality. This emphasizes the critical role of government in developing policies that not only promote innovation but also protect citizens from potential adverse effects.

A successful example of collaboration between the public and private sectors is seen in the partnership between the UK government and technology firms in crafting ethical AI guidelines. The UK established the Centre for Data Ethics and Innovation (CDEI) to facilitate dialogue among stakeholders. By engaging companies in discussions about ethical practices and data usage, the CDEI ensures that technological progress aligns with societal values. This collaborative framework promotes transparency and accountability among private entities while offering essential guidance from public authorities.

Public-private partnerships are also key in funding initiatives that advance AI research. By pooling resources from both sectors, collaborative funding models can support projects with significant societal implications. In healthcare, for instance, pharmaceutical companies often partner with government health agencies to leverage AI for drug discovery or diagnostic improvements. Such collaborations can accelerate developments that enhance public health outcomes while maintaining a focus on ethical standards.

And, these partnerships extend into education and workforce training programs. Equipping future generations with relevant skills is essential for meeting the demands of an AI-driven economy. Private firms can collaborate with educational institutions to develop curricula that prepare students for emerging roles in technology—such as internships or mentorship programs that foster practical skills alongside academic learning.

There is also a growing recognition of the importance of diverse stakeholder involvement in shaping AI policies. Engaging a variety of community voices—from industry leaders to local residents—ensures that a broad range of perspectives is considered when formulating regulations. This inclusivity helps bridge the gap between elite technologists and everyday users affected by technological changes.

International cooperation further strengthens the alignment between public and private sector efforts on a global scale. Challenges such as cybersecurity threats or climate change require unified approaches that transcend borders. Collaborative platforms like the Global Partnership on Artificial Intelligence facilitate knowledge sharing and promote coordinated strategies to address global challenges through technology.

When public policy aligns with private sector innovation, it cultivates an environment conducive to responsible growth within the AI landscape. This synergy reflects a commitment to shared goals—protecting individual rights while driving technological advancement that supports economic growth.

As we navigate the complex interplay between these sectors, it is vital for both public institutions and private enterprises to prioritize collective well-being over individual interests.

Striking a balance between competitiveness and social responsibility will ultimately shape how society embraces the transformative potential of artificial intelligence—not just as consumers but as informed participants guiding its future direction.

By fostering these collaborative efforts, we can pave the way for not only economic progress but also social equity as we adapt to the rapid changes brought by AI technologies. Uniting forces across sectors positions us strategically within this evolving landscape, ready to collectively tackle challenges while advancing our shared aspirations for a better future powered by artificial intelligence.

Navigating Policy Changes and Advocacy

Navigating the evolving landscape of artificial intelligence (AI) policy requires a multifaceted approach that balances innovation with ethical considerations. As technology and regulation intersect, it becomes imperative for all stakeholders to engage proactively rather than merely reactively. This dynamic interaction shapes the development, implementation, and regulation of AI technologies, affecting crucial areas such as privacy rights and economic equity.

Regulatory bodies play a vital role in establishing frameworks that not only encourage innovation but also prioritize ethical and social implications. Policymakers face the daunting task of keeping pace with rapid technological advancements while ensuring robust protections for public interests. For example, data protection laws like the General Data Protection Regulation (GDPR) in Europe set essential standards for how personal data is used by AI systems, reflecting a commitment to transparency and accountability that can foster public trust in these technologies.

However, effective policy development cannot occur in isolation. Collaborative dialogue among industry leaders, government officials, and civil society organizations is essential for fostering a comprehensive understanding of the complexities involved in AI adoption. Engaging diverse perspectives—from technologists to ethicists—enables policymakers to craft regulations that address both innovative potential and societal concerns. This inclusivity is particularly important given that AI's impacts can differ significantly across various demographics and communities.

Initiatives like the AI Now Institute exemplify advocacy efforts aimed at promoting fairness and inclusivity in AI applications. By focusing on research related to algorithmic bias and its societal effects, this organization highlights critical issues that might be overlooked by those concentrated solely on technological advancement. Advocacy groups play a crucial role in raising awareness about potential pitfalls while championing regulatory measures designed to protect marginalized communities disproportionately affected by automated systems.

Educational campaigns are also key to demystifying AI for the general public. By increasing awareness of how AI works and its implications, individuals can engage more meaningfully with technology and advocate for their rights. Workshops, seminars, and public forums provide platforms for citizens to voice concerns and contribute ideas toward shaping the future landscape of AI governance.

The collaboration between academia and industry is equally important for developing informed policies. Research institutions can supply empirical data that enrich legislative discussions about AI's impact on employment trends or consumer behavior. Their findings help craft evidence-based policies that address both current challenges and future possibilities.

A compelling example of successful advocacy is seen in efforts to promote inclusive AI practices within city governance. In cities like New York, local governments have initiated programs aimed at ensuring community voices are integral to discussions about smart city technologies. Engaging residents through town hall meetings allows officials to gather valuable input on how these technologies should be implemented responsibly while reflecting community values.

On a global scale, international collaboration is becoming increasingly vital as countries grapple with shared challenges such as cybersecurity threats and climate change. Initiatives like the Global Partnership on Artificial Intelligence underscore the importance of coordinated efforts across borders to leverage technological innovation in addressing pressing global issues.

successfully navigating policy changes related to AI hinges on the recognition that regulations must evolve alongside technological advancements. Continuous engagement with stakeholders—whether they represent industries impacted by automation or communities affected by emerging technologies—ensures that policies remain relevant and effective.

As we enter this era of rapid transformation driven by artificial intelligence, fostering an environment conducive to advocacy enhances our collective adaptability. Empowering citizens through education and encouraging active participation in policymaking will enable society to shape its future in meaningful ways.

To wrap things up, navigating the complexities of AI policy demands a commitment to inclusivity, transparency, and accountability from all parties involved. By prioritizing these principles, we can pave the way for responsible innovation that not only fuels economic growth but also enhances social equity as we move forward together in this evolving landscape.

The Role of Public Sector AI Adoption

The adoption of artificial intelligence (AI) by public sector entities marks a significant shift in the delivery and management of government services. As these organizations harness AI to boost efficiency, enhance decision-making, and drive innovation, they encounter unique challenges that require careful consideration. The public sector's role in this AI evolution is vital; it must serve as both a catalyst for progress and a guardian of ethical standards.

Integrating AI into government operations typically starts with pinpointing areas where technology can streamline processes or improve citizen services. Take this example, AI algorithms can analyze extensive datasets to identify trends in public health or traffic patterns, enabling city planners to make informed decisions that enhance urban living. A notable example is the use of predictive analytics by law enforcement agencies, which allows for more effective resource allocation and proactive measures against crime spikes in specific neighborhoods. However, these applications must be approached with caution, as they may also raise concerns regarding surveillance and civil liberties.

As public sector organizations embrace AI, they face the dual challenge of implementing new technologies while managing ethical considerations. Striking a balance between the benefits of increased efficiency and the potential biases inherent in AI systems is crucial. For example, if an AI model trained on historical data reflects societal biases, its deployment could unintentionally perpetuate discrimination. To address such risks, public entities must prioritize transparency and fairness in their algorithms. This requires robust auditing processes that examine the data feeding into AI systems and the outcomes produced.

Collaboration is essential for advancing AI adoption within the public sector. Governments frequently partner with academia and private industry to tap into expertise and resources that may not be available internally. For example, local governments might work alongside tech firms to develop smart city applications that enhance resource management or citizen engagement. These partnerships can foster innovative solutions while sharing the responsibility of addressing ethical implications, ensuring a comprehensive approach to implementation.

Public awareness and education are critical for facilitating successful AI integration. Engaging citizens through outreach initiatives helps demystify AI and fosters understanding of its potential benefits and inherent risks. Workshops explaining how data informs decision-making processes not only clarify technology's role but also empower citizens to critically engage with their government's use of AI. Take this example, by informing communities about data-driven policing practices, officials can build trust and invite feedback on effectiveness and fairness.

Additionally, policymakers have a responsibility to establish regulatory frameworks that guide the responsible use of AI technologies in public administration. These regulations should reflect a commitment to accountability and citizen welfare while remaining adaptable to rapid technological changes. Some governments have begun forming ethics boards tasked with evaluating new technologies before implementation—an essential step in ensuring alignment with societal values.

International cooperation is another key component for successful AI adoption in the public sector. Countries facing similar technological challenges can benefit from shared insights and best practices. Initiatives like the OECD's AIGO (Artificial Intelligence Governmental Observatory) provide platforms for nations to exchange knowledge on governance frameworks, enriching their approaches through collaboration.

Real-world examples underscore these principles in action. In Canada, for instance, the government initiated an effort to leverage AI for public health monitoring during the COVID-19 pandemic. By employing machine learning algorithms on health data, officials identified outbreaks more swiftly than traditional methods allowed—showcasing both innovation and an effective response to urgent needs.

integrating AI into the public sector necessitates ongoing dialogue among technology developers, government officials, civil society groups, and citizens themselves. Recognizing this collaborative dynamic is crucial for shaping policies that uphold public interests while fostering technological advancement.

Navigating this landscape requires flexibility; as situations evolve and new challenges emerge, strategies for implementing AI must adapt accordingly. A commitment to fostering an inclusive environment where all voices are heard will empower public sector entities to serve their constituents more effectively while fully harnessing the potential of artificial intelligence in their operations.

By focusing on ethical principles and engaging meaningfully with all stakeholders involved in AI policy development, governments can pave the way for responsible innovation —one that supports societal welfare alongside technological advancement without compromising their foundational responsibilities as stewards of public trust.

Preparing Society for AI Transformation

Integrating artificial intelligence into our daily lives presents not just a technical challenge, but a societal one as well. Preparing society for this transformation goes beyond merely equipping individuals with new skills; it calls for a comprehensive approach that takes into account cultural, economic, and ethical factors. This responsibility falls on the shoulders of not only tech developers and policymakers but also educators, community leaders, and citizens.

Education is central to this preparation. It is crucial to rethink curricula to include digital literacy from an early age, focusing not only on technical skills but also on critical thinking and ethical considerations surrounding AI technologies. For example, schools can implement modules that explore the implications of AI in everyday life—such as how algorithms shape news feeds, job searches, and even health diagnoses. This foundational understanding empowers students to recognize both the benefits and risks associated with AI, equipping them to navigate the future landscape thoughtfully.

In addition to education, fostering public discourse around AI is essential. Communities should engage in discussions about the technology's impact on employment, privacy, and ethical boundaries. Establishing forums where diverse perspectives are shared can facilitate these conversations, bringing together technologists, ethicists, business leaders, and everyday citizens to voice their hopes and concerns about AI's role in society. Such dialogue can empower communities to advocate for policies prioritizing transparency and accountability in AI development.

Collaboration across sectors is vital for effective preparation. Governments must partner with private enterprises to create initiatives that enhance awareness and understanding of AI technologies among various demographics. Take this example, local governments could sponsor workshops that allow citizens to interact with AI tools hands-on—demystifying the technology while providing practical skills relevant to the job market. In turn, companies can contribute by offering training programs tailored to different skill levels, ensuring accessibility for all community members.

Legislation will also play a critical role in navigating this transformation. Policymakers need to develop frameworks that promote innovation while safeguarding citizens' rights. This includes establishing guidelines for data privacy and security as well as addressing issues of bias within AI systems. Involving citizens in shaping these regulations through public consultations or town hall meetings ensures that their voices are heard in decisions that directly affect their lives.

As society braces for the changes brought by AI, cultivating adaptability becomes increasingly important. Individuals must embrace a mindset of lifelong learning—an openness to continually acquire new skills and knowledge throughout their careers. Organizations should support this by providing access to training resources and fostering environments where learning is an integral part of the corporate culture.

Simultaneously, it is crucial to create support systems for those displaced by technological advancements. Transition programs can assist workers in moving from roles that may become obsolete into new opportunities generated by AI-driven industries. These initiatives could include retraining programs or partnerships with educational institutions aimed at reskilling individuals for emerging fields.

As we move toward a more automated future, emphasizing ethics remains paramount. Public education efforts must include discussions about responsible AI use, ensuring society understands how these technologies should serve humanity rather than undermine it. Building frameworks that prioritize ethical considerations will help instill trust among citizens regarding how AI systems function within their lives.

preparing society for the transformation brought by AI is not just about embracing new technology; it is about crafting a future where technology enhances human capabilities while upholding the values fundamental to our communities—equity, justice, and dignity must remain at the forefront of our collective progress. By prioritizing education, fostering cross-sector dialogue, developing supportive policies, and encouraging adaptability among individuals, we can lay strong foundations for a future workforce capable of thriving amid the changes brought by artificial intelligence.

Engaging Citizens in AI Policy Discussions

Engaging citizens in discussions about AI policy is essential for nurturing a democratic approach to technological advancement. These conversations must be inclusive and participatory, ensuring that a wide range of voices are heard and considered. Without public engagement, policies risk reflecting the interests of a privileged few rather than those of the broader population, which can lead to distrust and disillusionment with AI technologies.

One effective way to foster citizen engagement is through community forums, where individuals can share their perspectives on the implications of AI in their lives. These gatherings provide a platform for open discussions that demystify complex technologies, allowing participants to voice their concerns and aspirations. Take this example, a town hall meeting could focus on how AI might impact local job markets, prompting questions such as: How will automation affect employment opportunities in our community? What safeguards do we need to protect our privacy? Such dialogues can cultivate a sense of ownership over AI-related policies.

To further enhance these discussions, local governments can utilize technology itself. Online platforms can facilitate ongoing conversations, allowing citizens who cannot attend in-person events to contribute their thoughts. Cities could create interactive websites where community members submit questions or ideas regarding AI developments and policy proposals. This approach not only broadens participation but also helps officials understand public sentiment and priorities regarding AI's integration into society.

Collaborating with educational institutions and nonprofits is another effective strategy. By hosting workshops that educate citizens about AI—covering topics like the basics of machine learning, ethical implications, and data privacy—these initiatives empower individuals to engage more confidently in policy discussions and advocate for their interests.

Harnessing the power of storytelling can also emotionally engage citizens with the subject matter. Sharing real-life examples of how AI technologies have transformed lives—both positively and negatively—can deepen understanding among community members. Take this example, a video series featuring local entrepreneurs who have successfully integrated AI into their businesses could inspire others while also highlighting the challenges they faced along the way.

As discussions around AI policy evolve, prioritizing transparency in governmental processes becomes crucial. Citizens should have access to information about how decisions regarding AI regulations are made. Establishing accessible channels for public feedback on proposed policies fosters trust and encourages active participation. When people see that their input leads to tangible changes, they are more likely to stay engaged in future discussions.

Partnerships between governments and civil society organizations can further enhance outreach efforts. These organizations often have established networks within communities and can play a vital role in bringing underrepresented voices into the conversation about AI policy. They can help organize events that focus on marginalized groups who might be disproportionately affected by AI developments, ensuring all perspectives are considered.

The media also plays a critical role in these engagements. Journalists can act as bridges between policymakers and the public by reporting on emerging technologies and their societal impacts. In-depth articles or investigative reports about local AI projects can spark interest and inform citizens about important issues surrounding technology deployment in their areas.

Finally, as citizen engagement becomes more robust, it is

imperative to continually evaluate its effectiveness. Collecting feedback from participants after events or initiatives allows organizers to refine their approaches based on what resonates with communities. This iterative process ensures that engagement strategies evolve alongside public understanding and sentiment regarding AI.

In summary, engaging citizens in AI policy discussions requires intentional efforts across various fronts: community forums for dialogue, educational workshops for knowledge-building, storytelling for emotional connection, transparency for trust-building, partnerships for outreach, media for information dissemination, and feedback mechanisms for continuous improvement. By embracing these strategies, we can cultivate an informed populace ready to navigate the complexities of an AI-driven future while advocating for equitable policies that serve everyone's interests.

CHAPTER 13: AI AND ECONOMIC INEQUALITY

The Impact of AI on Income Distribution

The impact of AI on income distribution prompts essential questions about equity and economic stability in an ever-evolving job market. As artificial intelligence becomes increasingly integrated into various industries, its effect on the disparity between high- and low-income workers grows more complex. While AI has the potential to boost productivity, enhance efficiency, and create new job opportunities, it also carries the risk of widening income inequality if not managed thoughtfully.

A significant way that AI influences income distribution is through automation. As machines take over tasks traditionally performed by humans—particularly in sectors like manufacturing and services—wage pressure mounts for lower-skilled jobs. Take this example, in the retail sector, self-checkout kiosks and automated inventory systems have streamlined operations but diminished the demand for human cashiers and stock clerks. That's why, those who remain in similar roles often face wage stagnation or reductions.

Conversely, AI has spurred the growth of high-skilled job opportunities that typically offer substantially higher wages. Roles in data analysis, machine learning engineering, and AI ethics are becoming increasingly important; however, they usually require specialized training and education. This shift creates a growing divide between individuals equipped with the skills needed to thrive in an AI-driven economy and those who lack such qualifications. A case study from a leading tech firm illustrates this trend: as it transitioned to an AI-centric model, it experienced a significant increase in demand for data scientists while simultaneously eliminating numerous entry-level positions.

Geographic disparities further complicate the relationship between AI advancements and income distribution. Urban areas with access to technological infrastructure and educational resources tend to attract investments that generate high-paying tech jobs. In contrast, rural regions often struggle to provide the training programs necessary for workers to reskill for these new opportunities. This disconnect between urban prosperity and rural stagnation is evident in employment rates; cities with robust tech sectors frequently experience job growth while rural areas grapple with rising unemployment due to automation's impact.

In this context, education emerges as a crucial factor influencing income distribution. Policymakers must prioritize creating pathways for reskilling and upskilling initiatives aimed at displaced workers. Programs offering vocational training alongside access to technology can empower individuals to transition effectively into emerging job markets. For example, community colleges across the United States have begun providing certifications in AI-related fields, helping workers pivot into new careers instead of being left behind.

And, we must consider the role of policy intervention in addressing inequalities exacerbated by AI integration. Governments have a responsibility to implement regulations that promote fair labor practices within the AI ecosystem. This includes establishing minimum wage standards that reflect the cost of living and protecting workers from unjust layoffs resulting from automation. Countries like Finland have started exploring universal basic income models as potential solutions for tackling income disparities—an idea gaining traction amid growing concerns about automation.

The necessity for inclusive growth cannot be overstated; businesses must adopt policies that promote diversity and representation within their workforces as they leverage AI technologies. Implementing diverse hiring practices not only fosters innovation but also ensures that various perspectives shape how these technologies are developed and deployed.

navigating the impacts of AI on income distribution requires collaborative efforts from governments, businesses, educational institutions, and civil society organizations. By fostering equitable access to education and training while encouraging policy frameworks that support fair labor practices, we can begin bridging the widening economic divides created by technological advancements.

As we explore this critical aspect of our future workforce landscape, it becomes clear that strategic actions must be taken now to reshape our understanding of work and wealth distribution amidst growing technological influences. Thoughtfully addressing these issues will help ensure that all segments of society can benefit from advancements rather than struggle against them.

Potential for Job Polarization

The emergence of job polarization in the age of AI highlights a landscape marked by significant contrasts. As artificial intelligence reshapes industries, the workforce increasingly divides into two categories: high-skill, high-wage positions and low-skill, low-wage jobs. This division raises pressing concerns about economic stability and the sustainability of our labor markets.

At the heart of job polarization is the rapid advancement of technology that favors automation. Many sectors are witnessing the automation of routine tasks, leading to the displacement of workers who traditionally occupied these roles. Take this example, in manufacturing, the rise of robotics has drastically reduced the need for assembly line workers while simultaneously increasing demand for robotics engineers and AI specialists. This shift underscores a growing disparity in job prospects for lower-skilled workers, often resulting in heightened unemployment or underemployment.

Conversely, high-skilled positions that require advanced education and specialized training are flourishing. The demand for data scientists, AI trainers, and software developers is surging, with a leading consulting firm projecting that jobs requiring advanced technical skills will grow by over 20% in the next decade. This growth not only promises substantial financial rewards but also exacerbates the skills gap between those prepared to thrive in the new economy and those who are not.

Geographical disparities further deepen job polarization. Urban centers with vibrant tech ecosystems attract talent and investment, fostering environments rich in opportunities. In these cities, tech startups thrive alongside established corporations, creating a cycle of growth that boosts demand for skilled workers. In contrast, rural areas often struggle with limited access to high-speed internet and educational resources essential for workforce development. That's why, residents in these regions face restricted employment options, leading to economic stagnation and a widening gap between urban and rural communities.

Education plays a crucial role in mitigating this polarization. To counteract the effects of automation on low-skilled jobs, educational institutions must adapt by offering training programs aligned with emerging job markets. Coding bootcamps and online courses have become effective avenues for individuals seeking to rapidly upskill. For example, a community college in Ohio recently revamped its curriculum to include AI-related coursework, resulting in graduates successfully transitioning into tech roles that were previously considered unattainable without a four-year degree.

Policy interventions are vital for addressing job polarization as well. Governments must establish frameworks that promote equitable labor practices and support displaced workers through reskilling initiatives. Innovative policies, such as providing income support during transition periods, can offer a safety net for those affected by automation. Countries like Germany are already implementing such measures, funding retraining programs through public-private partnerships aimed at reskilling workers facing job displacement due to technological advancements.

And, companies must take responsibility in this evolving landscape. By actively engaging in reskilling efforts—whether through mentorship programs or direct training initiatives—businesses can play a pivotal role in bridging the skills gap. This collaborative approach not only fosters employee loyalty but also ensures that companies have access to a diverse talent pool capable of driving innovation.

addressing job polarization requires an integrated effort involving various stakeholders. Educators, policymakers, businesses, and community organizations must work together to create pathways for all workers to succeed in an AI-driven economy. By prioritizing inclusive practices and expanding access to quality education and training opportunities, we can pave the way for a more equitable future where everyone has the chance to thrive amid rapid technological change.

The implications of job polarization extend far beyond individual experiences; they reverberate through entire communities and economies. Recognizing these dynamics within our workforce landscape makes it clear that proactive measures must be implemented now to ensure equitable access to opportunities created by technological advancements—transforming potential challenges into collective successes.

Addressing Wage Stagnation

The challenges of wage stagnation in today's economy are deeply connected to the broader issue of job polarization. As AI and automation transform industries, workers are confronted with the unsettling reality of stagnant wages, even as productivity rises. This disconnect prompts urgent questions about the sustainability of economic growth and the overall well-being of the workforce.

Wage stagnation primarily impacts low- and middle-income workers, who find themselves caught between soaring living costs and limited opportunities for income advancement. The rise of automation has replaced many routine tasks, placing these workers in a precarious position where they must adapt to new roles or risk being left behind. For example, retail jobs—once considered stable sources of income—have been drastically affected by automation technologies such as self-checkout systems and online shopping platforms. While these innovations boost efficiency, they simultaneously restrict wage growth for frontline employees.

The repercussions of wage stagnation are particularly pronounced in sectors that rely heavily on low-skilled labor. Take the fast-food industry: companies benefit from lower labor costs due to automation, yet workers see minimal wage increases. A 2022 report noted that despite record profits reported by fast-food chains during the post-pandemic recovery, average wages for entry-level positions remained flat. This disconnect fosters frustration among workers, who increasingly feel their contributions go unrecognized.

To address this pressing issue, we must explore proactive solutions that tackle both wage stagnation and the necessity for skill advancement. A key strategy is to enhance access to vocational training and higher education opportunities tailored to today's job market demands. Community colleges and trade schools are stepping up with innovative programs focused on relevant skills—such as coding, data analysis, and digital marketing—offering individuals pathways to better-paying jobs.

Consider a successful tech initiative in San Francisco where local nonprofits partnered with educational institutions to establish an apprenticeship program for underrepresented communities. Participants gained hands-on experience alongside established tech companies while earning stipends that alleviated financial pressures during their training period. This model not only provided individuals with valuable skills but also addressed immediate economic needs —demonstrating how targeted training can effectively combat wage stagnation.

In addition to education and training, policy measures are crucial in mitigating the effects of wage stagnation. Raising the minimum wage can directly empower low-income workers while stimulating consumer spending within local economies. And, as evidenced by various states that have enacted "living wage" laws, businesses often find that higher wages lead to improved employee retention and productivity —creating a win-win situation.

Also, technology itself offers potential solutions for addressing wage concerns. Companies can harness AI tools to identify inefficiencies within their workforce structures and optimize roles accordingly—ensuring that human labor is complemented rather than replaced by technology. Take this example, organizations employing data analytics to monitor employee performance may uncover areas where additional training could significantly enhance productivity without further straining budgets.

Combating wage stagnation requires multifaceted strategies involving collaboration among educators, policymakers, businesses, and communities alike. By collectively investing in upskilling initiatives while enacting policies that safeguard worker rights and promote fair compensation practices, we can establish a foundation for equitable growth in an AI-driven economy.

addressing wage stagnation goes beyond improving individual circumstances; it is essential for fostering broader economic health. Ensuring that all workers have access to fair wages reflects our commitment to social equity— a cornerstone of sustainable progress as we navigate these turbulent times shaped by rapid technological advancements.

The Role of Social Safety Nets

The effectiveness of social safety nets is increasingly critical in a landscape where economic volatility and technological disruption have become the norm. As industries evolve under the influence of AI and automation, traditional job security diminishes, making these safety nets not just helpful but essential for maintaining societal stability. Their primary role is to cushion individuals against various shocks—such as job loss, unexpected medical expenses, or economic downturns —ensuring that basic needs are met even in times of drastic change.

Central to this discussion is the understanding that social safety nets must adapt to the realities of a transforming job market. For example, unemployment benefits should not only provide immediate financial relief but also include elements that encourage skill development and reemployment. A noteworthy example is Germany's initiative, which successfully integrates training programs into its unemployment insurance system. Here, beneficiaries receive financial support while also enrolling in courses designed to enhance their employability in fields experiencing growth due to technological advancements.

Access to healthcare is another pivotal aspect of effective social safety nets. Health-related expenses can consume a significant portion of an individual's income, leading to financial strain that exacerbates economic insecurity. Countries with universal healthcare systems often demonstrate lower rates of bankruptcy due to medical bills, illustrating how a strong health safety net can prevent individuals from falling into poverty during unforeseen medical crises. This support allows them to focus on career transitions without the looming threat of financial ruin.

Childcare assistance further enhances workforce participation rates, particularly among low-income families. When parents have access to affordable childcare, they can pursue job opportunities without the burden of balancing work and family responsibilities. Research indicates that states with comprehensive childcare support programs see higher employment rates among single parents. This not only empowers families economically but also contributes positively to child development outcomes, underscoring that investments in social safety nets yield multifaceted benefits.

As gig work and freelance roles become increasingly prevalent, there's an urgent need for social safety measures specifically tailored for these workers. Unlike traditional employees who benefit from employer-sponsored protections like health insurance and retirement plans, gig workers often lack such safeguards. Innovative solutions like portable benefits—where entitlements follow workers regardless of their employment status—can bridge this gap. Take this example, states like Illinois are exploring policies that allow gig workers access to health insurance and retirement savings plans akin to those enjoyed by traditional employees.

Economic mobility is another crucial factor influenced by effective social safety nets. Programs designed to assist individuals through educational grants or subsidies empower marginalized communities and facilitate upward mobility. A notable example is the Tennessee Promise program, which offers free community college tuition to recent high school graduates. By eliminating financial barriers to education, it significantly increases enrollment rates among low-income students, equipping them with skills necessary for in-demand jobs.

However, the conversation surrounding social safety nets cannot overlook the importance of funding and political willpower. Policymakers must prioritize these frameworks within national budgets while ensuring they remain resilient against economic downturns. During crises—such as the COVID-19 pandemic—countries with robust social safety nets were better positioned to mitigate economic fallout compared to those lacking such support structures.

To wrap things up, strengthening social safety nets involves more than just providing financial aid; it requires creating a holistic framework that empowers individuals to navigate an uncertain job economy effectively. By investing in comprehensive systems that include unemployment benefits, healthcare access, childcare support, and education initiatives tailored for gig workers, societies can foster resilience among their populations. This approach not only enhances individual well-being but also cultivates a more robust economy capable of weathering future challenges posed by technological advancements and shifting labor markets.

Education and Training for Economic Mobility

Education and training are essential drivers of economic mobility, particularly in a world increasingly shaped by rapid technological advancements. As AI and automation continue to transform industries, individuals must equip themselves with relevant skills and knowledge that align with the evolving job landscape. This necessity calls for a dual approach: while traditional education remains important, innovative training methods that accommodate diverse learning styles and career paths are equally vital.

Formal education serves as a foundational element for many, providing essential qualifications that open doors to various career opportunities. However, the traditional educational model often struggles to keep pace with the rapid changes driven by technology. To address this challenge, educational institutions need to adopt a more flexible approach, offering courses that adapt to market demands. Take this example, many universities now collaborate with tech companies to design curricula that reflect real-world needs, ensuring graduates possess the skills that employers are actively seeking.

In addition to formal education, vocational training and apprenticeships present alternative pathways for those pursuing economic mobility. These programs offer hands-on experience in specific trades or industries, allowing participants to acquire valuable skills while earning a wage. Countries like Switzerland have successfully implemented apprenticeship models where businesses partner with educational institutions to train young people in various trades. This collaboration not only addresses skill gaps in the labor market but also enables individuals to transition smoothly into well-paying jobs without incurring significant student debt.

The rise of online learning platforms has further revolutionized access to education, dismantling barriers related to location and cost. Platforms such as Coursera and edX allow individuals to pursue courses from top universities at their own pace and often at a fraction of the traditional tuition cost. This democratization of knowledge empowers learners from all backgrounds to invest in their personal development and adapt to changing job requirements. For example, someone interested in data analysis can take specialized online courses, gaining credentials that enhance their employability without needing a formal degree.

And, companies play a crucial role in promoting workforce adaptability through continuous employee training programs. Organizations that invest in their employees' professional development not only enhance individual skills but also foster a culture of innovation and retention within their workforce. Take this example, tech giants like Google and Amazon have established internal training initiatives aimed at upskilling employees for emerging roles within their organizations. These efforts underscore a commitment to maintaining a skilled workforce while providing employees with clear pathways for advancement.

Mentorship and coaching can further enrich educational experiences by offering personalized guidance tailored to individual career aspirations. Engaging with mentors who have navigated similar challenges can provide invaluable insights and support. Initiatives like SCORE—which offers mentoring for entrepreneurs—illustrate how experienced professionals can help newcomers navigate the complexities of career development.

Community colleges are increasingly focusing on partnerships with local businesses to create tailored training programs that meet specific industry needs. This collaboration ensures that graduates are well-prepared for local job markets, thereby enhancing their prospects for economic mobility. For example, some community colleges have developed fast-track programs aimed at training healthcare workers in response to regional demands.

The integration of technology into education and training is also critical for effective skill acquisition. Techniques such as gamification make learning more engaging while simulating real-world scenarios that enhance retention. Tools like coding boot camps utilize interactive learning environments where students practice coding on real-time projects—effectively bridging the gap between theory and application.

Importantly, ongoing education should be viewed as a lifelong pursuit rather than a one-time achievement. As job roles evolve due to technological advancements, individuals must remain proactive in updating their skill sets regularly. Cultivating a habit of continuous learning enables workers to stay relevant and competitive in an ever-changing job market.

In summary, education and training for economic mobility hinge on adaptability and innovation. By embracing diverse learning methods—whether through formal education, vocational training, online courses, or corporate upskilling—individuals can equip themselves with the tools necessary to thrive amid change. As societies prioritize these initiatives, they foster environments where economic mobility is attainable for all, ultimately contributing to more resilient communities prepared for future challenges.

Public Perception and Trust in AI

Public perception and trust in artificial intelligence (AI) are crucial factors that will shape the future of the workforce. As AI technologies become more integrated into our daily lives and professional environments, understanding how people perceive these advancements is vital for fostering acceptance and effective collaboration between humans and machines. The narratives surrounding AI—both positive and negative—directly influence individuals' approaches to their work, their openness to adopting new technologies, and ultimately, the success of AI initiatives.

Trust in AI is built on several key dimensions, including transparency, reliability, and perceived fairness. Take this example, when companies use AI tools for hiring or performance evaluations, concerns about bias can arise if the algorithms are not well understood or are perceived as opaque. A study by MIT researchers highlighted racial and gender biases in facial recognition systems, which heightened public skepticism regarding their use in sensitive contexts like law enforcement. This emphasizes the need for organizations to clearly communicate how their AI systems function and to ensure that these systems are designed to effectively mitigate bias.

Transparency involves more than just explaining how algorithms work; it also requires openness about the data used to train these models. Individuals are more likely to trust AI when they understand its foundations—how data is sourced, processed, and utilized. For example, a financial institution that shares information about its machine learning models for credit scoring can help alleviate customer concerns regarding potential discrimination based on race or socioeconomic status. By openly discussing these aspects, organizations can build rapport with stakeholders and foster trust.

Reliability also plays a significant role in shaping public perception. If an AI system consistently delivers accurate results, users are more likely to feel confident relying on it in their daily tasks. Conversely, frequent inaccuracies can lead to frustration and distrust. Tesla's Autopilot feature serves as an illustrative case: while many users praise its capabilities, others remain cautious due to reported incidents where the system failed to perform as expected. To mitigate such risks, developers must prioritize rigorous testing and validation processes before deploying AI technologies in real-world settings.

Perceived fairness in AI decision-making processes further impacts trust. Stakeholders must believe that AI systems operate without favoritism or bias; otherwise, even well-functioning technologies may face pushback. Take this example, when an insurance company introduces an AI-driven policy pricing tool, it should clearly outline how premiums are calculated based on individual risk factors rather than arbitrary decisions that could lead to unfair treatment of specific groups.

Education is also essential in shaping public perceptions of AI. As individuals become more informed about the technology's potential benefits—such as enhanced efficiency and reduced human error—they may be more inclined to embrace it. Community workshops or online webinars discussing practical applications of AI can demystify its operations and demonstrate its relevance across various industries. For example, a local government might host sessions highlighting how AI improves traffic management systems or optimizes waste collection routes, showcasing tangible benefits for residents.

And, media representation of AI significantly influences public opinion. Sensationalist narratives that focus on dystopian futures can provoke fear and resistance toward technological advancements. In contrast, success stories where AI has positively impacted sectors like healthcare—through predictive analytics that improve patient outcomes—can shift perspectives toward optimism and acceptance.

Social media also plays a powerful role in shaping perceptions of AI technology. Positive testimonials from users can enhance acceptance, while widely shared negative experiences can exacerbate mistrust. Companies must actively manage their online presence by engaging with users' concerns and highlighting positive outcomes achieved through their technologies.

The role of policymakers is another critical aspect of this discussion. As governments consider regulations surrounding AI deployment, they must establish frameworks that promote ethical practices while fostering innovation.

Collaborative efforts between tech companies and regulatory bodies can create guidelines that enhance transparency and accountability without stifling progress.

building public trust in AI requires a concerted effort across various sectors—education initiatives to improve understanding of technology's capabilities, transparent communication from organizations about their implementation strategies, fair decision-making practices in algorithm design, responsible media portrayals, and effective policy frameworks.

As we advance into an era defined by artificial intelligence, cultivating a public perception rooted in understanding rather than fear will be essential for harnessing the full potential of this transformative technology. Trust is not merely an abstract concept; it forms the foundation upon which successful human-AI collaboration will be built—a collaboration poised to redefine industries and create new opportunities for economic growth and innovation.

Addressing Disparities Across Industries

Disparities in the adoption of artificial intelligence (AI) across industries are becoming increasingly pronounced, highlighting differences in readiness, resource allocation, and cultural acceptance. While some sectors quickly embrace AI and enjoy significant benefits, others lag behind due to various barriers that impede their progress. Understanding these disparities is vital for stakeholders who seek to bridge gaps and foster equitable growth in the evolving job market.

The technology sector is leading the way in AI adoption, utilizing sophisticated algorithms to enhance productivity and streamline operations. Companies like Google and Amazon leverage AI not only to improve efficiency but also to innovate products and services that transform consumer behavior. Take this example, Amazon's recommendation engine personalizes shopping experiences by analyzing user data to suggest relevant products, significantly boosting sales and customer satisfaction. In contrast, industries such as agriculture face challenges in adopting similar technologies, primarily due to limited resources and inadequate technological infrastructure. Although AI has the potential to revolutionize farming—through precision agriculture techniques that optimize crop yields—the high costs associated with implementation often deter many farmers from making the necessary investments.

Manufacturing illustrates another stark difference in AI utilization. Advanced factories equipped with robotics and machine learning algorithms exemplify the future of production, increasing throughput and minimizing waste. Tesla's Gigafactory serves as a prime example, where automated processes drive innovation at scale. However, small to medium-sized enterprises (SMEs) often struggle to compete, lacking the capital needed for such investments. This divide underscores a systemic issue: larger corporations that successfully harness AI can outpace SMEs, which are essential for job creation in local economies.

Healthcare presents both the promise of AI and the obstacles that persist. On one hand, AI-driven diagnostic tools have revolutionized patient care; algorithms can analyze medical images faster than some human radiologists. Yet, many healthcare institutions remain hesitant to adopt these technologies due to concerns over data privacy and ethical considerations regarding algorithmic biases—issues made more pressing by the high stakes involved in patient outcomes. The absence of standardized guidelines complicates the integration of AI in healthcare settings, leaving some facilities entrenched in traditional practices while others advance into new territories.

The education sector reveals another layer of disparity in AI adaptation. While elite universities invest heavily in research and offer specialized programs that prepare graduates for tech-driven roles, community colleges often lack the resources to develop similar curricula. This educational gap perpetuates an imbalance in the workforce's ability to meet future demands; students from underfunded institutions may miss out on lucrative opportunities in tech-centric industries.

The financial sector has also undergone significant transformation through AI, yet it faces challenges reminiscent of those in other industries. Algorithms enable accurate fraud detection and risk assessment; however, smaller banks may find it difficult to adopt these tools due to the high operational costs tied to integrating advanced technologies into legacy systems. Additionally, concerns about algorithmic transparency raise questions about trustworthiness when it comes to decisions made by machines—a worry that echoes across various sectors.

Addressing these disparities necessitates an understanding of how cultural attitudes toward technology influence industry responses to AI adoption. In regions where skepticism toward automation is prevalent—often fueled by fears of job displacement—the path forward becomes more intricate. Grassroots initiatives aimed at promoting technology literacy can help cultivate acceptance by demonstrating how AI can enhance human roles rather than replace them.

Collaboration among industry leaders can also play a crucial role in leveling the playing field. Joint ventures between established firms and startups can create environments conducive to resource sharing while driving innovation in sectors that might otherwise stagnate. For example, partnerships between tech companies and educational institutions can accelerate workforce readiness by aligning curricula with real-world skill demands.

Government policy must also rise to the occasion to effectively address these disparities. Incentives designed to encourage investment in AI technologies among smaller enterprises could stimulate broader participation across various sectors. Also, regulatory frameworks that promote fair competition will ensure all organizations—regardless of size—can adapt without compromising ethical standards or stifling innovation.

tackling disparities across industries requires a comprehensive approach that engages stakeholders from all sectors: businesses must invest in workforce training and development; educational institutions need support to create relevant programs; and policymakers should craft regulations that encourage equitable access to technology—all while fostering a culture that embraces innovation rather than resists it.

As we consider this complex landscape shaped by differing levels of readiness for AI integration, it becomes clear that collaborative efforts are essential for overcoming barriers to widespread adoption. By embracing diversity—not only within our workforces but also in our approaches to technology—we can create an environment where all industries are equipped not just to survive but to thrive amid the sweeping changes ushered in by artificial intelligence.

Inclusive Growth Strategies

Inclusive growth strategies are essential for ensuring that the benefits of artificial intelligence (AI) reach all segments of society, helping to mitigate the risk of widening inequalities. To achieve this, we must shift our focus from simply integrating AI technologies to creating environments where diverse communities can thrive alongside these advancements. This commitment to inclusivity necessitates collaboration across sectors, innovative policy frameworks, and proactive community engagement.

A key component of inclusive growth is the development of training programs specifically designed for underserved populations. For example, coding boot camps that emphasize digital skills can empower individuals from lower-income backgrounds to enter the tech workforce. In recent years, these boot camps have proliferated, providing intensive training in programming languages and software development. A successful case is General Assembly, which has equipped thousands with high-demand tech skills. Such initiatives not only provide participants with critical competencies but also promote diversity within the tech industry, enriching it with a wider array of perspectives and innovations.

To amplify these efforts, partnerships between public institutions and private organizations are vital. Local governments can collaborate with tech companies to establish scholarships for aspiring coders from marginalized communities. This approach opens doors for individuals who may lack financial means while allowing companies to access untapped talent pools. The result is an inclusive workforce that better reflects the diversity of society.

However, skill-building initiatives alone are insufficient; we must also address infrastructural disparities that hinder technology adoption in less advantaged areas. Broadband access remains a significant barrier for many rural and low-income urban communities. Initiatives aimed at expanding internet access—such as community-funded networks or government subsidies—are crucial for bridging this divide and ensuring that everyone has the opportunity to engage with AI technologies.

Additionally, creating mentorship programs that connect industry veterans with newcomers can provide invaluable guidance for those entering the field. These mentorship opportunities could include shadowing experiences or regular skill-sharing sessions where seasoned professionals share their insights on navigating AI-driven environments. Programs like Year Up have successfully linked young adults with mentors who help them develop both soft and hard skills necessary for successful careers.

Cultural attitudes toward technology also play a pivotal role in fostering acceptance and innovation among diverse groups. Outreach efforts aimed at demystifying AI can alleviate fears associated with job displacement while highlighting how AI complements human capabilities rather than replaces them. Community workshops showcasing practical AI applications —such as automation tools that enhance productivity or predictive analytics that improve customer service—can effectively demonstrate the potential benefits of technology.

And, inclusive growth strategies must extend beyond individual skill development to encompass corporate responsibility regarding ethical AI deployment. Companies should adopt frameworks prioritizing fairness in algorithmic decision-making processes and actively seek input from diverse stakeholders when designing their products or services. Engaging a wide range of voices will help mitigate biases often present in AI deployment, ensuring that technologies serve all demographic groups equitably.

As we navigate an era defined by rapid technological advancement, it is evident that proactive measures are necessary to foster inclusivity within the AI landscape. Collaborative frameworks that bridge government support, private sector innovation, community engagement, and educational initiatives will build resilience against potential inequalities created by these advancements.

By embracing holistic strategies rooted in shared responsibility among stakeholders—from businesses prioritizing ethical practices to educators fostering accessible learning pathways—we can pave the way for a future where everyone has equal opportunities to thrive amidst the transformative impact of artificial intelligence on our economies and societies.

our vision transcends mere survival; it aims for collective flourishing as we responsibly harness technology's full potential. By inviting every member of our communities into this dynamic narrative of progress, we not only empower individuals but also enhance our collective capacity for innovation and resilience against future challenges in an evolving job economy driven by artificial intelligence.

Case Studies of AI and Economic Inequality

Case studies of AI and economic inequality reveal both the transformative potential of technology and the risks that can worsen disparities if not managed thoughtfully. Various sectors demonstrate that AI can either bridge or widen economic gaps, largely depending on the strategies employed. By examining real-world examples, we gain valuable insights into the nuanced effects of AI integration across diverse communities, highlighting both best practices and cautionary tales.

In the healthcare sector, one striking example illustrates the positive impact of AI. A partnership between a tech company and a community health organization focused on underserved populations led to the development of an AI-driven platform designed to predict health risks and streamline access to preventive care. This initiative not only improved patient outcomes but also equipped local clinics with actionable data that informed their services. By addressing specific community needs through technology, this approach fostered greater equity in healthcare delivery.

In contrast, another case highlights the potential for widening inequality when AI is deployed without adequate consideration for all stakeholders. A large financial institution implemented an automated loan approval system aimed at speeding up processing times. Although initially regarded as a significant innovation, it inadvertently perpetuated bias against applicants from certain neighborhoods due to historical data that reflected socio-economic disparities. This situation underscores the critical importance of fairness in algorithmic decision-making processes. To avoid reinforcing existing inequalities, companies must actively engage with diverse communities during system development.

The education sector offers further examples of AI's varying impacts on economic equity. At a public university, a successful program utilized machine learning algorithms to tailor educational content to individual student needs, dramatically improving retention rates among first-generation college students. This personalized learning experience proved effective in leveling the academic playing field, showcasing how targeted technology use can empower marginalized learners.

Conversely, some online education platforms have faced criticism for accessibility issues related to cost and internet availability. Students in rural areas often struggle to access high-speed internet necessary for fully engaging with these resources, limiting their ability to benefit from such innovations. This scenario emphasizes that while technology has the potential to democratize learning, addressing infrastructural barriers is essential for ensuring equitable access.

The gig economy serves as another compelling case study that reflects both promise and peril. Platforms like Uber and Lyft have transformed job opportunities for many; however, they also expose economic vulnerabilities tied to algorithm-driven work conditions. Take this example, drivers often face unpredictable income due to fluctuating demand dictated by algorithms that prioritize efficiency over job security. These challenges raise important questions about how gig workers can be protected in an increasingly automated landscape while still benefiting from its opportunities.

And, collaboration between private companies and non-profits presents pathways for mitigating inequalities in gig work. Initiatives that provide training programs focused on digital literacy skills specifically designed for gig workers have emerged as effective strategies for enhancing job stability and earning potential. These collaborations equip individuals to navigate a rapidly changing landscape while improving their adaptability across various roles.

Policy also plays a crucial role in shaping how AI impacts economic equality across different demographics. Cities implementing inclusive policies—such as grants or training programs aimed at supporting small businesses—have witnessed increased entrepreneurial activity among diverse populations. These initiatives highlight how intentional policy frameworks can create environments conducive to equitable growth while leveraging technological advancements.

Together, these varied case studies reveal that while AI holds significant promise for driving economic development, its benefits are not automatic or universal. Active engagement from all stakeholders—government agencies, businesses, educational institutions, and communities—is vital for creating a balanced landscape where everyone can thrive amidst technological advancements.

As we consider these examples collectively, they illuminate pathways forward that prioritize inclusivity alongside innovation. By fostering shared responsibility among all sectors involved in AI development and deployment, society can harness technology's capabilities while building resilience against emerging inequalities within this new economy shaped by artificial intelligence.

CHAPTER 14:
CASE STUDIES IN
AI WORKFORCE
TRANSFORMATION

*Success Stories in AI-
Driven Industries*

S uccess stories from AI-driven industries illustrate the transformative potential of technology when implemented thoughtfully and inclusively. Each example highlights how strategic applications can enhance various sectors, improve outcomes, and foster resilience amid rapid change. By examining these instances, we can glean valuable insights into successful AI integration and its role in driving progress.

Consider the agricultural sector. A pioneering farm in California embraced AI-powered analytics to optimize crop yields while minimizing resource use. By employing machine learning algorithms that analyzed weather patterns, soil conditions, and market trends, farmers received actionable insights to guide their planting decisions. This approach not only boosted productivity but also lessened environmental impact by enabling more precise applications of water and fertilizers. This initiative serves as a prime example of how AI can facilitate sustainable practices that benefit both farmers and the broader ecosystem.

Similarly, the manufacturing industry is undergoing a renaissance thanks to AI-enhanced automation. A mid-sized automotive company introduced robotics powered by AI to streamline assembly processes, leading to remarkable efficiency gains: production times fell by 30%, and defects were significantly reduced. Crucially, the company invested in retraining its workforce for new roles that required human oversight of these machines, promoting a culture of continuous learning and adaptability among employees. This scenario exemplifies how technology can complement human skills rather than replace them.

The retail sector also demonstrates how AI can reshape customer experiences. A well-known fashion retailer leveraged predictive analytics to personalize shopping across its platforms. By analyzing customer behavior data, the retailer tailored product recommendations to individual preferences, which resulted in increased sales and enhanced customer satisfaction rates. This success underscores the importance of understanding consumer insights through AI as a means to drive business growth while bolstering brand loyalty.

However, it is equally important to recognize instances where AI implementations have faced challenges or failed to deliver equitable benefits. In the hospitality industry, a hotel chain employed an AI-based pricing model that optimized room rates based on demand fluctuations. While this strategy boosted revenue during peak times, it alienated price-sensitive customers who felt marginalized by dynamic pricing. This case highlights the necessity of maintaining customer trust through transparent practices when utilizing advanced technologies.

Healthcare presents another critical arena for observing both successes and pitfalls in AI integration. A large health system adopted an AI-driven tool for early disease detection, significantly improving patient outcomes in chronic care management. By leveraging electronic health records and machine learning algorithms to proactively identify at-risk patients, healthcare providers could intervene earlier and tailor treatment plans effectively.

Yet the same sector has encountered stark disparities when deploying similar technologies without addressing accessibility issues—particularly for underserved populations who may lack internet access or familiarity with digital health tools. These contrasting scenarios remind us that while innovation can lead to remarkable advancements in care delivery, equitable access is essential.

Examining these narratives collectively reveals key takeaways regarding effective strategies for harnessing AI's potential across diverse industries:

1. Investing in Workforce Development: Both manufacturing and agriculture examples demonstrate that equipping employees with new skills ensures they remain vital players in an evolving technological landscape.

2. Fostering Inclusivity: Engaging diverse communities during implementation allows businesses to create solutions that address real needs instead of imposing generic technologies.

3. Prioritizing Customer Experience: The retail success story emphasizes the importance of understanding consumer behavior; utilizing data-driven insights ethically fosters loyalty while driving revenue.

4. Ensuring Equitable Access: The healthcare sector

illustrates the necessity of designing inclusive technologies so that all populations can benefit from innovations without exacerbating existing disparities.

These narratives not only highlight successful outcomes but also offer cautionary lessons about the complexities inherent in implementing AI solutions responsibly. They remind us that thoughtful integration requires ongoing dialogue among stakeholders—business leaders must actively listen to communities affected by their innovations if they hope to achieve meaningful progress.

As we advance into an increasingly automated world shaped by artificial intelligence, these stories stand as beacons of hope—demonstrating what is possible when ambition meets responsibility—and they underscore our shared responsibility in shaping a future where technology uplifts everyone involved.

Lessons from Failed AI Implementations

The journey to harness the transformative power of artificial intelligence has been marked by both triumphs and challenges for various organizations. The lessons learned from failed AI implementations are especially valuable, providing essential insights for businesses navigating this complex landscape. Understanding these pitfalls is crucial for developing resilient strategies that align technology with human values.

Take, for instance, a retail giant that made a substantial investment in an AI-driven customer service chatbot. Initially, there were high expectations; the chatbot was designed to enhance customer experience by delivering instant responses and round-the-clock service. However, the implementation did not meet these expectations due to a lack of sufficient training data. Customers frequently faced frustrating interactions, as the bot struggled to comprehend their inquiries and often misinterpreted requests. This dissatisfaction led to a backlash, prompting the company to revert to traditional customer service methods. This case highlights the importance of robust training and ongoing refinement in AI applications—neglecting these elements can significantly hinder user experience and tarnish brand reputation.

In another scenario, an insurance company sought to streamline its claims processing using an AI system intended to analyze documentation and expedite approvals. While the technology showed promise during its pilot phase, it encountered significant challenges when scaled across all operations. The system faltered with unusual cases that required human discretion, resulting in delays and increased frustration for policyholders. This example underscores a critical lesson: although automation can improve efficiency, it cannot replace the nuanced judgment needed for complex decision-making without substantial oversight.

The healthcare sector has also faced challenges in integrating AI effectively. A hospital implemented predictive analytics to optimize resource allocation during peak times. The intention was commendable—leveraging data to forecast patient influx and allocate staff accordingly. However, the model relied on historical data that overlooked external factors like public health emergencies or seasonal fluctuations. So, hospitals found themselves ill-prepared during unexpected surges in patient numbers, leading to overcrowding and compromised care delivery. This situation illustrates that effective AI solutions must incorporate real-time data and adaptive models rather than relying solely on historical trends.

Similarly, a major tech firm introduced an AI tool for talent acquisition that automated resume screenings to quickly identify qualified candidates. However, it soon became clear that the algorithm exhibited bias toward certain educational backgrounds and demographics rooted in historical hiring practices embedded within its training data. That's why, diverse candidates were frequently overlooked, raising ethical concerns about fairness in recruitment processes. This incident serves as a stark reminder that without careful attention to bias mitigation strategies during development, AI applications can perpetuate inequalities instead of alleviating them.

These cautionary tales highlight several key considerations for organizations embarking on AI integration:

1. Thorough Testing Before Scaling: Rigorous testing under varying conditions is essential before rolling out an AI solution on a large scale to identify and proactively address potential weaknesses.

2. Continuous Learning Mechanisms: Systems should include feedback loops that enable ongoing learning from user interactions and outcomes, allowing models to adapt accordingly.

3. Human Oversight is Essential: While automation can streamline operations, maintaining human oversight is crucial when decisions affect individual lives or require ethical considerations.

4. Addressing Bias Proactively: Organizations should prioritize developing algorithms with fairness in mind by employing diverse datasets and regularly auditing their outputs for unintended bias.

5. Flexible Adaptation Strategies: Acknowledging external variables—such as market shifts or societal changes—is vital for designing resilient systems capable of dynamic adjustments.

By examining both failures and successes in AI implementation, organizations can gain a comprehensive understanding of what constitutes effective integration across industries. Recognizing missteps not only equips businesses with insights necessary for overcoming challenges but also underscores their broader responsibility to ensure technology serves humanity equitably.

As industries evolve under the influence of artificial intelligence, learning from both successes and failures offers pathways toward creating solutions grounded in ethical principles. This approach ultimately shapes a future where technology benefits society at large while mitigating the risks associated with rapid innovation.

Transformations in Healthcare

The integration of artificial intelligence (AI) into the healthcare sector marks one of the most significant transformations of our time. As health systems around the globe strive to enhance patient care and improve operational efficiency, AI technologies are leading this evolution. Their applications range from diagnostics to treatment protocols, making a profound impact on various aspects of healthcare.

Imagine a hospital employing machine learning algorithms to boost diagnostic accuracy. By analyzing extensive datasets from medical records, imaging studies, and genetic profiles, these algorithms can uncover patterns that might elude human clinicians. Take this example, an AI model trained on thousands of radiology images can identify subtle indicators of conditions such as lung cancer or pneumonia with greater precision than traditional methods. This integration not only facilitates early diagnosis but also empowers healthcare professionals to make informed decisions about patient treatment plans.

However, the path forward is not without challenges. A notable example is an AI system designed to predict patient outcomes based on historical treatment data. Initially hailed for its potential to personalize medicine, the system faced significant difficulties when applied in real-world scenarios. It struggled with diverse patient populations since it had been trained primarily on data from a specific demographic. This limitation resulted in less reliable predictions for patients outside that group, underscoring the necessity for diverse training datasets in creating robust AI solutions.

The pharmacy sector further exemplifies how AI is transforming healthcare delivery. Automated systems can enhance inventory management by predicting medication demands based on patient admission rates and prescription trends. Take this example, one pharmacy chain implemented such a system but encountered accuracy issues due to unpredictable supply chain disruptions caused by external factors like global events or seasonal flu outbreaks. This situation highlights the need for flexible AI models that can adapt to changing circumstances and incorporate real-time data for more accurate forecasting.

Telemedicine has also undergone a revolution thanks to AI-powered virtual assistants that triage patients before they see a physician. These systems collect symptoms through chat interfaces or voice commands and provide initial recommendations based on algorithms crafted by medical experts. While this innovation significantly improves accessibility—especially in rural areas—it raises important questions about data privacy and security. Balancing the use of patient information for enhanced care with the need to protect individual privacy remains a critical concern.

Another exciting application of AI lies in drug discovery, where technologies can rapidly analyze molecular databases far more efficiently than traditional research methods. For example, one biotech company utilized machine learning to sift through billions of compounds swiftly, drastically reducing the time needed to identify promising candidates for clinical trials. However, even within this promising domain, ethical implications arise regarding intellectual property rights and potential biases against unconventional approaches that could yield breakthroughs.

The integration of AI also faces regulatory hurdles as healthcare increasingly relies on these tools. Regulatory bodies must ensure that AI technologies meet rigorous safety standards while fostering innovation in the industry. This requires ongoing collaboration between technologists, healthcare professionals, and policymakers to establish frameworks that support responsible deployment without hindering advancements.

To successfully navigate these complexities, healthcare organizations should prioritize several key strategies:

1. Multidisciplinary Collaboration: Engage teams from technology development, clinical practice, and policy-making early in the design process to effectively address real-world challenges.

2. Diverse Data Collection: Actively seek inclusive datasets that represent varied patient demographics to improve algorithm accuracy across populations.

3. Transparency in Algorithms: Develop clear protocols outlining how algorithms make decisions; transparency fosters trust among providers and patients regarding AI recommendations.

4. Ongoing Monitoring: Implement systems for continuous assessment of AI performance after deployment; regular audits help quickly identify biases or inaccuracies.

5. Regulatory Engagement: Involve regulatory bodies early in development discussions to ensure compliance with evolving standards while promoting innovation opportunities.

By thoughtfully and ethically leveraging these strategies, healthcare organizations can harness the transformative power of AI while navigating its inherent complexities.

successful implementation not only enhances efficiencies but also improves patient outcomes—a shared goal among all stakeholders in this vital sector.

As technology continues to reshape our world, understanding how best to adapt within industries like healthcare serves as a valuable blueprint for other sectors poised for transformation through innovations in artificial intelligence.

The Retail Sector and Automation

The retail sector is on the verge of a revolution, propelled by automation and artificial intelligence (AI). As consumers increasingly seek seamless shopping experiences, retailers must adapt to remain relevant. This transformation goes beyond merely implementing technology; it requires a fundamental rethinking of retail operations, encompassing everything from inventory management to customer engagement.

One notable area of change is the adoption of AI-driven inventory systems. Retailers can utilize machine learning algorithms to analyze sales patterns and customer behaviors. For example, a leading grocery chain recently implemented an AI platform that predicts product demand by considering historical sales data, seasonal trends, and even local events. By optimizing inventory levels in real-time, this approach not only reduced waste but also enhanced stock availability, demonstrating how automation can lead to more efficient operations while better meeting customer needs.

Nonetheless, the path to automation is fraught with challenges. A major clothing retailer, for instance, adopted an automated supply chain system to streamline order fulfillment. Initially promising significant efficiency gains, the system faltered when faced with sudden surges in online orders during peak shopping seasons—like Black Friday—resulting in delays and stockouts. This shows the importance of flexibility in AI solutions; systems must be designed to quickly adapt to unpredictable market conditions rather than relying solely on historical data.

Customer interactions have also transformed thanks to AI technologies such as chatbots and virtual assistants. These tools engage customers on e-commerce sites around the clock, answering queries and offering product recommendations based on browsing history and preferences. A prime example is a beauty retailer that successfully integrated a chatbot into its website, allowing customers to receive personalized skincare advice while shopping online. This significantly enhanced the user experience and boosted conversion rates. However, this innovation raises questions about AI's ability to replicate human empathy in customer service—an essential element for building brand loyalty.

Beyond direct consumer interactions, AI is reshaping marketing strategies within retail environments. Predictive analytics enables retailers to create personalized marketing campaigns tailored to individual shopper behaviors. Take this example, a popular fashion brand used data analytics tools to identify key trends from social media discussions surrounding their products. They then launched targeted advertising campaigns that resonated with specific demographics, resulting in increased engagement and sales conversions.

However, the reliance on data analytics also raises ethical concerns regarding privacy and consent. As retailers gather extensive amounts of personal data from customers, transparency becomes crucial. Implementing clear policies on data usage fosters trust among consumers who are increasingly concerned about how their information is handled.

The impact of automation extends beyond consumer-facing applications; it is also transforming backend operations like logistics and distribution networks. Autonomous robots are becoming commonplace in warehouses, picking items for orders with remarkable speed and accuracy compared to human workers alone. For example, one global logistics firm reported significant improvements in order processing times after introducing robotic systems alongside human workers —a model known as "cobotics." This successful integration of human intuition with robotic efficiency illustrates that automation does not necessarily mean job displacement but rather job enhancement through collaboration.

To effectively harness the potential of automation in retail while addressing inherent challenges, companies should consider several key strategies:

1. Investing in Employee Training: Equip employees with the skills needed to work alongside automated systems; understanding how to leverage technology enhances both job satisfaction and productivity.

2. Fostering an Agile Mindset: Encourage teams to embrace change by cultivating a culture that values adaptation; this mindset enables quicker responses to market shifts.

3. Integrating Customer Feedback Loops: Regularly collect insights from customers about their experiences with AI tools; this feedback can guide ongoing improvements in service delivery.

4. Ensuring Data Protection Compliance: Develop robust measures for protecting consumer data while adhering to regulations such as GDPR or CCPA— building trust through responsible practices.

5. Continuous Innovation: Stay informed about technological advancements by fostering partnerships with tech firms or investing in research initiatives aimed at exploring new applications for AI in retail.

By adopting these strategies thoughtfully, retailers can position themselves at the forefront of this evolving landscape while delivering enhanced value for both their customers and themselves. The integration of automation into retail operations signifies not just a shift towards efficiency but also an opportunity for deeper engagement between businesses and consumers—a relationship that thrives on adaptability amid constant change.

As they navigate this new terrain marked by rapid technological advancement, learning from both successes and setbacks will be essential for those aiming not only to survive but also to thrive within the modern retail ecosystem shaped by automation's transformative influence.

AI Innovations in Manufacturing

AI innovations are reshaping the manufacturing landscape, leading to significant improvements in productivity, efficiency, and quality. In an industry traditionally marked by manual processes and inflexible workflows, AI introduces a level of agility that was previously thought unattainable. Smart factories are transitioning from mere concepts to reality as companies increasingly leverage advanced analytics, machine learning, and automation technologies to optimize their operations.

One of the key advancements is the implementation of predictive maintenance systems driven by AI algorithms. These systems analyze real-time data from machinery to identify patterns and potential failures before they happen. For example, General Electric (GE) employs machine learning models to forecast when parts are likely to fail based on sensor data from their turbines and jet engines. This proactive approach not only reduces downtime but also significantly cuts maintenance costs. Research shows that predictive maintenance can save manufacturers up to 12% in maintenance expenses while boosting productivity by 20%.

Another factor propelling this transformation is the rise of collaborative robots, or cobots. Unlike traditional industrial robots that operate independently at high speeds for repetitive tasks, cobots are designed to work safely alongside human operators. Companies such as Universal Robots have developed lightweight robotic arms that can be deployed across various settings, enhancing production line flexibility. Take this example, a small electronics manufacturer successfully integrated a cobot into its assembly process to assist with soldering components onto circuit boards, resulting in a remarkable 50% increase in throughput while maintaining high-quality standards.

Data-driven decision-making is yet another critical area where AI is making significant strides in manufacturing. Organizations now have access to vast amounts of operational data—from supply chain logistics to customer feedback. By implementing AI analytics tools, manufacturers can uncover deeper insights into operational inefficiencies and customer preferences. Siemens exemplifies this by using AI to analyze data from its supply chain networks, optimizing inventory levels and minimizing waste by predicting demand fluctuations more accurately. This capability not only enhances customer satisfaction through timely deliveries but also streamlines resource allocation.

And, AI is advancing product design and development through generative design processes. This innovative approach allows engineers to input desired specifications into an AI system that explores numerous design alternatives within those parameters, often producing solutions that a human designer might overlook. Autodesk has pioneered this technology within its Fusion 360 software suite, enabling users to generate hundreds of potential designs for components based on constraints like weight or material usage. This accelerates the design phase and often results in lighter, more efficient products.

The integration of artificial intelligence into manufacturing also underscores the importance of sustainability—a growing concern for companies facing pressure from consumers and regulators alike. By optimizing energy usage through smart grid technologies and minimizing waste with better material utilization practices, manufacturers can significantly reduce their environmental impact. For example, employing AI algorithms to manage energy consumption patterns can lead to reductions of up to 30% in energy costs while sustaining production levels.

As these technological advancements unfold, training employees for new systems remains essential; the workforce must adapt to effectively operate alongside advanced technologies. Companies like Bosch are investing heavily in reskilling initiatives by providing immersive learning experiences through virtual reality (VR) platforms that simulate real-world scenarios involving complex machinery or robotics operation.

Embracing these AI innovations requires more than just technological upgrades; it necessitates a cultural shift within organizations toward agility and continuous improvement. Leaders must cultivate an environment that encourages experimentation—viewing failures as opportunities for learning rather than setbacks.

As manufacturers navigate this transformative era fueled by artificial intelligence, those who embrace change will not only survive but thrive amid disruption—a testament to the power of innovation reshaping entire industries for years to come.

Finance and AI: Evolution and Challenges

The financial sector is experiencing a profound transformation fueled by the integration of artificial intelligence (AI) technologies. This shift extends beyond the mere adoption of new tools; it fundamentally alters how financial institutions operate, manage risk, and engage with clients. AI is unlocking possibilities that once seemed like science fiction, significantly enhancing efficiency and accuracy across various operations, from trading to customer service.

One of the most notable impacts of AI in finance is its capacity to analyze vast datasets at incredible speeds. Traditional data analysis methods are quickly becoming outdated as AI algorithms can process millions of transactions per second, uncovering patterns and anomalies that human analysts might overlook. For example, JPMorgan Chase has developed a program called COiN that employs machine learning to review legal documents, reducing the review time from thousands of hours to just seconds. This transformation not only boosts productivity but also minimizes human error, allowing financial professionals to concentrate on more strategic initiatives.

AI is also making significant strides in risk management. Financial institutions are increasingly using AI-driven predictive analytics to better forecast market trends and evaluate credit risk. By analyzing historical data alongside current market conditions, machine learning models empower firms to make informed decisions regarding lending and investment strategies. A prime example is American Express, which utilizes AI algorithms to monitor transaction patterns in real-time, swiftly identifying fraudulent activities before they escalate. This proactive approach to risk management saves companies millions in potential losses.

In addition to improving operational efficiency, AI is revolutionizing customer engagement within the finance industry. Chatbots powered by natural language processing (NLP) are enhancing customer service experiences by delivering instant responses to inquiries and providing personalized recommendations based on user behavior. Bank of America's virtual assistant, Erica, exemplifies this trend; it helps customers manage their finances by offering insights into spending habits and suggesting savings strategies. As these AI systems learn from interactions, they become increasingly sophisticated, fostering more meaningful engagements over time.

However, the integration of AI into finance presents its own set of challenges. Regulatory compliance remains a crucial concern as financial institutions navigate a complex landscape of laws while striving for transparency in their algorithms. Take this example, if an AI model makes a biased decision regarding loan approvals, it could attract regulatory scrutiny and harm reputations. In response, organizations like Goldman Sachs are investing in governance frameworks that prioritize ethical AI practices, including regular audits and impact assessments of their algorithms.

Additionally, the workforce must evolve in tandem with these technological advancements. As AI takes over repetitive tasks, professionals will need to cultivate skills centered on strategic thinking and complex problem-solving. This transition calls for ongoing education and training initiatives within financial institutions. Companies such as Citibank have launched programs aimed at upskilling their employees in data analytics and machine learning principles, preparing them for a future where collaboration with AI systems will be essential.

Looking ahead, the challenge lies in balancing innovation with responsibility. While the potential benefits of AI in finance are immense, careful implementation is crucial to avoid pitfalls associated with ethical concerns and compliance issues. Financial leaders must cultivate a culture that embraces continuous learning while prioritizing operational integrity.

In this rapidly evolving landscape where technology advances at breakneck speed, those who effectively leverage AI will enhance operational efficiency and drive meaningful changes in customer experiences. The journey toward an AI-augmented financial future is not just about technology;

it involves reimagining what finance can achieve when combined with human ingenuity. This convergence of advanced technology and traditional practices is paving the way for a resilient and adaptive financial ecosystem capable of thriving amid uncertainty and change.

AI Integration in Media and Communication

The media and communication sector is experiencing a profound transformation as artificial intelligence (AI) becomes increasingly integrated into its core processes. This shift goes beyond merely adopting new technologies; it represents a fundamental reimagining of how information is produced, distributed, and consumed. As AI rises to prominence, traditional media paradigms are being challenged, creating unprecedented opportunities for innovation and engagement.

Central to this transformation is AI's remarkable ability to analyze and generate content on an extraordinary scale. Algorithms can now autonomously create news articles, generate social media posts, and even produce video content with minimal human intervention. A notable example is the Associated Press, which employs AI to automatically generate thousands of earnings reports each quarter. This capability not only accelerates content creation but also allows journalists to devote more time to in-depth investigative reporting, ultimately enhancing the overall quality of news coverage.

In addition to content generation, AI-driven insights are reshaping how media companies understand their audiences. By utilizing machine learning techniques to analyze viewer preferences and behavior patterns, organizations can customize their content strategies to better meet specific consumer needs. Platforms like Netflix illustrate this trend; through sophisticated algorithms that monitor user interactions, they offer personalized recommendations that boost engagement and satisfaction. This data-driven approach is essential for media companies striving to remain competitive in a rapidly changing marketplace.

AI is also playing a pivotal role in advertising by optimizing campaigns through the analysis of vast amounts of data to identify trends and forecast consumer behavior. This helps advertisers to target their audiences with precision, crafting highly relevant advertisements that resonate with potential customers. Take this example, companies like Google leverage machine learning algorithms to scrutinize search behaviors, allowing advertisers to refine their strategies based on real-time data feedback. The outcome is a more efficient allocation of resources and a higher return on investment for marketing efforts.

However, the integration of AI into media and communication brings forth significant ethical considerations. The emergence of deepfake technology—where AI generates hyper-realistic fake videos—has intensified concerns about misinformation. Navigating this challenge requires the development of robust frameworks that promote responsible AI use while safeguarding freedom of expression. Media organizations must prioritize transparency in their AI practices by clearly indicating when content has been generated or altered by algorithms.

And, the workforce within media organizations faces the urgent need to adapt alongside these technological advancements. As automation takes over routine tasks such as editing and basic reporting, traditional roles are evolving. Professionals must commit to continuous learning, developing skills in data analytics and digital strategy —areas where human insight can effectively complement AI capabilities. For example, training programs focused on understanding AI tools can empower journalists to harness these technologies creatively rather than perceiving them as threats.

Looking ahead, the intersection of AI technology and media presents tremendous potential for innovation but requires careful navigation of ethical landscapes. The future will likely feature enhanced collaboration between humans and machines—a partnership where creativity meets computational power. As this dynamic unfolds, forward-thinking organizations will leverage AI not just as a tool for efficiency but as an enabler of richer storytelling and deeper audience connections.

The integration of AI into media and communication marks a critical juncture where tradition meets innovation. Those who adapt quickly will not only survive but thrive in this new environment, crafting compelling narratives while remaining vigilant stewards of truth and integrity in storytelling. As we delve deeper into this transformative era, it becomes evident that embracing the possibilities of AI means reshaping our understanding of communication itself, paving the way for a more informed society enriched by diverse voices and perspectives.

Public Sector AI Successes

The public sector is currently experiencing a significant transformation, with artificial intelligence (AI) emerging as a pivotal force in enhancing government operations and service delivery. This integration of AI goes beyond mere efficiency; it fundamentally redefines how public institutions interact with citizens, manage resources, and tackle societal challenges. Success stories from various sectors highlight the profound impact that thoughtful AI applications can have.

A notable example is the use of AI in predictive analytics for crime prevention. Cities like Los Angeles have adopted machine learning algorithms to analyze historical crime data, enabling law enforcement to anticipate potential crime hotspots. By incorporating these insights into their resource allocation strategies, police departments can optimize patrol routes and deploy officers more effectively. This proactive approach not only enhances public safety but also builds community trust by showcasing a commitment to data-driven decision-making.

Healthcare in the public sector has also benefited greatly from AI integration. The National Health Service (NHS) in the UK is leading the way in utilizing AI to improve patient outcomes. Take this example, AI algorithms analyze patient records to identify individuals at risk of chronic diseases, allowing healthcare providers to intervene early. This capability not only enhances individual health outcomes but also reduces long-term healthcare costs, demonstrating how AI can contribute to more sustainable public health systems.

AI is also revolutionizing the way governments engage with citizens. Chatbots are becoming increasingly common on government websites, providing instant responses to inquiries and streamlining access to information. In Singapore, for example, these digital assistants handle thousands of queries daily, ensuring that citizens receive timely assistance while alleviating the burden on human staff. This innovation not only boosts citizen satisfaction but also enables government employees to concentrate on more complex issues requiring human judgment.

However, deploying AI in the public sector presents challenges that cannot be overlooked. Ethical considerations surrounding privacy and bias are critical as governments navigate this new landscape. While algorithms can enhance efficiency, they must be designed with transparency and accountability in mind. Initiatives like the "Algorithmic Accountability Act" aim to ensure that government agencies conduct regular audits of their AI systems to mitigate biases that could negatively impact marginalized communities.

Additionally, training and upskilling the workforce are essential for successful AI integration within public institutions. As routine tasks become automated, there is an urgent need for public servants to acquire new competencies in data analysis and technology management. Programs designed to equip employees with these skills are vital; they empower staff to utilize AI tools effectively rather than fearing job displacement. Take this example, a city might offer workshops focused on data literacy, enabling employees to understand and leverage insights generated by AI systems.

As we observe these successes across various sectors of public administration, it becomes clear that the future will require a collaborative approach between technology and human expertise. The integration of AI presents an opportunity for governments not only to enhance efficiency but also to promote democratic engagement by fostering transparent communication channels with citizens. This alignment between innovation and responsibility will pave the way for a new era where governmental processes are more responsive and inclusive.

the journey toward embracing AI in the public sector is ongoing and multifaceted. Success depends on balancing technological advancements with ethical considerations and workforce preparedness. Those who navigate this landscape thoughtfully will emerge not just as leaders in innovation but also as stewards of public trust—crafting policies that reflect a commitment to serving all constituents effectively and equitably. As we delve deeper into this evolving narrative, it becomes increasingly evident that harnessing AI's potential offers a pathway toward more effective governance and improved societal outcomes for all citizens.

Global Comparisons in AI Adoption

The landscape of AI adoption varies dramatically across the globe, influenced by cultural, economic, and political factors. Each country approaches AI integration with distinct strategies that reflect its unique challenges and aspirations.

For example, while the United States and China are making aggressive investments in AI technologies, European nations are navigating regulatory frameworks aimed at balancing innovation with ethical considerations.

In the U.S., the tech sector is a key driver of AI advancement. Silicon Valley remains a hub for startups exploring diverse AI applications, from healthcare diagnostics to financial services. This competitive environment encourages rapid development, allowing companies to iterate quickly and test new solutions in real-time market conditions. A notable illustration of this agility is OpenAI's ChatGPT, which has been integrated into various platforms for customer service automation and content generation. While this dynamism positions U.S.-based firms as leaders in global technological adoption, it also raises important questions about ethical use and accountability.

Conversely, China's approach emphasizes state-led initiatives that prioritize both technological superiority and socio-economic advancement. The government heavily invests in AI to enhance capabilities across sectors such as manufacturing and transportation. Smart cities like Shenzhen serve as practical examples of this strategy, utilizing AI for traffic management and urban planning. However, this top-down model also raises concerns regarding privacy and data governance—issues that remain pressing as global norms continue to evolve.

Europe presents a different narrative, where ethical considerations take precedence amid ambitious AI initiatives. The European Union has been proactive in establishing comprehensive regulations that govern AI deployment to ensure transparency and safeguard citizens' rights. Initiatives like the General Data Protection Regulation (GDPR) set standards that could influence global practices in data handling for AI systems. Take this example, France has launched programs aimed at promoting responsible AI innovation by providing funding and support to startups that adhere to ethical guidelines.

Meanwhile, developing countries encounter their own unique challenges and opportunities when adopting AI technologies. In Africa, nations are increasingly leveraging AI to tackle local issues—from enhancing agricultural productivity through precision farming to improving educational access via personalized learning platforms powered by machine learning algorithms. In Kenya, for example, mobile technology combined with AI enables farmers to make data-driven decisions regarding crop management, showcasing how local contexts can shape tailored innovative solutions.

Despite these promising developments, the path toward robust AI integration is fraught with difficulties worldwide. Many countries struggle with inadequate infrastructure or a shortage of skills necessary for effectively harnessing advanced technologies. In regions where educational resources are limited or digital literacy is low, implementing complex systems can be particularly challenging— highlighting the need for capacity building alongside technology deployment.

As we examine these diverse paths toward adopting AI technologies, it becomes clear that there is no one-size-fits-all solution. Each nation's strategy must take into account its unique social fabric and existing technological landscape while engaging citizens in ways that resonate with their values and needs. Emphasizing local adaptation is crucial; communities should have a say in how technology intersects with their lives.

This understanding encourages us to consider collaborative efforts between nations to share best practices and ensure equitable access to emerging technologies. International partnerships can facilitate knowledge transfer—countries learning from each other's successes and failures can accelerate progress while mitigating risks associated with unregulated innovation.

In summary, insights gained from global comparisons in AI adoption reveal how diverse strategies influence outcomes across regions. These lessons underscore the importance of aligning technology deployment with societal needs and ethical frameworks—an essential endeavor as we navigate an increasingly automated world together. Countries that engage thoughtfully in these discussions will not only advance technological progress but also create environments where innovation serves broader humanitarian goals—ensuring that all citizens benefit from the transformative potential of artificial intelligence.

CHAPTER 15:
SOCIETAL SHIFTS
AND AI

Changes in Consumer Behavior

C onsumer behavior is undergoing significant transformation as artificial intelligence becomes an integral part of daily life. This shift goes beyond mere technological advancement; it marks a fundamental change in how consumers engage with products, services, and brands. As AI systems grow more sophisticated, they are reshaping expectations and experiences, prompting businesses to rethink their strategies.

One notable development is the rise of personalized marketing. With AI's capacity to analyze vast amounts of consumer data, companies can now customize their offerings with unprecedented precision. Instead of receiving generic advertisements, consumers are met with recommendations that closely align with their individual preferences and behaviors. For example, streaming platforms like Netflix utilize algorithms that assess viewing habits to suggest content, significantly enhancing user satisfaction. So, consumers no longer see themselves as passive recipients of marketing messages; they feel understood and valued.

However, this personalization introduces its own challenges. As brands harness AI to anticipate and influence purchasing decisions, concerns about privacy become more pronounced. Consumers are increasingly wary of how their data is collected and utilized. Businesses must tread carefully in this landscape, striving to balance the desire for personalization with the need for transparency. A prominent example is Apple's emphasis on privacy as a key selling point—its marketing highlights user control over personal data while still providing tailored experiences through its services.

The pandemic further accelerated shifts in consumer behavior that might have otherwise taken years to emerge. Lockdowns prompted a surge in online shopping, compelling businesses to adapt swiftly to changing demands. E-commerce giants introduced AI-driven chatbots for customer service, ensuring consumers received immediate assistance even during peak traffic times. These chatbots not only enhanced efficiency but also redefined consumer expectations regarding response times and service availability.

As we observe these changes, it's crucial to recognize how emerging technologies impact purchasing decisions on a deeper level. AI-driven analytics enable companies to track consumer sentiment in real time through social media monitoring and sentiment analysis tools. Brands can gauge reactions to new product launches almost instantly, allowing them to adjust marketing strategies based on feedback from potential customers.

The integration of AI also promotes greater convenience—consumers now expect seamless interactions across various touchpoints. Voice-activated assistants like Amazon's Alexa or Google Assistant exemplify this trend by providing users quick access to information and facilitating transactions effortlessly. Such convenience fosters loyalty; if consumers can reorder products simply by speaking a command, they are more likely to remain loyal to that brand.

Nonetheless, this technological ease does not diminish the importance of human connection in the consumer experience. While AI effectively handles routine inquiries, there remains a strong demand for authentic human interaction in complex or emotionally charged situations. Businesses must find a balance between automation and personal engagement—recognizing when it's advantageous to leverage technology versus when it's essential to provide a human touch.

Additionally, consumers are becoming increasingly socially conscious as they interact with brands. Many now evaluate products not only based on quality but also on ethical considerations such as sustainability and corporate responsibility. Companies that utilize AI for supply chain optimization can enhance transparency regarding sourcing practices—an increasingly important factor influencing purchase decisions among ethically-minded consumers.

As these behavioral shifts continue to unfold, brands must adopt agile strategies that reflect an understanding of evolving consumer values and priorities. Businesses that leverage AI effectively will be those that anticipate changes rather than react after the fact—proactively adapting product offerings and customer engagement tactics based on insights drawn from data analytics.

This evolving landscape presents opportunities for businesses willing to embrace innovation while remaining attuned to the nuances of consumer expectations. Recognizing that AI is not just about technology but also about fostering connections will empower organizations to navigate these changes successfully.

these transformations highlight an essential truth: consumers today seek more than just products; they desire meaningful interactions that resonate with their values and lifestyles. By reimagining their strategies around these insights, organizations position themselves not merely as sellers but as partners in creating positive consumer experiences within an increasingly automated world.

AI and Cultural Transformations

The influence of artificial intelligence (AI) extends far beyond consumer interactions; it deeply affects the very fabric of our culture. As AI continues to weave itself into various aspects of daily life, it drives cultural transformations that reshape societal norms, values, and expectations in significant ways. This integration challenges traditional notions of creativity, identity, and community.

One prominent change is in the production and consumption of culture. In creative industries, AI is increasingly regarded as a collaborator rather than merely a tool. Musicians, for example, are harnessing AI algorithms to generate new sounds or even entire compositions, giving rise to innovative genres and styles. This fusion of human creativity and machine learning is not just about efficiency; it pushes the boundaries of artistic expression. Artists like Taryn Southern have leveraged AI technology to co-create music that embodies both human emotion and algorithmic precision, effectively blurring the lines between human and artificial artistry.

As AI-generated content becomes more prevalent, it raises critical questions about authorship and authenticity. The debate over whether an algorithm can be considered creative prompts us to reflect on what it means for human artists when their work can be mimicked or augmented by machines. This evolution compels us to rethink our understanding of originality and intellectual property, prompting both creators and consumers to reevaluate their relationships with art.

Social media's role has also transformed dramatically in this AI-enhanced environment. Algorithms not only dictate what content we encounter but also shape cultural trends by promoting certain narratives over others. Viral challenges on TikTok or trending topics on Instagram often emerge from algorithmic recommendations favoring specific types of engagement. So, cultural phenomena can spread rapidly but may lack depth or authenticity; popularity can become a byproduct of machine-driven engagement rather than genuine resonance.

AI's impact further extends to entertainment consumption patterns. Streaming services have evolved from mere content repositories into active architects of viewing habits through sophisticated algorithms that analyze user behavior. Features like "You might also like" create personalized experiences that keep viewers engaged for longer periods, yet they risk creating echo chambers where diverse perspectives are overlooked. Audiences may find themselves exposed predominantly to content that aligns with their preferences, potentially stifling broader cultural dialogues.

Education is another domain experiencing transformation driven by AI technologies. Personalized learning platforms employ adaptive algorithms to customize educational experiences for individual students, enhancing engagement and retention. However, this innovation raises concerns about equity; students from varied backgrounds may not have equal access to these technologies, leading to disparities in educational outcomes.

And, as companies increasingly rely on AI for decision-making processes—from hiring practices to market predictions—ethical considerations become paramount within cultural contexts. The decisions made by algorithms must be scrutinized for potential biases that could reinforce systemic inequalities or misrepresent diverse communities. Organizations have a responsibility to ensure that their AI systems embody inclusive values and do not perpetuate existing stereotypes or prejudices.

In response, culturally conscious brands are adopting ethical frameworks for AI use that emphasize transparency and accountability. Initiatives aimed at diversifying data inputs are being implemented to mitigate the biases inherent in machine learning systems. Take this example, companies like IBM are working towards developing fairness-aware algorithms that evaluate and adjust for bias in the data sets used for training AI models.

As we observe these cultural shifts instigated by advancements in AI, it becomes clear that technology acts as both a reflection and a shaper of societal values. It mirrors our desires while simultaneously molding them, creating a dynamic interplay between innovation and tradition. The challenge lies in achieving a balance where technological progress enhances our cultural fabric rather than dilutes it.

This ongoing dialogue underscores the need for thoughtful engagement from stakeholders across industries—creators, consumers, and policymakers alike—as we navigate the implications of AI's integration into culture. By working together, we can foster cultural transformations that honor human creativity while embracing the transformative potential of technology.

In this evolving landscape, businesses must view AI not merely as a tool for efficiency but as a catalyst for cultural evolution. By prioritizing ethical considerations alongside technological advancements, organizations can contribute positively to discussions surrounding identity, authenticity, and community in an increasingly automated world. This shift empowers individuals to redefine their roles within society—encouraging them not only to adapt but also to actively shape the future cultural landscape influenced by artificial intelligence.

Redefining Human-AI Collaboration

The relationship between humans and artificial intelligence

(AI) is evolving into a complex partnership that redefines collaboration in remarkable ways. This transformation prompts us to reevaluate the roles of both parties within the workspace. As AI increasingly takes on tasks once performed by humans, our collaboration shifts from a transactional dynamic to a more synergistic relationship, where each contributes unique strengths.

In various fields, professionals are now leveraging AI not merely for automation but as an active participant in the creative process. Take this example, designers utilize AI tools to generate design concepts informed by user preferences and historical trends. This collaborative effort allows them to focus on refining ideas and enhancing aesthetics, freeing them from repetitive tasks. Here, AI acts as an idea generator, offering fresh perspectives that can spark innovative outcomes.

Similarly, in marketing, AI's role extends to analyzing consumer behavior and predicting trends. By processing vast amounts of data quickly, AI uncovers insights that human analysts might overlook. Businesses can harness predictive analytics to tailor strategies based on emerging consumer patterns identified by AI algorithms. This collaborative approach enables marketers to make data-driven decisions with greater accuracy and confidence.

However, redefining human-AI collaboration is not just about task allocation; it fundamentally alters workplace dynamics. The integration of AI fosters enhanced teamwork by creating environments where human creativity is amplified through machine learning capabilities. For example, project management software that incorporates AI can streamline workflows by automating scheduling and resource allocation, allowing teams to concentrate on strategic planning and innovation rather than administrative details.

Yet this transformation brings forth important questions about job security and professional identity. As machines assume certain functions, individuals must adapt by cultivating skills that complement AI rather than compete with it. This shift highlights the necessity for upskilling—encouraging employees to develop competencies that enhance their value in a technology-driven landscape.

The challenge lies in finding a balance between leveraging AI's strengths and preserving the essential qualities that define human contribution: empathy, critical thinking, and ethical judgment. For example, while an AI system may analyze employee performance data objectively, it cannot grasp personal circumstances or emotional factors influencing those metrics. Human oversight remains crucial for interpreting insights and making nuanced decisions that account for broader implications.

And, as organizations deepen their reliance on AI, they must confront potential biases embedded within these systems. An algorithm trained on historical data may unintentionally perpetuate existing inequities if not closely monitored. Thus, collaboration between humans and machines necessitates vigilance regarding ethical considerations—ensuring that AI tools align with values of fairness and inclusivity.

As professionals navigate this new terrain, they should pursue interdisciplinary collaboration—drawing from fields such as ethics, psychology, and technology—to enrich their understanding of human-AI interaction. This holistic approach fosters innovative solutions and cultivates a culture of shared responsibility toward ethical AI deployment.

For organizations aiming to thrive in this evolving landscape, fostering an environment that encourages experimentation is crucial. Supporting teams in exploring novel applications of AI can lead to breakthrough ideas while reinforcing a mindset open to change and adaptation.

redefining human-AI collaboration challenges us to reimagine the future of work—a landscape where technology enhances human capabilities rather than diminishes them. Embracing this vision empowers individuals to see themselves not merely as employees but as co-creators within a rapidly evolving technological ecosystem.

As we adapt our professional practices around these innovations, we position ourselves at the forefront of shaping a future where humans and machines collaborate harmoniously—each contributing their unique strengths towards shared goals of creativity and progress.

Impact of AI on Community Forms

The impact of AI on community forms is fundamentally reshaping our interactions, connections, and collaborations in both personal and professional spheres. As AI technologies become increasingly integrated into our daily lives, they open up new avenues for community engagement, evolving traditional models into more dynamic and inclusive structures. Today, the essence of community transcends geographic boundaries; digital platforms enable diverse voices to come together around shared interests and goals.

Take, for instance, the emergence of online communities that gather around specific interests or challenges. These virtual spaces serve as hubs for knowledge exchange, collaboration, and support. Platforms like GitHub exemplify this trend by fostering vibrant communities where software developers from around the globe share code, troubleshoot issues together, and contribute to open-source projects. This collaborative spirit not only accelerates innovation but also nurtures a sense of belonging among participants who may never meet in person.

Social media channels have similarly transformed how communities rally around social causes or political movements. The #MeToo movement serves as a powerful illustration; it united individuals worldwide to share their experiences and advocate for change. AI tools have been crucial in amplifying these voices by swiftly analyzing trends and mobilizing support. Through techniques like sentiment analysis and predictive modeling, organizations can gain insights into public opinion and engage their communities more effectively.

Local neighborhoods are experiencing a similar transformation as AI-driven applications enhance connectivity among residents. Platforms such as Nextdoor facilitate neighborhood communication by enabling users to efficiently share information about local events, services, and safety concerns. These digital networks not only improve communication but also empower residents to collaborate on initiatives aimed at enhancing their communities. For example, local groups can coordinate efforts to organize events or advocate for neighborhood improvements through targeted outreach informed by AI insights.

In educational settings, AI is fostering collaboration among students from diverse backgrounds. Virtual learning environments are increasingly using adaptive learning technologies that cater to individual student needs while promoting collaborative group work. This approach encourages learners to engage with peers across different geographies and cultures, broadening their perspectives and enriching their educational experiences.

Nevertheless, as we embrace these new forms of community engagement enabled by AI, we must confront challenges related to inclusivity and accessibility. It is vital to ensure that everyone can participate in these digital spaces without facing barriers such as limited access to technology or lack of digital literacy skills. Non-profit organizations are stepping up by leveraging AI tools to assess community needs more effectively and design initiatives that address disparities in access to information or resources.

Additionally, ethical considerations must remain central

when developing AI systems that influence community interactions. If not carefully monitored, algorithmic biases can perpetuate stereotypes or exclude certain groups. Thus, it is imperative for developers and stakeholders alike to prioritize fairness when designing algorithms used within these community platforms.

Strengthening communities also involves embracing diverse perspectives through interdisciplinary collaboration. Engaging technologists alongside sociologists or ethicists can yield richer insights into how technology shapes human interactions. By incorporating different viewpoints, communities can co-create solutions that respect ethical standards while maximizing technological potential.

As the landscape of community forms continues to evolve under the influence of AI technologies, a shift toward greater transparency becomes essential. Building trust within these environments requires open dialogue about how data is collected and utilized while ensuring robust privacy protections.

Navigating this complex interplay between technology and human interaction calls for continuous learning and adaptability among community members. By fostering an environment where experimentation is encouraged—such as through pilot projects utilizing new digital tools—communities can explore innovative ways to strengthen connections while addressing emerging challenges head-on.

the impact of AI on community forms compels us to redefine what it means to be connected in today's world. As we embrace the collaborative opportunities technology offers while remaining vigilant about ethical implications, we pave the way for stronger bonds forged through shared experiences —a future where technology enhances our communal ties rather than diminishes them.

AI and the Future of Family and Social Structures

The impact of AI on family and social structures is profound and multifaceted, fundamentally altering how we engage within our closest circles and extending to broader social dynamics. As these technologies become more integrated into our daily lives, they offer new avenues for families to connect, communicate, and collaborate.

Take smart home devices, for example. Tools like Amazon Echo and Google Nest have revolutionized household management by providing convenience through voice-activated tasks while also fostering shared experiences—be it listening to music together or coordinating schedules. Imagine a family gathering around their smart speaker to ask about the weather as they plan a picnic. Each interaction becomes an opportunity for connection, weaving technology seamlessly into their daily routines. This integration goes beyond mere convenience; it cultivates a shared digital space that enhances communication among family members, particularly in homes with varied schedules or remote work arrangements. A simple reminder set by one member can keep everyone informed, eliminating the need for constant verbal updates.

AI-driven platforms are further redefining family dynamics by facilitating virtual gatherings that overcome geographical barriers. Families spread across cities or even countries can engage in real-time activities through video calls, gaming platforms, or shared online experiences like cooking classes or book clubs. Such virtual interactions can strengthen familial bonds, allowing members to maintain meaningful relationships despite physical distance.

However, with these technological advancements come challenges related to dependency and digital overload. The omnipresence of screens may lead to diminished face-to-face interactions at home. Parents often find themselves navigating how to balance technology use among their children while ensuring personal interactions remain vibrant and engaging. Establishing norms around tech usage—such as designating tech-free times during meals or encouraging outdoor activities—can help families prioritize personal connections over digital ones.

Looking at social structures more broadly, AI's impact is equally significant. Community engagement initiatives increasingly utilize AI tools to identify social issues and mobilize resources effectively. Take this example, AI algorithms can analyze local data to highlight areas experiencing food insecurity or inadequate healthcare access, enabling targeted interventions that make a real difference in people's lives.

In urban settings where diverse communities coexist, AI plays a crucial role in amplifying underrepresented voices through data analysis and advocacy campaigns fueled by social media insights. Organizations harness sentiment analysis to gauge community perspectives on various issues—from public safety to education—allowing policymakers to address concerns more directly and transparently.

Despite these benefits, ethical considerations surrounding privacy and surveillance remain pressing as we navigate this evolving landscape. Families must be vigilant about data security; understanding what information their devices collect is essential for protecting their personal lives from potential misuse. Likewise, as communities adopt AI tools for engagement, maintaining transparency regarding data usage is vital for fostering trust between citizens and institutions.

Cultural shifts resulting from AI integration are also evident in how we perceive relationships. Concepts like "friendship" have expanded beyond traditional boundaries; online platforms allow individuals to forge connections that may never materialize in person yet are enriched by shared interests and experiences cultivated through digital interactions.

As society adapts to these changes, the importance of emotional intelligence takes center stage. Understanding how technology influences our emotions—whether it's anxiety from constant connectivity or joy from virtual celebrations—is crucial for nurturing healthy relationships both at home and within our communities.

navigating the evolving landscape of family and social structures in an AI-driven world requires adaptability and open dialogue about technology's role in our lives. Families must develop practices that embrace innovation while remaining anchored in values of empathy and connection. Communities thrive when inclusivity is prioritized; encouraging diverse perspectives ensures that as we advance technologically, every voice is heard.

Looking ahead to a future shaped by artificial intelligence, the potential lies not only in technological advancements but also in our ability to strengthen human connections amid change. Through thoughtful engagement and an ethical approach to innovation, we can create environments where both families and communities flourish alongside technology rather than being overshadowed by it.

Navigating the Human Experience with AI

The integration of AI into everyday life is reshaping not only professional landscapes but also the very fabric of our personal and social interactions. As technology becomes an integral part of our human experience, the ways we connect, communicate, and collaborate are evolving. Exploring how families and communities adapt to these advancements reveals a landscape filled with both opportunities and challenges.

Smart home devices exemplify this transformation. Tools like Amazon Echo and Google Nest have revolutionized household management by enabling voice-activated commands for tasks such as setting reminders or adjusting lighting. Beyond their practical functionality, these devices create moments of shared engagement. Imagine a family cooking dinner together while their smart speaker plays music or suggests recipes; such interactions turn routine activities into collaborative experiences. This seamless integration of technology into daily life fosters familial bonds, particularly in a world where busy schedules often pull members in different directions.

However, the convenience of these technologies can lead to increased dependency, raising concerns about the decline of face-to-face interactions. Children may become engrossed in screens, prompting parents to confront the challenge of nurturing genuine connections amidst the digital noise. To counterbalance this trend, establishing tech-free zones or designated family times can be effective. By prioritizing quality time over digital engagements, families can create an environment that values both innovation and intimacy.

This evolving dynamic extends beyond individual families to encompass broader community structures. AI tools are proving invaluable in addressing social issues and facilitating engagement within communities. For example, algorithms can analyze data to identify areas experiencing food scarcity or healthcare disparities, allowing for targeted interventions that make a real difference in people's lives. Nonprofits that leverage these insights can mobilize resources more effectively, ensuring that assistance reaches those who need it most.

In diverse cities, AI also plays a crucial role in amplifying marginalized voices. Social media platforms act as conduits for advocacy campaigns powered by data analytics, reflecting community sentiments on critical issues like public safety or education reform. By embracing these technologies, policymakers gain access to nuanced perspectives that foster transparency in decision-making processes and build trust within communities.

Yet, this reliance on AI raises important ethical concerns regarding privacy and surveillance. Families must navigate the complexities of data security, making it essential to understand what information their devices collect to safeguard their privacy. Communities share the responsibility of ensuring transparency about how data is utilized in civic initiatives; building trust between citizens and institutions relies on ethical practices that prioritize consent and openness.

Culturally, AI's influence extends into how we define relationships themselves. Digital platforms enable friendships that transcend geographical boundaries, allowing individuals to form meaningful connections based on shared interests rather than proximity alone. While these online relationships enrich our lives, they also challenge traditional notions of intimacy and support systems.

Amidst these changes lies the importance of emotional intelligence—the ability to navigate our feelings about technology's pervasive presence is crucial for maintaining healthy relationships both at home and in public spheres. Recognizing when connectivity brings joy versus when it induces anxiety empowers individuals to make informed choices about their tech usage.

Navigating this new landscape requires adaptability and a commitment to ongoing dialogue about technology's role in our daily experiences. Families must establish practices that embrace innovation while remaining grounded in core values such as empathy and understanding. Communities thrive when diverse voices contribute to discussions about technological impact; fostering inclusivity ensures that everyone has a stake in shaping our collective future.

Looking ahead into an AI-driven future reveals the potential for enhancing human connections even as technology evolves rapidly. Through intentional engagement and ethical considerations surrounding innovation, we have the opportunity to create environments where families and communities prosper alongside advancing technologies rather than being overshadowed by them. Striking a balance between progress and purpose will determine not only how we coexist with AI but also how we thrive together in this new paradigm.

AI in Art and Entertainment

The art and entertainment sectors are experiencing a significant transformation, largely fueled by advancements in artificial intelligence. AI has evolved from being a mere tool to a collaborative partner, reshaping the landscape of creativity across music, visual arts, and interactive media. This shift prompts us to ponder important questions about authorship, originality, and the very essence of artistic expression.

In the realm of music, AI algorithms can sift through extensive libraries of sound to generate original compositions or assist human musicians in their creative endeavors. Take this example, platforms like Amper Music enable users to craft custom tracks by selecting preferred genres, moods, and tempos—often without requiring any formal musical training. This democratization of music production empowers aspiring artists who may lack traditional skills but possess unique visions. A musician can brainstorm ideas and leverage an AI tool to suggest chord progressions or melodies that align with current trends, effectively acting as a creative sounding board.

Visual arts are similarly enriched by this technological collaboration. AI-driven applications like DeepArt utilize neural networks to transform photographs into artworks that echo the styles of renowned artists. This allows creators to explore new dimensions within their work. Imagine an artist using this technology to produce a series that juxtaposes classic art styles with contemporary subjects; the outcome is not mere imitation but rather an innovative fusion that challenges viewers' perceptions of both historical works and modern culture.

Interactive media offers another exciting avenue for AI's influence. Video games are increasingly incorporating AI to develop adaptive narratives that respond to players' choices in real time. Picture a game where the storyline shifts based on players' decisions, leading to multiple possible endings shaped by their actions. This enhances player engagement and fosters deeper emotional connections with characters and narratives—an experience that was previously unimaginable in traditional gaming frameworks.

However, these innovations also raise important ethical questions regarding ownership and creativity. When AI generates art or music, who holds the rights? Is it the developer of the algorithm, the user directing it, or does ownership belong to the machine itself? This ambiguity complicates discussions about intellectual property rights within these industries.

And, as AI becomes more embedded in artistic processes, there is a concern that human creativity might be overshadowed by algorithmic outputs focused on commercial viability rather than authentic expression. While data-driven approaches can guide creators toward popular trends, they may inadvertently stifle innovation if artists start tailoring their work solely to algorithmic preferences instead of following their personal inspirations.

This interplay between technology and artistry also reshapes audience engagement. Social media platforms deploy sophisticated algorithms to curate content based on individual preferences, influencing how audiences discover and interact with art and entertainment. For example, recommendation systems on platforms like Spotify or Netflix analyze user behaviors to suggest personalized playlists or viewing options tailored specifically for each individual. While this enhances user experience by facilitating exploration, it risks creating echo chambers where diverse voices are overshadowed by mainstream choices.

As we navigate this evolving landscape where AI intersects with creativity, it is crucial for both artists and consumers to engage critically with these technologies. Artists should view AI as a collaborator while staying attuned to maintaining their unique voices amid algorithmic pressures. Consumers must cultivate discernment when interacting with content curated by machines—recognizing that behind every algorithm lies a set of choices reflecting human biases and societal trends.

integrating AI into art and entertainment presents vast potential for redefining creativity in our modern world. By fostering collaboration between human ingenuity and machine learning capabilities while remaining aware of ethical implications, we can create environments where both artists and audiences thrive alongside technological advancements rather than becoming passive observers.

This unfolding narrative not only shapes our approach to artistic endeavors but also influences how we connect with one another through shared experiences driven by innovation. As technology continues its rapid evolution within creative realms, our understanding of artistry will inevitably transform—inviting us into meaningful conversations about what it truly means to create and connect in an era defined by artificial intelligence.

Global Civil Movements and AI

Where X meets Y artificial intelligence and global civil movements is transforming the ways communities organize, advocate, and communicate. In recent years, we've seen social movements harness AI to amplify their voices, streamline their efforts, and connect with wider audiences. The potential of technology as a catalyst for change has never been clearer, as activists utilize data-driven insights to enhance their strategies and outreach.

One notable impact of AI is its role in mobilizing resources for humanitarian causes. Organizations like Amnesty International employ machine learning algorithms to analyze vast amounts of social media data, identifying trends in public sentiment and potential flashpoints for activism. This capability enables them to allocate resources more effectively and tailor their messages based on real-time feedback from supporters. Take this example, during the Arab Spring, activists used social media analytics to gauge public opinion and rally support for specific demands, showcasing how data can fuel grassroots movements.

Beyond resource mobilization, AI fosters the creation of networks among activists across geographical boundaries. Platforms such as Change.org allow individuals from diverse backgrounds to connect around shared causes, promoting collaboration that transcends borders. This global reach grants local movements international visibility, attracting potential allies from around the world. A prime example is the #MeToo movement, which originated in one country but quickly became a global phenomenon, illustrating how digital platforms can empower marginalized voices.

AI's capacity for processing large volumes of information also enhances transparency within civil movements. Innovations like blockchain technology are being explored for their ability to create tamper-proof records of donations and campaign finances. This guarantees accountability among organizations and builds trust within communities—essential elements for mobilizing collective action. When people have confidence that their contributions are being used effectively toward stated goals, they are more likely to engage in supporting these movements.

However, the integration of AI into civil activism presents challenges. As these technologies gain prevalence, concerns about surveillance and privacy infringements grow. Governments may exploit AI tools to monitor dissenting voices or suppress opposition—an issue highlighted by reports of state-sponsored cyberattacks on protestors during various uprisings worldwide. Activists must carefully navigate the use of technological advancements while remaining vigilant against potential misuse.

Additionally, algorithmic bias is a critical concern in this domain. If AI systems are trained on datasets that reflect societal prejudices or historical inequalities, they risk perpetuating those biases in decision-making processes related to resource allocation or campaign strategies. For example, an algorithm designed to identify areas in need of humanitarian aid may overlook marginalized communities if past data inadequately represented them. Therefore, incorporating diverse perspectives in the development of these technologies is crucial to achieving equitable outcomes.

As we delve deeper into the synergy between AI and civil movements, we must also confront the ethical considerations surrounding technology use in advocacy efforts. While AI can empower activists by enhancing outreach and providing analytical insights into effective strategies, it is essential that these tools uphold human values rather than undermine them. Engaging stakeholders—including community members affected by the issues at hand—in discussions about technology deployment can help ensure alignment with broader social goals.

In this rapidly evolving landscape where technology intersects with activism, one principle remains clear: embracing innovation should not compromise ethical integrity or community agency. By fostering collaborative relationships between technologists and advocates rooted in shared values —such as justice, equity, and inclusivity—we can responsibly harness AI's transformative power.

With careful consideration of both the opportunities and challenges presented by these innovations comes an exciting prospect: a future where humanity's collective efforts become even more impactful through the thoughtful integration of artificial intelligence into our shared journey toward social change.

The Sociological Impact of AI Technologies

The sociological impact of AI technologies reaches far beyond mere efficiency and productivity; it fundamentally reshapes the fabric of society, influencing everything from interpersonal relationships to community dynamics. Central to this transformation is the profound way AI alters communication patterns, enabling individuals to connect in unprecedented ways. Social media platforms, enhanced by AI algorithms, facilitate interactions that were unimaginable just a generation ago. These platforms not only serve as channels for information dissemination but also nurture new forms of community engagement and identity formation.

Take, for example, the emergence of virtual communities centered around shared interests or causes, often sparked by AI-driven recommendations. An individual passionate about environmental sustainability can connect with like-minded people across the globe within minutes, forming networks that transcend geographical barriers. This ability to forge connections enhances collective action and enables coordinated efforts in advocacy or social change initiatives. The Black Lives Matter movement serves as a powerful illustration of this phenomenon; localized events gained international traction thanks to social media's expansive reach and AI's role in amplifying messages.

As these connections deepen, they raise critical questions about authenticity and trust. The spread of misinformation —often fueled by AI-generated content—poses significant challenges for communities striving for genuine dialogue.

When algorithms prioritize sensationalism over accuracy, they can distort narratives and polarize opinions. Activists now face the dual challenge of combating misinformation while leveraging AI to enhance their credibility and outreach strategies. Building trust becomes essential; organizations must actively engage with their communities to verify information and maintain transparency.

Also, the integration of AI technologies into social structures invites scrutiny of power dynamics within these networks. Who controls the algorithms? What biases might be embedded within them? These questions are crucial as they pertain to access and representation in digital spaces. Take this example, marginalized groups may become further disenfranchised if AI systems prioritize content from more dominant voices or overlook their unique perspectives. Ensuring diverse representation among those developing these technologies is vital for fostering inclusivity and avoiding systemic biases.

The economic implications of AI are equally profound, reshaping labor markets and redefining job roles across sectors. As automation takes hold, traditional employment paradigms shift rapidly. Individuals must not only acquire new skills but also redefine their professional identities in a world increasingly influenced by technology. Embracing lifelong learning becomes crucial as workers navigate this evolving landscape; adaptability is no longer merely an advantage but a necessity for survival.

Workplace culture is also evolving, with remote work becoming more prevalent due to advancements in communication technologies driven by AI. While this shift offers flexibility and accessibility for many workers, it also blurs the lines between personal and professional lives. Organizations face the challenge of fostering a sense of belonging in virtual environments while ensuring employees remain engaged and supported despite physical distance.

Social equity remains at the forefront of discussions surrounding AI's societal impact. Although technological advancements have transformed lives for many, disparities persist that hinder access to these benefits for others. Initiatives aimed at promoting digital literacy among underserved populations are essential for leveling the playing field—ensuring that everyone can fully participate in this new economy shaped by AI innovations.

Finally, ethical considerations loom large as we explore the intersection of technology with societal values. As we develop increasingly sophisticated tools capable of influencing public opinion or shaping political landscapes, we must remain vigilant about their implications on democratic processes and individual freedoms. Engaging diverse voices—including ethicists, community leaders, technologists, and policymakers —in discussions about these technologies can guide us toward responsible innovation that respects human dignity while harnessing the potential of artificial intelligence.

Navigating these complex dynamics shaped by AI technologies reveals that our approach will determine whether this transformation leads us toward a more equitable future or exacerbates existing inequalities. The responsibility lies with all stakeholders—technologists must recognize their role in shaping societal norms while communities advocate for inclusive practices that reflect their values.

The journey ahead will require collaboration across disciplines as we seek solutions that honor both technological progress and social responsibility. Embracing this complexity invites us not only to envision a future intertwined with artificial intelligence but also to actively cultivate one rooted in shared humanity—a future where technology amplifies our collective potential rather than undermining it.

CHAPTER 16:
PREPARING FOR AI'S
LONG-TERM IMPACTS

Foresight and Scenario Planning

F oresight and scenario planning are essential tools for navigating the complexities of an AI-driven economy. As organizations confront unprecedented changes, the ability to anticipate future trends and adapt accordingly can serve as a significant differentiator. This approach goes beyond mere prediction; it focuses on creating a flexible framework that allows organizations to respond effectively to uncertainty.

To engage in effective scenario planning, the first step is identifying the key drivers of change within the industry. These drivers may include technological advancements, shifts in consumer behavior, regulatory changes, or economic fluctuations. For example, in the healthcare sector, one key driver could be the increasing demand for personalized medicine powered by machine learning algorithms. By understanding these drivers, professionals can develop scenarios that reflect potential outcomes based on various influencing factors.

Once the key drivers are identified, the next step is to develop plausible scenarios that encompass a range of possibilities, from best-case to worst-case outcomes. A healthcare organization might envision a future where AI significantly enhances patient outcomes while also grappling with ethical concerns related to data privacy. Alternatively, they could consider a scenario where resistance to AI implementation impedes progress due to regulatory hurdles. Exploring these diverse futures enables organizations to prepare for both opportunities and challenges.

A practical approach to scenario planning involves organizing workshops that bring together cross-disciplinary teams. These sessions can harness diverse perspectives, enriching discussions and uncovering blind spots that a homogeneous group might overlook. Take this example, during a workshop at a tech company focused on automation, participants engaged in role-playing exercises as different stakeholders —employees, customers, and regulators. This immersive method helped them identify critical factors influencing their decisions and anticipate reactions to AI technologies.

Effective foresight also hinges on continuous trend monitoring. Utilizing dashboards that aggregate relevant data can facilitate this process. For example, a dashboard might track developments in AI research publications, regulatory announcements, and market sentiment analysis from social media discussions. Regularly reviewing these indicators allows organizations to remain agile and adjust their strategies as needed.

Incorporating regular reviews into the planning cycle reinforces this agility. Establishing quarterly or biannual reviews enables teams to assess their assumptions against actual market developments. Flexibility becomes invaluable in this context; businesses must be willing to pivot their strategies based on real-world feedback rather than adhering strictly to initial forecasts.

Fostering an organizational culture that values foresight further enhances resilience. Encouraging employees at all levels to contribute ideas on emerging trends or potential disruptions not only cultivates an inclusive environment but also leads to innovative solutions. Companies like Shell have successfully implemented this approach through global scenario-planning exercises, drawing insights from across their workforce to navigate crises effectively.

foresight and scenario planning empower organizations to transform uncertainty into opportunity. They equip professionals with the mindset and tools necessary for proactive navigation of change rather than reactive responses. By embracing these practices, we position ourselves—and our organizations—for sustained success in an ever-evolving landscape shaped by artificial intelligence and other transformative technologies.

Predicting Disruptions in Emerging Markets

Disruptions in emerging markets often stem from a combination of technological advancements, economic shifts, and evolving consumer expectations. To navigate these changes effectively, professionals must keep a watchful eye on the horizon, as rapid developments can transform entire industries in the blink of an eye. In an AI-driven landscape, predicting these shifts goes beyond merely spotting trends; it requires recognizing patterns and making informed decisions that position one for success.

A compelling example of this dynamic can be found in the fintech sector, where innovations like blockchain and AI have fundamentally changed how financial services are delivered. Mobile banking applications, for instance, have gained tremendous traction in developing regions, providing consumers with unprecedented access to financial services while often circumventing traditional banking infrastructures. This shift has not only democratized finance but also opened up opportunities for startups to create tailored solutions for previously underserved markets. Professionals need to scrutinize these developments closely to understand how emerging technologies can disrupt established business models.

Engaging with local entrepreneurs offers valuable insights into the intricacies of market changes. By attending startup pitch events or visiting local innovation hubs, professionals can discern which ideas resonate with consumers and which face skepticism. Observing how local businesses adapt can uncover trends that larger corporations might overlook. For example, a Kenyan entrepreneur successfully launched a mobile payment service specifically designed for farmers needing quick access to funds for seeds and tools— highlighting how localized understanding can drive success in emerging markets.

It is equally important to remain vigilant about regulatory changes, as they often dictate the pace and effectiveness of technology integration within existing systems. A case in point is the European Union's introduction of stringent data protection regulations under GDPR, which forced companies to rethink their data strategies within a complex landscape. Similar regulatory frameworks are emerging worldwide, and professionals must evaluate how these laws could influence technological adoption in their sectors.

Also, predicting disruptions entails analyzing consumer behavior trends through data analytics and social listening tools. Companies that harness these technologies can gain real-time insights into consumer sentiments and preferences. Netflix serves as a prime example; its recommendation algorithms analyze viewer habits to effectively curate content, enhancing audience engagement and reducing churn rates. Professionals should consider implementing similar analytical approaches to better understand their target markets and refine their offerings accordingly.

In addition to technology and regulation, demographic shifts are crucial in shaping market dynamics. The rise of Generation Z as a significant consumer force is transforming industries from retail to entertainment. This generation prioritizes authenticity, sustainability, and seamless digital experiences, prompting businesses to rethink their strategies. Take this example, Glossier has successfully tapped into this shift by building a brand centered on community engagement and user-generated content—an approach that resonates deeply with younger consumers who favor relatability over traditional advertising.

As organizations strive to predict disruptions, cultivating an environment conducive to experimentation becomes essential. Encouraging teams to pilot new ideas without fear of failure fosters innovation amidst uncertainty. Google's "20% time" policy exemplifies this practice by allowing employees to dedicate one day a week to passion projects that could benefit the company—leading to significant breakthroughs like Gmail and AdSense.

To wrap things up, anticipating disruptions in emerging markets requires a blend of keen market observation with an understanding of technological trends and human behavior. Professionals armed with these insights will be better equipped to seize opportunities presented by disruption rather than merely reacting to them. By embracing curiosity, engaging with local entrepreneurs, analyzing data trends, remaining aware of regulatory environments, and nurturing an experimental culture within their organizations, individuals can navigate the complexities of change with agility and foresight. In doing so, they will not only survive but thrive in an ever-evolving landscape shaped by technological innovation and shifting consumer dynamics.

Adapting to Technological Singularities

Technological singularities, moments when the speed of technological advancement exceeds human comprehension, present both challenges and opportunities for professionals across various fields. To effectively adapt to these shifts, a proactive approach that emphasizes agility, strategic foresight, and continuous learning is essential. While technology can reshape landscapes at an unprecedented pace, it is human ingenuity that remains the driving force behind successful integration.

Take, for instance, the impact of artificial intelligence (AI) on healthcare. The emergence of machine learning algorithms that can diagnose diseases with remarkable accuracy is revolutionizing patient care. However, healthcare professionals must adjust their workflows to seamlessly incorporate these technologies. A doctor utilizing AI-driven diagnostic tools not only improves patient outcomes but also needs to develop the skills to interpret AI-generated insights effectively. This shows the importance of training programs that combine medical expertise with technological proficiency.

Similarly, the financial sector illustrates how adaptation to technological singularities can unfold through innovations like blockchain technology. This development has transformed transactions and introduced decentralized finance (DeFi) platforms, necessitating a new set of skills from traditional bankers and financiers. Professionals in this field must evolve by understanding concepts such as smart contracts and digital currencies—once seen as abstract but now integral to their roles. Recognizing this shift, many financial institutions have begun offering educational resources designed to equip employees with the knowledge needed to thrive in a blockchain-centric environment.

The rapid pace of change also demands an agile mindset among leaders tasked with guiding their teams through uncertainty. Take this example, a leader in the tech industry might face disruptions from breakthroughs in quantum computing—a field that could make traditional computing methods obsolete in just a few years. Embracing change requires fostering an organizational culture that encourages experimentation and resilience. Leaders who promote open communication about fears and uncertainties empower their teams to explore innovative solutions without hesitation.

Adaptability extends beyond individual skills; it encompasses the entire organizational structure. Companies must reevaluate their hierarchies to facilitate collaboration between technical and non-technical departments. For example, bringing data scientists together with marketing teams can generate valuable insights into customer behavior, driving targeted campaigns based on predictive analytics. Such interdepartmental collaboration not only enhances creativity but also ensures that diverse perspectives inform technological implementations.

Amidst these rapid advancements, ethical considerations are equally crucial. As we adapt to new technologies, particularly those involving AI, establishing clear ethical guidelines becomes paramount. How do we ensure algorithms do not perpetuate biases? How can organizations maintain transparency while leveraging data? Addressing these questions should be central to any adaptation strategy, ensuring responsible innovation.

Engagement with external thought leaders and communities is vital for effectively navigating these singularities. Professionals can learn from various sectors by participating in networking events or collaborative projects that encourage innovative ideas outside conventional silos. Conferences focused on emerging technologies serve as fertile ground for exchanging insights on best practices and lessons learned from other industries facing similar challenges.

In this context, the ability to pivot quickly cannot be overstated. Adopting an iterative approach allows organizations to test hypotheses in real-time rather than relying solely on long-term forecasts—an approach championed by companies like Amazon through their "fail fast" philosophy. This not only encourages innovation but also fosters a culture that views setbacks as valuable opportunities for growth.

As individuals and organizations navigate the complexities brought about by technological singularities, embracing lifelong learning becomes essential. Professionals should actively seek courses or workshops related to emerging technologies relevant to their fields—whether it's machine learning certification for engineers or leadership training focused on digital transformation strategies for executives.

adapting to technological singularities involves recognizing their transient nature while cultivating the skills necessary for immediate application today—and foresight for tomorrow's innovations yet unrealized. Those equipped with a blend of technical acumen, ethical awareness, and a collaborative spirit will not only keep pace with rapid advancements but also lead initiatives that define future success within their industries.

By adopting this multifaceted approach—integrating knowledge acquisition with ethical practices and collaborative efforts—the landscape shaped by technological singularities transforms into one filled with opportunity rather than mere disruption or uncertainty.

Long-term Career Planning in AI

In the rapidly evolving AI landscape, long-term career planning has become a dynamic exercise that requires both flexibility and foresight. Professionals must look beyond traditional notions of job security and envision career trajectories that are resilient in the face of technological advancements. To navigate this effectively, individuals should begin by identifying their core competencies while remaining open to acquiring new skills that align with emerging industry demands.

For example, consider a marketing professional with expertise in digital campaigns. As AI tools increasingly automate tasks like data analysis and customer segmentation, understanding these technologies becomes essential. This doesn't mean abandoning your existing skills; rather, it involves enhancing them by incorporating AI knowledge into your repertoire. Enrolling in courses focused on AI in marketing can provide valuable insights and help you leverage these tools effectively, ensuring you remain relevant and competitive.

Additionally, effective career planning requires an awareness of industry trends. Continuous market analysis is crucial for identifying sectors poised for growth as AI transforms various fields. Take healthcare, for instance—this sector is on the brink of significant change as AI-driven diagnostics and telemedicine reshape patient care. Professionals within this field can benefit from training programs that merge clinical expertise with technological insights, thereby positioning themselves as indispensable assets to their organizations.

Networking also plays a vital role in long-term career strategy. Engaging with professionals from diverse domains fosters opportunities for collaboration and knowledge sharing. By participating in forums, webinars, or even casual meetups, individuals can gain insights into how others are integrating AI into their careers. Attending industry conferences, for instance, allows you to hear firsthand experiences from leaders who have successfully pivoted their careers towards AI applications, providing valuable lessons and potential mentorship.

Setting specific, measurable goals is another crucial aspect of career planning. Aligning these goals with personal aspirations and market realities can help clarify your path. Utilizing the SMART criteria—Specific, Measurable, Achievable, Relevant, Time-bound—can guide professionals in mapping out their objectives. For example, if you aim to transition into a data analytics role within two years, outline actionable steps: complete relevant certification courses during the first year, pursue internships for practical experience in the second year, and actively seek mentorship from established data analysts throughout this journey.

Also, developing a personal brand that reflects your evolving skills and expertise is key in today's digital age. Investing time in curating online profiles that showcase your capabilities is essential. Creating content around AI applications relevant to your field not only positions you as a thought leader but also facilitates connections with like-minded individuals who share similar interests or career aspirations.

While careful planning is important, maintaining adaptability is equally vital as circumstances change. The unpredictable nature of technology means new roles may emerge at any moment; professionals who remain attuned to these shifts can seize opportunities quickly. Regularly reading industry publications and following thought leaders on social media can keep you informed about market developments.

Organizations also play a critical role in fostering environments conducive to growth. Companies can implement mentorship programs or continuous learning initiatives that encourage employees to explore new technologies without fear of failure. By investing in their workforce's adaptability through ongoing education and skill development, firms enhance employee satisfaction while cultivating a culture of innovation that benefits everyone involved.

effective long-term career planning in an AI-driven economy relies on a proactive mindset combined with strategic foresight. By prioritizing continuous learning, setting clear goals, leveraging networking opportunities, and embracing adaptability to change, professionals can successfully navigate their careers amid technological disruption. Rather than viewing AI as a threat to job security, embracing it as an ally will empower individuals not just to survive but to thrive on their paths toward future success.

Interdisciplinary Research and Collaborations

Interdisciplinary research and collaboration are becoming essential strategies for navigating the complexities of an AI-driven economy. As technology evolves rapidly, no single discipline can claim to have all the answers. Instead, the most innovative solutions emerge from the intersection of diverse fields. For example, when computer scientists collaborate with sociologists, they can create AI systems that not only function effectively but also address ethical implications and social impacts. This fusion of expertise results in more comprehensive approaches to multifaceted challenges.

In the healthcare sector, advancements in AI are transforming patient care through collaborative efforts among medical professionals, data scientists, and ethicists. Together, they have developed AI algorithms that can diagnose diseases with remarkable accuracy. These interdisciplinary teams evaluate both the technical performance of the algorithms and their ethical implications, ensuring responsible handling of patient data and preventing biases from influencing clinical decision-making. By working together, these experts enhance patient outcomes while upholding ethical standards.

Another compelling example can be found in environmental science, where researchers from various fields—such as climate science, economics, and urban planning—are increasingly leveraging AI to address climate change challenges. AI models can predict urban heat islands or optimize energy consumption in smart cities by analyzing extensive datasets that encompass meteorological patterns and urban infrastructure. Such interdisciplinary projects not only yield impactful insights but also support informed decision-making for sustainable urban development.

To foster these collaborative efforts, organizations can establish cross-functional teams that bring together representatives from different domains. Creating spaces for open dialogue encourages knowledge sharing and ignites creativity. Regular brainstorming sessions can lead to breakthroughs as team members contribute their unique perspectives and expertise. Additionally, hosting hackathons or innovation challenges focused on real-world problems can stimulate collaboration, inviting participants from diverse backgrounds to devise creative solutions using AI.

Educational institutions also play a crucial role in promoting interdisciplinary research. Programs that encourage students from various fields to work together equip future professionals with a broader understanding of both technical capabilities and societal needs. Take this example, engineering students paired with psychology majors might collaborate on designing user-friendly interfaces for mental health applications. Such experiences cultivate empathy while enhancing technical skills—an invaluable combination for addressing contemporary challenges.

The emphasis on collaboration extends beyond academia into corporate environments as well. Businesses that prioritize an interdisciplinary culture often experience heightened innovation and problem-solving capabilities among their teams. Encouraging employees to engage in joint projects with colleagues from different departments fosters an environment where diverse ideas can flourish. This practice not only enhances internal knowledge sharing but also positions organizations as leaders in innovation.

Technology plays a pivotal role in facilitating these interdisciplinary efforts; digital platforms enable collaborations like never before. Tools such as collaborative software streamline communication across geographical boundaries, allowing teams to work together efficiently regardless of location. Cloud-based storage solutions ensure easy access to shared resources, while virtual reality environments offer immersive experiences for team members tackling complex problem-solving tasks.

As professionals increasingly recognize the value of interdisciplinary approaches, they must remain open-minded and adaptable in their collaborations. Embracing diverse viewpoints broadens perspectives on problem-solving and fosters creativity—a crucial element when addressing intricate issues shaped by AI advancements. The willingness to learn from others nurtures a collaborative spirit that transcends individual expertise.

In this evolving landscape, leaders within organizations should champion interdisciplinary initiatives by allocating resources toward training programs focused on collaboration skills and cross-disciplinary methodologies. Encouraging employees to attend industry conferences or workshops emphasizing collaborative practices can further enhance their ability to navigate an interconnected world.

Monitoring AI and Job Market Trends

Monitoring AI and job market trends is crucial for individuals and organizations striving to succeed in an economy increasingly shaped by technological advancements. By understanding these trends, professionals can anticipate changes, adapt their skills, and align their career paths with emerging opportunities. As the work landscape evolves rapidly, staying informed about both AI technology developments and shifts in labor demand becomes essential.

A strong starting point for tracking these trends involves utilizing data analytics tools that provide insights into industry developments. Platforms such as LinkedIn Insights and Glassdoor can offer valuable information about in-demand skills and job postings that highlight specific qualifications sought by employers. Regularly reviewing these platforms not only keeps you updated on employer expectations but also helps you identify any skill gaps in your own repertoire that need addressing.

Take this example, if data indicates a rising demand for machine learning professionals, it would be prudent to invest time in online courses or workshops focused on this area. Websites like Coursera and Udacity provide structured learning paths that cover everything from foundational concepts to advanced applications. Completing these courses can enhance your competitiveness in a job market where employers increasingly prioritize candidates proficient in AI technologies.

Networking is another vital component of staying attuned to job market trends. Engaging with industry peers through events, webinars, or professional associations allows professionals to share insights and discuss emerging technologies firsthand. Participating in specialized forums or groups on platforms like Slack or Discord can also foster real-time discussions about AI developments and their impact across various sectors. Such interactions often yield perspectives that traditional news sources may overlook.

Staying connected with thought leaders in the field is an effective strategy for tracking advancements and anticipating future demands. Following experts on social media platforms like Twitter or LinkedIn exposes you to cutting-edge research and expert opinions regarding industry shifts. Additionally, subscribing to relevant newsletters or podcasts ensures a continuous flow of information directly from those at the forefront of AI discussions.

The contributions of research institutions and think tanks are also significant; they frequently publish reports analyzing current trends and offering forecasts based on rigorous methodologies. Reports from organizations like McKinsey Global Institute or PwC provide deep insights into how AI is set to reshape various industries over the next decade. Familiarizing yourself with these findings helps contextualize changes within your own industry, enabling informed decisions about your career trajectory.

Employers should consider implementing internal systems for monitoring AI integration within their organizations as well. Regular assessments of workforce capabilities against emerging technologies can help identify areas needing upskilling. Conducting employee surveys regarding comfort levels with new tools can inform tailored training programs designed to bridge any knowledge gaps effectively.

Establishing key performance indicators (KPIs) related to AI adoption within teams also facilitates ongoing evaluation of how well these technologies enhance productivity and efficiency. This proactive approach ensures that organizations remain agile, adapting swiftly as new tools emerge or as job functions evolve due to automation.

As companies embrace the changes brought about by AI, it's crucial for employees not only to enhance their technical skills but also to cultivate complementary soft skills—such as adaptability, creativity, and collaboration. Understanding how human skills intersect with technological capabilities will further solidify one's position in this evolving landscape.

In navigating this rapidly changing terrain shaped by AI advancements, staying vigilant about market trends becomes not just an advantage but a necessity. By actively seeking information through various channels—be it data analytics platforms, networking opportunities, expert insights, or organizational assessments—you position yourself at the forefront of opportunity rather than being left behind by change. Embracing a mindset geared towards continuous learning and adaptability ensures that you are equipped not just for today's challenges but also for those yet to come— enabling sustained growth in an era defined by technological transformation.

Cultivating Future Leaders in AI Ethics

Cultivating future leaders in AI ethics requires a comprehensive approach that addresses not only the technical aspects of artificial intelligence but also emphasizes moral philosophy and social responsibility. As AI technology continues to advance, it becomes increasingly vital for those in leadership positions to possess a nuanced understanding of ethical frameworks and their implications. This knowledge is essential for navigating the complexities of deploying AI solutions that have far-reaching societal impacts.

At the heart of developing leaders in AI ethics is an educational foundation that integrates ethical considerations into technical training. Traditional computer science curricula often focus heavily on algorithms, coding, and system architecture, frequently overlooking the broader implications of technology on society. Programs that incorporate ethical discussions throughout their coursework equip students with the skills needed to analyze potential impacts before they materialize. Take this example, integrating case studies that explore AI failures stemming from ethical oversights—such as biased algorithms or privacy violations—can provide real-world context and stimulate critical thinking among future technologists.

Mentorship also plays a crucial role in this developmental process. Experienced professionals should actively engage with emerging leaders, sharing insights into the ethical challenges they have faced and strategies for addressing them. Mentorship can occur in both formal and informal settings; casual conversations over coffee or discussions during industry events can yield valuable lessons. By fostering environments where seasoned practitioners share their experiences, mentees learn to anticipate ethical dilemmas and develop effective frameworks for decision-making.

Encouraging interdisciplinary collaboration is another effective strategy. Ethics does not exist in isolation; it intersects with law, sociology, psychology, and other fields. By bringing together students and professionals from diverse backgrounds, we can enrich discussions around AI ethics with varied perspectives. Hackathons or workshops focused on ethical AI design provide spaces for these dialogues, allowing participants to brainstorm solutions while considering multiple viewpoints.

Organizations must also take proactive steps to instill a culture of ethical awareness within their teams. Establishing dedicated ethics committees or task forces can facilitate ongoing discussions about AI's implications at every level of decision-making. These groups can provide guidelines and best practices that align with both organizational goals and societal norms. When employees see that ethical considerations are prioritized, they are more likely to adopt similar values in their work.

Training programs aimed at enhancing ethical decision-making skills are essential as well. Workshops that simulate real-world scenarios where participants must navigate complex choices can mirror the pressures faced in actual projects. Role-playing exercises enable individuals to step into the shoes of various stakeholders—users, developers, regulators—allowing them to understand differing perspectives on responsible AI use.

In parallel with these initiatives, organizations should encourage public engagement around AI ethics. Hosting webinars or community forums allows leaders to share knowledge while soliciting input from diverse audiences affected by AI technologies. Direct engagement with users fosters trust and transparency, highlighting the importance of user perspectives in shaping responsible practices.

Additionally, staying attuned to global dialogues around technology ethics is vital for developing leaders informed by diverse cultural perspectives. Following international debates on AI regulation—such as those emerging from the European Union's Artificial Intelligence Act—can illuminate varying approaches to ethics across different regions. Understanding these differences prepares leaders to operate effectively in a globalized economy where local nuances significantly influence technology adoption.

To further solidify this cultivation process, promoting thought leadership through writing and public speaking empowers emerging leaders to articulate their visions for ethical AI practices. Publishing articles on platforms like Medium or participating in panels at industry conferences enhances visibility while demonstrating a commitment to the cause. When these individuals share their insights publicly, they contribute to a larger movement advocating for accountability within technology development.

cultivating future leaders in AI ethics encompasses educating individuals about the interplay between technology and society while fostering environments rich in mentorship and collaboration. By emphasizing ethical awareness from education through professional development, we can ensure that those shaping tomorrow's technologies do so with an informed conscience—a prerequisite for sustainable innovation in our rapidly evolving world. Building this foundation today will not only address current challenges but also prepare us for unforeseen dilemmas tomorrow, nurturing a generation equipped to lead responsibly amid ongoing technological transformation.

Creating Futurist Roadmaps

Creating futurist roadmaps necessitates an understanding

that the choices we make today will shape the workforce of tomorrow. This process combines foresight, technological expertise, and adaptability. It begins with identifying emerging trends in technology and society that will influence job roles, skill requirements, and workplace dynamics.

To start, analyze current advancements in artificial intelligence (AI) and their implications across various industries. For example, AI-powered tools are transforming sectors such as healthcare, finance, and logistics. In healthcare, predictive analytics can improve patient outcomes by identifying potential health issues before they occur. So, professionals in this field must not only refine their technical skills but also deepen their understanding of data interpretation and the ethical considerations surrounding patient privacy.

Following this analysis, engage in scenario planning to envision multiple futures based on varying levels of technological adoption and societal responses. This method enables organizations to explore "what if" scenarios—such as the effects of widespread AI integration on employment rates or the creation of entirely new job categories driven by automation. By imagining these possibilities, companies can devise strategies to mitigate risks associated with job displacement while simultaneously fostering innovation in emerging fields.

Collaboration is essential in developing these roadmaps. Involve stakeholders from different levels within the organization, as well as external experts from academia and industry. Facilitated workshops or brainstorming sessions can bring diverse perspectives on anticipated challenges and opportunities. Take this example, at a recent industry summit focused on AI in manufacturing, participants identified potential productivity gains from automation alongside the pressing need for reskilling initiatives to help workers transition smoothly into new roles.

Another crucial component in crafting futurist roadmaps is the effective use of data analytics. Organizations should leverage existing workforce data to identify skill gaps and predict future needs based on projected trends. Advanced analytics can provide insights into which skills are becoming obsolete while highlighting those that will remain valuable or grow in demand. A practical approach might include developing a dashboard that tracks industry changes against internal skill sets, empowering leaders to make informed decisions regarding training investments.

Incorporating a culture of continuous learning will ensure that employees are not only prepared for current demands but also equipped for future shifts. This may involve forming partnerships with educational institutions to create customized training programs tailored to evolving industry needs. For example, tech companies have started collaborating with universities to design curricula focused on machine learning applications within business contexts, ensuring graduates are ready to contribute meaningfully from day one.

As organizations develop these futurist roadmaps, they must also prioritize ethical considerations alongside technological advancements. Engaging with frameworks that emphasize social responsibility helps ensure that the implementation of AI solutions aligns with broader societal goals—such as equity and inclusion—rather than exacerbating existing inequalities. This could involve conducting regular ethical audits of AI systems used in business processes or establishing community advisory boards to guide responsible practices.

Establishing metrics for success is crucial when implementing futurist strategies. Clearly defined key performance indicators (KPIs) can help organizations track progress towards their vision while maintaining flexibility to adapt as new insights emerge. These metrics might include employee satisfaction after training initiatives, efficiency gains from newly adopted technologies, or societal impacts measured through community feedback channels.

Finally, fostering an environment where innovation thrives encourages proactive contributions from all employees towards achieving these futuristic visions. Empowering team members to experiment with new ideas without fear of failure cultivates a culture where creative solutions flourish —essential for navigating the uncertainties that accompany rapid technological change.

By weaving together insights from various sources—including data analysis, stakeholder engagement, and continuous learning opportunities—organizations can craft robust futurist roadmaps that effectively navigate both anticipated challenges and unforeseen opportunities. Emphasizing flexibility ensures these plans remain relevant amid the rapidly changing landscape driven by advances in artificial intelligence and related technologies, ultimately positioning organizations for success in a collective advancement across industries.

Engaging with Future Studies Institutes

Engaging with future studies institutes offers professionals and organizations a strategic advantage in navigating the complexities of an AI-driven landscape. These institutes focus on analyzing trends and predicting future scenarios, providing valuable insights that enhance decision-making processes. By collaborating with these entities, companies can tap into a wealth of knowledge that supports strategic planning, talent development, and risk management.

To effectively engage with future studies institutes, start by identifying key organizations renowned for their research and foresight expertise. The Institute for the Future (IFTF), for example, has played a crucial role in developing frameworks that help businesses anticipate changes in technology and society. Attending their workshops or webinars provides firsthand exposure to methodologies used in scenario planning. Companies should consider sending team members to these events not only to learn but also to build relationships with futurists who can offer tailored insights relevant to specific industries.

Beyond workshops, collaborating on research projects can yield substantial benefits. Organizations might partner with future studies institutes to conduct joint studies on emerging trends pertinent to their sector. Take this example, a financial services firm could team up with an institute to explore the implications of blockchain technology on traditional banking models. Such collaborations can result in reports or white papers that enhance internal understanding and position the organization as a thought leader within its industry.

Leveraging insights from future studies also plays a critical role in workforce planning. Understanding anticipated shifts —like automation's impact on job roles—enables organizations to prepare strategically for their talent needs. For example, if research indicates an impending demand for data literacy skills across multiple sectors due to AI integration, companies can proactively implement training programs aimed at enhancing their workforce's competencies in this area.

Networking opportunities abound within the realm of future studies as well. Engaging with experts at conferences or informal meet-ups grants access not only to knowledge but also to potential collaborators. Professionals should actively seek out such events, participating in discussions about technological advances and societal shifts that will shape work environments. These interactions often spark innovative ideas and open doors for collaborations that might otherwise remain inaccessible.

As organizations integrate insights from future studies into their operational strategies, they must prioritize adaptability. A well-crafted foresight strategy includes continuous feedback loops where information gathered from ongoing research informs real-time decisions. Take this example, if emerging data suggests changing consumer behaviors toward sustainability practices due to AI advancements, businesses should be prepared to adjust their offerings accordingly.

The engagement process is further enhanced by creating interdisciplinary teams within organizations that draw from various expertise areas—marketing, technology, operations— to foster innovative thinking informed by external insights. By blending internal knowledge with findings from future studies institutes, companies can improve their ability to innovate effectively while remaining aligned with anticipated market demands.

Cultivating a culture of curiosity around futures thinking is equally important, encouraging employees at all levels to think critically about upcoming challenges and opportunities driven by technological advancements. Initiatives such as "futures lunch-and-learns" or internal hackathons focused on solving anticipated problems empower staff members and contribute significantly toward creating an agile organizational environment ready for any eventuality.

By establishing connections with future studies institutes and integrating foresight methodologies into daily practices, organizations become better equipped not only to respond but also to thrive amidst the rapid changes brought about by AI and other technologies shaping tomorrow's workplace landscape. This proactive approach ultimately builds resilience against uncertainty while fostering innovation at every operational level.

CHAPTER 17: TOOLS AND RESOURCES FOR AI ADAPTATION

Comprehensive List of Learning Platforms

L earning platforms have become indispensable for anyone aiming to excel in the rapidly evolving AI job market. They offer a vast array of resources that empower professionals to enhance their skills, stay updated on technological trends, and adapt to changing market demands. Below is a comprehensive overview of notable learning platforms, each with unique features that cater to different learning styles and career aspirations.

Coursera is particularly noteworthy for its collaborations with prestigious universities and organizations worldwide. It provides courses covering a variety of topics, such as AI, machine learning, and data science. With opportunities to earn certificates and degrees from accredited institutions, Coursera not only helps individuals sharpen their skills but also strengthens their resumes. For example, a learner can enroll in Stanford University's "Machine Learning" course and obtain a certificate that holds considerable value in tech hiring processes.

Similarly, Udacity has gained popularity for its Nanodegree programs that focus on essential tech skills like AI programming and data analysis. These programs are developed in partnership with industry leaders such as Google and Facebook, ensuring the curriculum meets real-world demands. A notable success story involves students who completed Udacity's Data Analyst Nanodegree landing positions at major companies like IBM shortly after graduation, thanks to their hands-on projects that demonstrate practical experience.

edX offers comparable advantages with courses from esteemed institutions like Harvard and MIT. A standout feature of edX is its MicroMasters programs, which allow learners to delve deeper into specific subjects. Take this example, someone interested in AI ethics might pursue the MicroMasters in Artificial Intelligence from Columbia University, gaining both theoretical insights and practical knowledge relevant to the ethical dilemmas emerging in technology.

LinkedIn Learning integrates professional development seamlessly into users' daily routines by leveraging LinkedIn's extensive network. It focuses on short courses designed for busy professionals seeking quick learning opportunities. Topics vary from essential Excel functions for data management to advanced Python programming techniques crucial for machine learning projects. By completing courses on LinkedIn Learning, individuals can easily showcase new skills on their LinkedIn profiles, enhancing visibility to recruiters.

Skillshare distinguishes itself with an emphasis on creative skills alongside traditional tech competencies. Users can explore topics such as design thinking or creative coding

—fields increasingly sought after as organizations look for innovative problem solvers who can tackle challenges from diverse perspectives. For example, someone interested in blending graphic design with data visualization can find classes specifically tailored to these intersections.

Khan Academy provides free educational resources across a broad spectrum of subjects beyond technology. With interactive exercises and instructional videos available at no cost, it serves as an excellent supplementary resource for those seeking foundational knowledge before tackling more advanced topics elsewhere.

For those looking for certifications or specialized training without hefty fees, Google Career Certificates offer an accessible pathway into tech fields like IT support or data analytics. Designed by industry experts, these certificates equip graduates with essential skills needed for entry-level roles, ensuring they are workforce-ready upon completion.

The rise of MOOCs (Massive Open Online Courses) has further democratized education; platforms like FutureLearn allow users from diverse backgrounds access high-quality content delivered by top universities worldwide while facilitating discussions among learners—a key element of collaborative learning environments.

Engaging with multiple platforms enables learners to customize their educational journeys while integrating diverse perspectives into their skill sets. By combining knowledge gained from various sources—such as taking a programming course on edX followed by exploring design principles through Skillshare—individuals become well-rounded professionals prepared for the multifaceted challenges posed by advancements in AI.

investing time in these various learning platforms fosters resilience against the rapid changes characteristic of technology-driven job markets. Continuous upskilling not only boosts employability but also cultivates confidence in navigating future career shifts—a crucial asset in an increasingly unpredictable world shaped by AI innovations and ongoing digital transformation across industries.

Recommended Books and Journals

Books and journals are essential tools for deepening understanding and broadening perspectives in the rapidly evolving landscape of artificial intelligence (AI). They provide valuable insights, case studies, and critical analyses that empower professionals navigating this transformative job economy. A thoughtfully curated selection of literature can inspire innovation, encourage ethical considerations, and showcase real-world applications across various industries.

One notable title is "Artificial Intelligence: A Guide to Intelligent Systems" by Michael Negnevitsky. This comprehensive text explores the principles and methodologies of AI, offering readers both theoretical foundations and practical insights. Take this example, it explains concepts such as fuzzy logic and neural networks in an accessible manner, making it suitable for newcomers while also providing seasoned professionals with valuable knowledge. The inclusion of case studies further illustrates how these techniques can be applied in real-world scenarios, effectively bridging the gap between theory and practice.

For a more focused examination of AI ethics, Cathy O'Neil's "Weapons of Math Destruction" offers a compelling critique of algorithmic bias. O'Neil argues that many AI systems perpetuate inequality by prioritizing efficiency over fairness. By highlighting specific examples from finance and education, this book encourages readers to critically consider the ethical implications of their work in AI, fostering a deeper commitment to responsible development in the field.

Beyond individual titles, academic journals like "Artificial Intelligence" and the "Journal of Machine Learning Research" are invaluable for staying informed about cutting-edge research and trends. These publications often feature peer-reviewed articles that explore innovative algorithms and applications across various sectors. For example, an article discussing reinforcement learning techniques could provide insights applicable in fields such as robotics or autonomous systems, enhancing the reader's understanding of current methodologies shaping the industry.

The emerging field of data science is well represented by "Data Science for Business" by Foster Provost and Tom Fawcett. This book emphasizes the importance of data-driven decision-making in modern enterprises, equipping professionals with frameworks for effectively leveraging data analytics. It addresses practical issues such as model evaluation and predictive analytics while contextualizing these concepts within broader business strategies—essential reading for anyone looking to make a significant impact in an AI-centric workplace.

On a more conceptual level, "Human Compatible: Artificial Intelligence and the Problem of Control" by Stuart Russell examines the future relationship between humans and AI systems. Russell discusses the necessity of aligning AI goals with human values—an increasingly important consideration as technology advances at a rapid pace. The provocative questions raised in this work stimulate discussions about the control mechanisms needed to ensure safe integration into society.

As we explore diverse sources to enhance our expertise, "The Second Machine Age" by Erik Brynjolfsson and Andrew McAfee sheds light on how digital technologies are reshaping economies worldwide. The authors analyze both the opportunities presented by technological advancements and the challenges posed by labor market displacement, prompting readers to reflect on their roles within this shifting paradigm.

Equally noteworthy are industry-specific journals like "Machine Learning," which focus on theoretical developments alongside significant advancements relevant across sectors —ideal for professionals seeking both technical depth and applied knowledge.

Engaging with this spectrum of literature not only builds a rich foundation of knowledge but also fosters critical thinking skills essential for addressing the challenges posed by rapid technological change.

For those eager to expand their horizons beyond traditional resources or formal education settings, recommended readings should be complemented by active participation in community discussions around these texts through online forums or local meetups. This approach promotes networking while reinforcing learning through conversation.

immersing oneself in these recommended books and journals cultivates not only awareness but also a proactive mindset towards navigating the complexities inherent in the evolving AI job economy—an invaluable asset when striving for success amid ongoing transformation.

Industry Conferences and Workshops

Engaging with industry conferences and workshops is a powerful catalyst for professional growth in the evolving landscape of artificial intelligence. These events unite thought leaders, innovators, and practitioners who share insights, explore emerging trends, and showcase groundbreaking technologies. Attending such gatherings not only broadens one's knowledge but also opens invaluable networking opportunities that can lead to collaborations and mentorships.

Take this example, the annual AI Summit serves as a notable platform where professionals come together to discuss advancements in artificial intelligence across various sectors. Attendees have the opportunity to hear from industry pioneers like Andrew Ng and Fei-Fei Li, gaining access to keynotes that provide actionable strategies for implementing AI solutions within their organizations. Participants often leave with fresh perspectives on how AI can tackle pressing business challenges, and the networking opportunities at these summits frequently result in fruitful connections— many attendees find themselves collaborating on projects or exploring new career prospects soon after.

Workshops complement conferences by offering a different yet equally enriching experience. These hands-on sessions often delve into specific tools or techniques, such as machine learning frameworks or data visualization software. For example, a workshop led by TensorFlow experts might guide participants through the step-by-step process of building a predictive model. This immersive learning experience equips individuals with practical skills they can immediately apply in their current roles, thereby enhancing their employability in an ever-evolving job market.

And, many conferences emphasize inclusivity by featuring panels that address diverse perspectives on AI's impact. Events like the Women in Data Science Conference highlight the contributions of women and underrepresented groups in tech. By attending these discussions, participants gain insight into the unique challenges faced by diverse voices in AI development while learning about initiatives aimed at increasing representation in technology fields. These conversations are vital; they not only inspire attendees but also encourage organizations to cultivate more inclusive environments.

Incorporating participation in conferences into a professional development plan necessitates strategic planning. Setting clear objectives before attending helps focus efforts on what one aims to achieve—whether acquiring new skills, identifying potential collaborators, or seeking inspiration for innovative projects. After attending an event, taking time to reflect on key takeaways reinforces learning and aids in determining how best to integrate newfound knowledge into existing workflows.

The rise of virtual conferences has significantly expanded accessibility in recent years. Online platforms now host global gatherings that bring together experts who might otherwise be unreachable due to geographical barriers or budget constraints. For example, participating in a virtual data science conference allows individuals to watch presentations from world-class researchers and engage with them through live Q&A sessions—all from the comfort of their home office.

To deepen engagement within the community surrounding AI technology, active involvement is essential. Volunteering as a facilitator during workshops or leading discussion groups helps professionals establish themselves as knowledgeable contributors within their networks. Sharing insights gained during these interactions fosters relationships built on mutual respect and expertise.

As we navigate our professional journeys in this rapidly changing world of artificial intelligence, ongoing education remains crucial—whether through structured programs like certifications or spontaneous discoveries made at innovative events. The exchanges fostered at these gatherings empower individuals while propelling collective progress toward ethical advancements in technology that align with societal values.

The dynamic environment created by industry conferences and workshops nurtures continual evolution not just within individual careers but also across broader organizational practices. This synergy paves the way for successfully integrating artificial intelligence into our working lives—a goal that grows increasingly vital as we collectively embrace this era of transformation.

Online Communities and Forums

Online communities and forums have become essential

resources for professionals navigating the complexities of the AI landscape. These platforms foster discussion, collaboration, and the real-time sharing of experiences, allowing individuals to connect with peers who share similar interests. This engagement is vital for staying updated on the latest developments and trends in artificial intelligence, especially in a field that evolves so rapidly.

Consider platforms like GitHub and Stack Overflow, where developers and data scientists congregate to exchange knowledge. On GitHub, for instance, users can contribute to open-source projects, gaining hands-on experience while expanding their professional networks. A developer contributing code to a machine learning project may encounter collaboration opportunities that could lead to job offers or partnerships in future endeavors. This collaborative spirit fosters innovation, creating an ecosystem where ideas can flourish and be tested against real-world challenges.

Forums such as Reddit's r/MachineLearning or specialized groups on LinkedIn enhance this learning experience by allowing members to pose questions and seek advice from seasoned experts. For example, a user might inquire about optimizing a neural network architecture and receive valuable feedback from professionals at leading tech companies. Such interactions often spark deeper discussions that not only address technical concerns but also explore strategic considerations when implementing AI solutions in business settings.

Beyond technical knowledge sharing, online communities also serve as crucial support systems during career transitions. Individuals looking to pivot into AI-related fields can find mentorship opportunities through these networks. Platforms like Meetup often host events where members can connect in person or virtually, fostering relationships that may lead to valuable guidance or job referrals. A marketing professional aiming to leverage AI tools for analytics might attend a local data science meetup and discover mentors willing to share insights on necessary skills or training resources.

The diversity within these online forums provides broader perspectives on AI's implications across various industries and demographics. Engaging with varied viewpoints helps professionals understand how AI technologies impact societal structures, ethical considerations, and job markets differently depending on context. Participating in discussions about ethical AI practices or inclusive technology design not only enhances understanding but also encourages critical thinking about one's role in the evolving ecosystem.

To maximize the benefits of these communities, consistent participation is crucial. Regular engagement—through commenting on threads, sharing articles of interest, or asking thoughtful questions—builds visibility and credibility within the network. Setting specific goals for each interaction can enhance this experience; for instance, aiming to contribute at least one meaningful comment per week or initiating discussions around emerging AI trends fosters deeper relationships over time and solidifies one's position as an active contributor.

Building personal connections within these communities can also open additional avenues for growth, such as access to exclusive webinars or workshops that may not be widely advertised. Many forums host expert-led sessions that delve into advanced topics like reinforcement learning or ethical algorithm design; attending these events can be instrumental in developing specialized skills that set one apart in a competitive job market.

And, many online communities feature dedicated channels for job postings specific to AI roles—a particularly valuable resource given the high demand for skilled professionals in this field. Monitoring these listings not only provides insights into market demands but also offers direct access to employment opportunities that align with one's skill set.

As professionals navigate an evolving job landscape shaped by artificial intelligence, their involvement in online communities will be critical for staying informed and engaged. The synergy created through shared knowledge enhances individual careers while contributing to the development of an informed community ready to tackle future challenges together. this collective effort reinforces the ethical integration of AI into society's fabric as we move forward into this new era of work.

Volunteer Opportunities for Skill Development

Volunteering offers a powerful way to enhance your skills while positively impacting your community. Many organizations actively seek volunteers, and these roles can provide unique experiences that are often unavailable in traditional employment settings. For example, local non-profits focused on education, healthcare, or technology can offer valuable opportunities. Volunteering with such organizations allows you to gain practical experience in real-world applications of AI and data management—areas that are increasingly relevant in today's job market.

Consider the experience of volunteering at a local coding bootcamp where you assist instructors and mentor students. This not only deepens your understanding of programming languages but also sharpens your communication skills. You'll learn how to explain complex concepts in an accessible way—an invaluable skill when collaborating with diverse teams or clients. And, mentoring others fosters leadership qualities that employers highly value.

In addition to local opportunities, online platforms also provide a wealth of volunteer options that can enhance your professional repertoire. Websites like Catchafire connect skilled volunteers with non-profits seeking specific expertise, such as digital marketing or web development. Take this example, if you have a background in graphic design, you might assist a small charity in revamping its website or creating marketing materials. Each project challenges you to apply your knowledge creatively while refining your problem-solving skills.

It's important to incorporate these experiences into your resume as they demonstrate initiative and a commitment to personal growth. Crafting compelling narratives around your volunteer work allows you to showcase not only the skills you've developed but also the impact you've made. Whenever possible, use metrics—such as "increased social media engagement by 30%" or "trained over 50 students in basic coding"—to provide tangible evidence of your contributions.

Networking is another significant advantage of volunteering. You'll likely meet professionals from various fields who share similar interests and values. These interactions can lead to job referrals or collaborative projects down the line. It's common for connections made during volunteer work to evolve into mentorships or even job offers—relationships built on mutual respect and shared goals.

Additionally, aligning your volunteer work with your career aspirations is crucial. If you're aiming for a career in AI ethics, for example, seek out organizations focused on responsible AI use or digital rights advocacy. Engaging in discussions about ethical implications while volunteering positions you as someone attuned to contemporary issues in the field, thereby enhancing your credibility when applying for jobs or networking with industry leaders.

Finally, remember that volunteering is not just about acquiring skills; it also offers personal fulfillment. Engaging with diverse communities enhances emotional intelligence —a vital soft skill in today's workforce. Understanding different perspectives and working towards common goals fosters empathy and adaptability—traits highly sought after by employers navigating the complexities of an AI-driven economy.

By immersing yourself in varied volunteer roles, you're not only developing hard skills but also cultivating a well-rounded professional identity rooted in service and collaboration— qualities that will distinguish you in the competitive job market ahead.

Accessing Government Resources and Grants

Accessing government resources and grants can significantly enhance your professional development, particularly in the rapidly evolving AI job market. Recognizing the urgent need to prepare the workforce for new technologies, many governments have established various programs to support individuals aiming to improve their skills.

A key avenue for this support is funding for educational programs focused on AI and technology. Numerous national and local governments offer grants to both individuals and organizations that promote skill development in these critical areas. For example, in the United States, the Workforce Innovation and Opportunity Act (WIOA) allocates funds to training programs designed to help job seekers acquire in-demand skills. Individuals can apply for these grants through their local workforce development boards, which provide guidance on eligibility requirements and application processes.

In Canada, initiatives like the Canada Job Grant provide financial assistance for training expenses. This program allows employers to access funding for training employees or potential hires in essential skills needed in today's job market. Such initiatives not only enhance workforce capabilities but also ensure that individuals seeking employment receive tailored training aligned with industry demands.

To effectively tap into these resources, it is crucial to engage with local government initiatives actively. Attend workshops or information sessions hosted by workforce agencies; these events often spotlight available funding opportunities and offer insights into best practices for securing grants. Connecting with representatives from these agencies can yield valuable advice tailored to your specific circumstances, thereby increasing your chances of success.

Online platforms have become indispensable for locating government-supported programs. Websites like Grants.gov serve as centralized databases where you can search for federal grant opportunities across various sectors, including education, technology, and workforce development. Utilizing filters based on your interests or location can simplify the process of finding relevant grants.

Additionally, many organizations publish newsletters or maintain active social media channels that share updates on available resources. Subscribing to these communications keeps you informed about new opportunities as they arise, including details about deadlines and specific requirements that could impact your eligibility for funding.

Collaborating with community colleges or universities can further broaden your access to governmental resources. These institutions often partner with government entities to provide specialized training programs funded by state or federal grants. Participating in such programs not only equips you with essential skills but also connects you with networks that may lead to internships or job placements.

Networking within professional organizations related to AI and technology is equally important when seeking governmental support. Members frequently share insights about grants they have accessed, offering valuable tips on successful applications or collaborative projects funded by government resources. Engaging in forums or local chapters of these organizations positions you among peers who are navigating similar paths toward skill enhancement and career advancement.

As you explore these avenues, documenting your progress is vital. Keep a record of applications submitted, deadlines met, and skills acquired through funded training programs. This documentation serves as both a personal motivator and a tangible asset when discussing your qualifications during interviews or networking events.

In summary, leveraging government resources requires proactive engagement—actively seeking information about available grants and participating in training initiatives empowers you in a landscape increasingly shaped by AI advancements. The benefits extend beyond mere funding; they foster a culture of continuous learning and adaptability that is crucial in today's economy. By immersing yourself in these opportunities, you not only enhance your own skill set but also contribute to building a more robust workforce ready to tackle the challenges posed by emerging technologies.

Personal Development Plans

Creating a personal development plan (PDP) is crucial for anyone navigating the complexities of the AI job economy. This strategic framework serves as both a roadmap for skill acquisition and career progression while fostering accountability. In a landscape characterized by rapid technological change, a well-structured PDP empowers you to stay ahead, ensuring that your professional journey remains intentional and aligned with industry demands.

At the heart of an effective PDP is self-assessment. Begin by evaluating your current skills, experiences, and interests. This reflection offers clarity on what you bring to the table and identifies any gaps. Take this example, if you excel in project management but lack technical skills in AI, recognizing this gap allows you to focus your learning efforts. Tools like SWOT analysis (Strengths, Weaknesses, Opportunities, Threats) can be invaluable during this phase. By mapping out these elements, you gain insights that inform your goals and spotlight areas needing attention.

After completing your self-assessment, it's time to set clear, achievable goals. These should be specific, measurable, attainable, relevant, and time-bound (SMART). For example, if your goal is to become proficient in machine learning within a year, outline specific milestones—such as finishing an introductory course by the end of the first quarter and completing at least two practical projects by mid-year. This structured approach not only provides direction but also simplifies tracking your progress.

The resources you choose to incorporate into your PDP are vital for achieving these goals. Identify educational platforms and learning materials that align with your objectives. Online courses from platforms like Coursera or edX offer valuable content on AI and data science that can enhance your knowledge base. Additionally, participating in workshops or boot camps can provide hands-on experience that theoretical learning alone cannot offer. Seeking mentorship from experienced professionals can also deliver insights and guidance tailored to your unique circumstances.

Turning plans into reality hinges on actionable steps. Break down each goal into manageable tasks to maintain momentum. For example, if you aim to learn Python for data analysis, start with simple tasks such as completing an online tutorial or reading relevant chapters from a programming book. As you build confidence, gradually increase the complexity of your tasks. Tracking these actions reinforces discipline and offers opportunities for self-reflection on which methods work best for you.

Regularly reviewing your progress ensures that your PDP remains dynamic and responsive to both personal aspirations and industry trends. Set aside time monthly or quarterly to assess what you've accomplished against your established milestones. This practice encourages adaptability; if a particular strategy isn't yielding results or if new AI technologies emerge requiring immediate attention, revising your plan becomes essential.

Incorporating feedback is another powerful aspect of refining your development plan. Share your goals with peers or mentors who can provide constructive criticism and insights into areas for improvement. Engaging in discussions about your progress fosters a support network that motivates you through challenges and celebrates achievements along the way.

As you develop and execute your personal development plan, remember that it is more than just a document; it's an evolving guide reflecting both personal growth and shifts within the job market influenced by AI advancements. Embrace flexibility within this framework—being adaptable allows you to pivot when unexpected opportunities arise or when obstacles emerge that necessitate reevaluating priorities.

committing to a personal development plan empowers you to take charge of your professional trajectory amidst the uncertainties presented by AI integration across various industries. By focusing on lifelong learning and actively engaging with the resources available in this evolving landscape, you position yourself not only to survive but also to thrive in an economy increasingly defined by technological innovation.

Guide to AI Job Boards and Application Tips

Navigating the job market in an AI-driven economy requires a strategic approach to job searching. The rise of AI technologies has not only changed the types of roles available but also transformed how employers assess candidates. Therefore, understanding where to find opportunities and how to effectively present yourself is crucial for success.

Begin your search with specialized AI job boards

tailored to tech-savvy professionals. Websites like AIJobs.com, DataJobs.com, and MachineLearningJobs.com feature positions ranging from data scientists to machine learning engineers. These platforms provide a focused search experience, connecting you directly with companies seeking expertise in artificial intelligence. If remote work is a priority, explore platforms such as Remote.co or We Work Remotely, which regularly list AI and tech jobs that offer flexibility.

In addition to dedicated job boards, mainstream platforms like LinkedIn have become essential tools for job seekers. Not only can you discover job postings directly on LinkedIn, but the platform also facilitates networking with industry professionals. When creating your profile, highlight your skills related to AI, being specific about your experience with relevant tools like TensorFlow or PyTorch. Tailor your resume and cover letter for each position, incorporating keywords from the job description to enhance your chances of passing through applicant tracking systems (ATS) that many companies utilize.

Understanding how to navigate these systems is vital. ATS scans resumes for specific phrases and qualifications before they reach human eyes. To improve your chances of being noticed, ensure your application materials are polished and optimized with relevant keywords. Take this example, if a job posting emphasizes "data visualization," make sure this phrase prominently appears in your resume alongside any corresponding experience you possess.

Networking remains an invaluable tool in the job-seeking process. Actively engage within professional communities both online and offline. Attend industry conferences or webinars where you can connect with thought leaders and potential employers. Platforms like Meetup.com host groups focused on AI topics that provide ample networking opportunities. These interactions can lead directly to referrals or unadvertised openings.

When preparing for interviews, seize the opportunity to demonstrate your knowledge of AI trends and practical applications during discussions with potential employers. Research common interview questions related to AI roles; be prepared to explain how you've applied machine learning techniques in past projects or navigated ethical considerations in implementing AI solutions.

Practice is key for technical interviews as well—consider participating in mock interviews that focus on both behavioral questions and technical problem-solving scenarios. Websites like Pramp offer free peer-to-peer mock interviews specifically tailored for tech roles, including those in AI.

Another crucial aspect is following up after applications and interviews. A well-crafted thank-you email can reinforce your interest and professionalism, helping you stay top-of-mind for hiring managers. This gesture not only expresses gratitude but also reiterates why you are an excellent fit for the position discussed.

Beyond direct applications and networking efforts, consider building a portfolio that showcases your work related to artificial intelligence projects—whether personal initiatives or contributions made during previous employment. Platforms like GitHub allow you to share code samples and project outcomes that effectively highlight your capabilities.

Emphasizing soft skills alongside technical knowledge will also give you an edge over other candidates who may have similar qualifications but lack interpersonal abilities. Highlight experiences where you've collaborated on cross-functional teams or managed projects requiring communication between technical and non-technical stakeholders.

As opportunities continue to evolve in this rapidly changing landscape shaped by AI advancements, staying proactive is vital. Regularly update your profiles on various job boards;

even small adjustments based on current industry trends can significantly enhance your visibility among recruiters seeking fresh talent.

By integrating these strategies into your job search within the context of the AI economy, you'll increase your chances of landing desirable positions and establish yourself as a knowledgeable candidate ready to tackle future challenges head-on. With effective preparation, both personal growth and career advancement await those who take initiative in this dynamic field.

CHAPTER 18: OVERCOMING BARRIERS TO AI INTEGRATION

Resistance to Technological Change

T he apprehension surrounding technological change has been a constant since the inception of technology itself. Take this example, when the steam engine was introduced, many laborers feared for their jobs, believing that automation would render their skills obsolete. Today, we find ourselves grappling with similar concerns regarding artificial intelligence (AI). This resistance often stems from fear—fear of job loss, fear of the unknown, and fear of inadequacy in adapting to new tools and processes.

Understanding this resistance is essential for anyone navigating the AI-driven job economy. It manifests in various ways, such as skepticism about AI capabilities, reluctance to engage with new tools, or outright dismissal of technology as a passing trend. Many individuals hold onto traditional methods because they are comfortable, familiar, and have served them well in the past. For example, a seasoned accountant might hesitate to embrace AI-driven financial tools that promise efficiency but require learning new software.

Addressing this resistance begins with education. Providing training on AI technologies can help alleviate concerns. When employees see tangible benefits—like reduced workloads or increased accuracy—they may become more inclined to embrace these advancements. Consider a company that integrated an AI-driven analytics platform. Initially met with skepticism by its marketing team, members quickly recognized how the tool provided deeper insights into customer behavior than traditional methods ever could. This shift not only enhanced their marketing strategies but also empowered team members to make data-driven decisions with greater confidence.

However, education alone is not enough; fostering a culture of innovation is equally vital. Organizations must create environments that encourage experimentation and risk-taking without fear of punitive consequences for failure. When employees feel supported in trying new things, they are more likely to enthusiastically adopt new technologies. Google's renowned "20% time" policy exemplifies this approach, allowing employees to dedicate a portion of their workweek to projects beyond their primary responsibilities. This practice has led to groundbreaking innovations like Gmail and Google News while nurturing a spirit of curiosity.

Leadership also plays a crucial role in overcoming resistance to technological change. Leaders should model the way by actively engaging with new technologies and demonstrating their value firsthand. By sharing their experiences— showcasing both successes and challenges—leaders humanize the technology and reduce anxiety around adoption. A notable example is IBM's Watson; when executives publicly demonstrated its capabilities by winning on Jeopardy!, it not only ignited excitement within IBM but also encouraged other industries to explore AI applications more seriously.

Involving employees in discussions about upcoming changes can further promote buy-in and mitigate resistance. Allowing team members to express concerns or suggestions fosters a sense of ownership over the transition process. Instead of imposing solutions from the top down, organizations can facilitate workshops where employees brainstorm potential applications for AI within their roles. This collaborative approach not only generates innovative ideas but also alleviates fears by showcasing how employees will be integral to shaping the integration process.

External factors can also contribute to resistance; for instance, economic uncertainty can intensify fears about job security amid automation advancements. It is essential for organizations to address these concerns transparently, clearly communicating how AI will be used and what safeguards exist to protect jobs or enhance roles rather than replace them outright. Demonstrating commitment through retraining programs or reskilling initiatives further reassures employees that their development remains a priority.

In summary, overcoming resistance to technological change in an AI-driven environment relies on education, engaged leadership, fostering an innovative culture, inclusive discussions about transitions, and clear communication regarding job security and retraining opportunities. By addressing these aspects directly, organizations can facilitate smoother transitions into adopting AI technologies while minimizing apprehension among their workforce.

Recognizing that resistance often stems from deeply rooted fears enables us to approach this challenge with empathy rather than frustration. As we advance into an era increasingly defined by artificial intelligence and automation, understanding these dynamics will be critical for both individuals and organizations seeking successful integration and adaptation in the evolving job landscape.

Bridging the Digital Divide

Bridging the digital divide is a critical task in our increasingly interconnected world, especially as we harness the advancements brought about by artificial intelligence. The term "digital divide" refers to the gap between those who have easy access to digital technology and the internet and those who do not. This divide can manifest in various forms, including geographical disparities, socioeconomic factors, educational inequalities, and even age-related gaps in tech savviness. Addressing these divides is essential to ensure that the benefits of AI and other technological advancements are equitably shared.

Access to technology is often perceived as a luxury rather than a fundamental right. In urban centers, high-speed internet may be readily available, while rural communities frequently grapple with slow connections or a complete lack of service. This disparity affects not only individual users but also entire economies. Take this example, small businesses in underserved areas may lack the necessary tools to leverage AI for marketing or customer engagement, putting them at a distinct disadvantage against competitors with better resources.

Education plays a pivotal role in bridging this gap. Schools equipped with modern technology can provide students with valuable skills that will serve them well in their future careers. However, many schools in low-income areas struggle with outdated technology and insufficient training for teachers on how to incorporate these tools effectively into their curricula. Successful initiatives like Google's "Grow with Google," which offers free training workshops aimed at improving digital skills among underserved populations, demonstrate how targeted interventions can empower individuals to navigate the digital landscape confidently.

Investing in community resources such as public libraries is another effective strategy for mitigating this divide. Libraries often serve as gateways to technology access; they provide computers and internet access while offering classes on everything from basic computer literacy to advanced topics like coding and data analysis. These programs not only equip individuals with essential tools but also create supportive environments where learning is encouraged.

Partnerships between private companies and public institutions can further help close the digital gap. For example, tech companies can collaborate with local governments or educational institutions to sponsor workshops or create mentorship programs that connect skilled professionals with eager learners. Initiatives where local businesses sponsor coding boot camps for youth from underserved backgrounds exemplify this collaboration; they not only teach technical skills but also inspire future generations to consider careers in tech fields that might otherwise seem out of reach.

In addition to education and resource allocation, addressing cultural attitudes toward technology is vital for fostering a more inclusive environment. Many individuals may feel intimidated by new technologies or doubt their ability to learn technical skills. Community leaders can play a significant role by advocating for technology use through local events or campaigns that celebrate digital literacy achievements within their communities.

Mentorship programs focusing on peer-to-peer support also offer effective strategies for alleviating apprehension surrounding technology adoption. When individuals see peers succeed—whether it's an older adult mastering social media or a young person launching an online business— they are more likely to believe they can succeed too. This communal approach fosters an atmosphere where learners feel empowered rather than isolated in their struggles.

Finally, addressing infrastructure challenges is essential when discussing how best to bridge the digital divide effectively. Governments must invest in high-speed internet accessibility as a public utility comparable to electricity or water services. Organizations like "EveryoneOn" advocate for equitable broadband access across regions while promoting programs designed specifically for low-income households.

The journey toward closing the digital divide requires concerted effort from all sectors of society—businesses must prioritize equitable access alongside innovation; governments need proactive policies ensuring infrastructure investment; and communities should cultivate environments that support learning without prejudice toward technological capabilities or background experiences.

bridging this divide enhances individual lives and strengthens economies by fostering inclusion and opportunity within an AI-driven job market where everyone has a stake in shaping our collective future.

Addressing Skills Mismatch

Addressing the skills mismatch in today's rapidly evolving job market is a critical challenge that requires urgent attention. As artificial intelligence and automation increasingly permeate various industries, a significant gap has emerged between the skills that workers possess and those that employers demand. This disparity not only hinders individual career advancement but also stifles overall economic growth, as companies struggle to find qualified candidates for essential roles.

To effectively bridge this gap, a multifaceted approach is essential. Understanding the specific skills in demand is a crucial first step. Take this example, in the tech sector, there has been a marked increase in the need for expertise in data analysis, machine learning, and cybersecurity. According to a report from the World Economic Forum, jobs requiring advanced digital skills are expected to grow significantly, while positions focused on routine tasks may decline sharply. Recognizing this trend enables educators and policymakers to design training programs that are closely aligned with market needs.

One proactive strategy involves fostering partnerships between educational institutions and industry leaders. Collaborations between companies and universities can lead to the development of curricula that reflect real-world applications and emerging technologies. Such partnerships often result in internships or co-op programs, allowing students to gain practical experience while pursuing their studies. Research shows that students who participate in internships are more likely to secure full-time positions after graduation, highlighting the value of experiential learning.

And, addressing the skills mismatch goes beyond formal education; it extends into the realm of lifelong learning. Professionals must embrace continuous education through online platforms that offer courses on emerging technologies. Websites like Coursera and Udacity have become essential resources for individuals looking to acquire new competencies at their own pace. By dedicating time each week to skill development—whether through coding boot camps or digital marketing workshops—workers can remain competitive amid ongoing changes in their industries.

Regular assessments of workforce capabilities within organizations can also be an effective strategy. Companies can conduct surveys or workshops to identify gaps between employee skills and those required by their evolving business models. For example, a healthcare organization may discover that its staff lacks adequate training in telehealth technologies, a need that has become increasingly important due to the shift toward remote consultations during the COVID-19 pandemic. Recognizing these gaps allows management teams to invest strategically in targeted training initiatives that enhance staff expertise and improve patient care.

Mentorship programs further contribute to alleviating skills mismatches by pairing less experienced employees with seasoned professionals. This supports knowledge transfer within organizations and enhances overall competency levels among team members. A case study from a Fortune 500 tech company demonstrated that establishing mentorship pairs improved technical proficiency across teams as junior staff benefited from their mentors' insights and experiences.

Government involvement is also crucial in facilitating access to training opportunities for underrepresented populations facing systemic barriers due to historical inequities. Community colleges often provide affordable skill development programs tailored to local job markets, offering courses ranging from basic computer skills to advanced AI analytics.

Private sector investment plays an important role as well; businesses should consider funding scholarships or grants aimed at supporting workforce development initiatives designed to close skills gaps within their communities. This investment not only nurtures a more skilled labor pool but also enhances companies' social responsibility profiles.

Finally, it is essential for workers themselves to take ownership of their professional development journeys. By proactively seeking out resources for skill acquisition—rather than waiting until demands arise—they can engage with online courses or industry-specific certifications that bolster their resilience against job market fluctuations.

To wrap things up, addressing the skills mismatch necessitates collaboration across multiple sectors: education providers must work closely with businesses; employers need to invest in ongoing training opportunities; governments must create policies that promote equitable access; and individuals must prioritize continuous learning throughout their careers. By collectively striving to bridge these gaps, we can empower workers and ensure that economies remain dynamic and innovative in the face of technological advancements reshaping our workplaces daily.

Strategies for Small and Medium Enterprises

Small and medium enterprises (SMEs) face distinct challenges in the rapidly evolving AI landscape, especially when it comes to integrating new technologies while maintaining a competitive edge. Unlike larger corporations that often have the resources for substantial investments in AI, SMEs can capitalize on their agility and innovative spirit to implement effective strategies. Embracing AI doesn't necessarily require a complete system overhaul; rather, it can be approached through incremental changes that deliver significant benefits.

One effective strategy for SMEs is to begin with small-scale initiatives by pinpointing specific processes that could benefit from AI integration. For example, automating customer service inquiries with chatbots can improve response times and boost customer satisfaction without requiring a major infrastructure investment. Solutions from companies like Drift and Intercom allow businesses to engage customers 24/7, providing immediate answers to frequently asked questions. This not only streamlines operations but also frees up staff to focus on more complex tasks that require human intervention.

In addition to starting small, forming partnerships with technology providers can enable SMEs to access advanced AI solutions at a fraction of the cost of developing them in-house. Collaborations with local tech startups or universities can yield customized solutions tailored to the specific needs of smaller businesses. Take this example, a small retail store might collaborate with a university's computer science department on an internship program aimed at developing predictive analytics tools that help forecast inventory needs based on sales trends. These partnerships foster innovation while providing students with valuable real-world experience and businesses with cutting-edge solutions.

Investing in employee training is another critical factor for SMEs navigating the AI landscape. By equipping their workforce with the skills needed to work alongside AI tools, businesses can maximize their return on investment. Online platforms such as LinkedIn Learning and Skillshare offer industry-specific courses that help employees enhance their capabilities in areas like data analysis or machine learning. Companies prioritizing workforce upskilling not only cultivate a culture of continuous improvement but also boost employee retention by investing in professional growth.

And, adopting a data-driven mindset is essential for any SME aiming to thrive amidst technological disruption. Collecting and analyzing data related to customer behavior, operational efficiency, and market trends can yield valuable insights that inform strategic decision-making. Tools like Google Analytics enable even the smallest enterprises to effectively track website performance and user engagement metrics. By harnessing data analytics, SMEs can tailor their marketing strategies more effectively, ensuring resources are allocated where they will yield the highest returns.

Building an adaptable organizational culture is vital for successfully integrating AI technologies within SMEs. Fostering an environment where experimentation is encouraged—where failures are viewed as learning opportunities—can lead to innovative solutions and creative problem-solving approaches. When employees feel empowered to suggest improvements or pilot new ideas without fear of repercussions, companies are more likely to discover effective ways of incorporating AI into their operations.

For those concerned about the costs associated with adopting new technologies, exploring government grants or subsidies designed to encourage technological advancements can provide much-needed financial support. Many regions offer funding programs specifically aimed at helping SMEs innovate through technology adoption. Researching these opportunities can make implementing cutting-edge solutions more feasible without straining budgets.

Lastly, engaging with industry networks or local business associations allows SMEs to share knowledge and resources while learning from peers facing similar challenges. Collaborating within these communities fosters an exchange of ideas that can lead to novel approaches in effectively leveraging AI technologies. Networking events or workshops focused on digital transformation offer platforms for sharing best practices and cultivating relationships that may evolve into beneficial partnerships in the future.

In summary, small and medium enterprises have various avenues available for navigating the complexities of AI integration without overwhelming themselves financially or logistically. By starting small with targeted initiatives, forming partnerships, investing in employee training, embracing data-driven decision-making practices, fostering an innovative culture, exploring funding opportunities, and engaging within industry networks, SMEs can create resilient organizations ready to tackle the future challenges posed by an increasingly automated world.

Cultivating an Innovative Mindset

Cultivating an innovative mindset is essential for small and medium enterprises (SMEs) looking to thrive in an AI-driven economy. This mindset not only nurtures creativity but also promotes proactive problem-solving, enabling businesses to adapt swiftly to the rapid changes within their industries. At its essence, an innovative mindset involves embracing experimentation and viewing challenges as opportunities for growth rather than obstacles.

To nurture innovation effectively, the first step is creating a safe environment where ideas can flourish. When employees feel secure in sharing their thoughts without fear of criticism, they are more likely to contribute creatively. Encouraging open dialogue within teams can lead to brainstorming sessions that yield novel solutions and strategies. Implementing regular "innovation huddles," for example, allows employees to gather and discuss new ideas or improvements, fostering a collaborative culture that fuels creativity.

Taking cues from the tech industry, SMEs can adopt practices such as hackathons or design sprints. These structured events challenge teams to address specific problems within a limited timeframe, often resulting in creative solutions that might not surface through traditional workflows. Take this example, a bakery could host a one-day event where staff brainstorm ways to enhance customer experiences or streamline operations using AI tools. The energy and urgency of these initiatives frequently lead to breakthrough ideas that can be tested and refined quickly.

Another key aspect of fostering innovation is encouraging a growth-oriented approach among employees. Businesses should emphasize learning from failures rather than penalizing mistakes. For example, if a marketing campaign utilizing AI analytics doesn't deliver the expected results, leadership can facilitate discussions about what went wrong and how similar issues can be avoided in the future. This approach not only builds resilience but also promotes continuous improvement.

Integrating diverse perspectives into decision-making processes further enriches creativity. Cross-functional teams allow for the merging of various skill sets and viewpoints, leading to comprehensive solutions that consider multiple angles of a problem. Take this example, a technology firm might bring together engineers, marketers, and customer service representatives to collaborate on developing an AI-driven product tailored to their target audience's needs.

Additionally, seeking external inspiration through partnerships or collaborations can significantly enhance innovation within SMEs. Engaging with startups or academic institutions allows companies to leverage fresh ideas and cutting-edge research. Such alliances often yield unique solutions that may not arise internally due to entrenched perspectives or established processes.

Investing time in ongoing professional development also signals a commitment to innovation. Providing training opportunities related to emerging technologies ensures employees stay informed about advancements relevant to their roles. Platforms like Coursera offer courses on AI applications tailored for different sectors; encouraging staff participation enhances their skills while sparking new ideas aligned with the organization's goals.

Establishing clear channels for feedback is crucial for nurturing an innovative culture as well. Regularly soliciting input from all levels within the organization enables leadership to gauge how well new initiatives are being received and whether adjustments are necessary. Take this example, after implementing an AI tool aimed at streamlining operations, gathering feedback from users can highlight areas needing enhancement or further training.

Patience is equally important; cultivating an innovative mindset requires time and consistency. Recognizing progress —even small victories—reinforces the value of creativity within the organization while motivating teams to continue exploring new ideas.

fostering an innovative mindset equips SMEs with the adaptability needed in today's fast-paced environment. By embracing experimentation and prioritizing collaborative problem-solving efforts infused with diverse perspectives and external insights, these firms are better positioned not only to survive but also to thrive amidst technological evolution.

With this foundational understanding of innovation embedded within their organizational culture, companies will be more adept at navigating the complexities associated with integrating AI technologies into their business models while reaping the rewards that come from creative engagement across all levels of operation.

Dispelling Myths about AI

Dispelling myths about AI is essential for both businesses and individuals as they navigate the complexities of an increasingly automated world. Misunderstandings surrounding AI can foster unnecessary fear and resistance to adopting new technologies. By addressing these misconceptions directly, we can cultivate a more informed perspective on how AI can enhance productivity, creativity, and job satisfaction.

One widespread myth is that AI will inevitably lead to massive job losses. While it's true that certain tasks may be automated, history demonstrates that technological advancements often create new roles even as they displace existing ones. Take this example, the rise of industrial automation resulted in job losses within manufacturing but simultaneously opened up opportunities in tech support, maintenance, and systems management. As AI continues to evolve, so too will the nature of work; many positions will transition towards roles that emphasize human intelligence, creativity, and emotional understanding—qualities machines cannot replicate.

In the healthcare sector, for example, AI tools are increasingly employed for diagnostics and data analysis. However, these advancements do not diminish the need for skilled healthcare professionals. Instead, they empower doctors to enhance their decision-making processes and devote more time to patient care rather than administrative tasks. A 2021 study found that physicians using AI-assisted diagnostic tools reported greater accuracy in patient evaluations and were able to spend more time interacting directly with patients.

Another common misconception is that only tech-savvy individuals can benefit from AI. In reality, user-friendly interfaces and intuitive designs have made these technologies accessible across various sectors. Platforms like Microsoft Excel now feature AI capabilities such as predictive analytics, allowing users without extensive technical backgrounds to analyze trends effortlessly. This democratization of technology means anyone willing to learn can effectively utilize these tools.

The belief that learning about AI is a one-time endeavor also stems from a fear of being outpaced by technology. In truth, staying relevant requires ongoing education and adaptation. Just as industries have evolved alongside technological advancements over decades or centuries, today's workforce must engage in continuous learning. Many organizations recognize this necessity; companies like Amazon provide employees with access to training programs focused on emerging technologies and skill development tailored to meet future demands.

Additionally, there's a misconception that all aspects of AI are inherently biased or flawed due to their reliance on data sets reflecting historical prejudices. While bias in algorithms is indeed a legitimate concern—especially when considering ethical implications—many researchers are actively working on methods to mitigate these biases through improved data curation techniques and transparency measures. Engaging diverse teams in the development process also ensures broader perspectives are considered when creating algorithms.

Concerns about data privacy also arise when discussing

AI capabilities. The narrative often portrays a surveillance-like environment where personal information is constantly monitored without consent. However, many organizations prioritize ethical practices surrounding data collection by implementing robust security measures and allowing users greater control over their information-sharing preferences.

By addressing misconceptions about artificial intelligence with factual narratives supported by evidence from various sectors—such as healthcare innovations enhancing care quality or educational platforms empowering individuals—we can shift the dialogue from fear-based resistance toward proactive engagement with technology's potential benefits. Embracing change while remaining grounded in an understanding of both the challenges posed by evolving technologies and the myriad opportunities they present for growth across disciplines will be essential moving forward.

cultivating an informed outlook regarding what AI truly represents—the fusion of machine efficiency with human creativity—enables individuals to approach this transformation not merely as passive observers but as active participants shaping their professional landscapes amidst unprecedented shifts driven by technological advancements.

Aligning AI Strategies with Business Goals

Aligning AI strategies with business goals extends beyond merely deploying technology; it involves weaving AI into the very fabric of an organization's mission and vision. Businesses that implement AI with a clear understanding of their overarching objectives can unlock its potential to deliver substantial value. A strategic framework for AI integration requires identifying key areas where AI can enhance operations, improve decision-making, and contribute to achieving business goals.

Take the retail sector as an example, where companies are increasingly utilizing AI for inventory management. Walmart exemplifies this approach by employing advanced algorithms to predict customer purchasing patterns and optimize stock levels. This alignment of AI capabilities with business objectives—such as cost reduction and improved customer satisfaction—illustrates how technology can facilitate operational efficiency while meeting specific market demands. By focusing on meaningful outcomes, organizations can steer clear of the common pitfall of adopting AI for its own sake.

To effectively integrate AI, organizations should first conduct a comprehensive assessment of their existing processes. This evaluation should identify pain points or inefficiencies that could benefit from automation or enhanced data analysis. Take this example, a manufacturing company may find that its supply chain management could greatly improve through predictive analytics, enabling it to anticipate disruptions before they impact production. By aligning these insights with strategic business goals—such as minimizing downtime or enhancing responsiveness—companies can develop a clear roadmap for effective AI integration.

Collaboration between technical teams and business leaders is also crucial for ensuring that AI initiatives remain aligned with organizational objectives. When IT professionals work closely with stakeholders from various departments—such as marketing, finance, and operations—they gain a deeper understanding of the specific challenges and opportunities each area faces. This collaboration fosters tailored solutions that not only leverage advanced technologies but also resonate with the company's mission.

An illustrative case is Netflix, which employs machine learning algorithms to analyze viewer preferences and behaviors. This data-driven approach informs content creation and marketing strategies that are directly linked to user engagement and subscription growth. By maintaining a feedback loop between AI insights and strategic goals, Netflix continually refines its offerings in response to evolving consumer interests.

Training employees to effectively leverage AI tools is another vital aspect of this alignment process. As organizations adopt new technologies, equipping staff with the necessary skills ensures they can fully utilize these innovations. For example, when a financial institution implements an AI-driven risk assessment tool, it must train analysts not only on how to use the software but also on interpreting the insights in relation to broader financial objectives such as risk management or regulatory compliance.

The importance of metrics in this context cannot be overstated; organizations should establish clear key performance indicators (KPIs) aligned with their business objectives. Regularly measuring progress against these KPIs allows companies to systematically evaluate the effectiveness of their AI initiatives. If a particular project isn't meeting expectations—such as an automated customer service chatbot not improving response times—it becomes essential for teams to refine their strategy based on real-world feedback.

Additionally, ethical considerations must be integrated into every aspect of AI deployment. Aligning strategies with corporate values around privacy, fairness, and transparency builds trust among stakeholders while mitigating risks associated with misaligned technology usage. Take this example, companies using facial recognition technology must ensure compliance with privacy regulations while respecting individual rights.

Finally, businesses should adopt an agile approach to aligning AI strategies with their goals. The rapidly evolving nature of technology demands ongoing adaptation and refinement of strategies as new capabilities emerge and market conditions change. This flexibility enables organizations to pivot quickly when unexpected challenges arise or new opportunities present themselves.

To wrap things up, successful alignment between AI strategies and business goals hinges on thoughtful integration across various organizational levels—from assessing current processes to fostering cross-departmental collaboration and continuous learning among employees. By grounding their approach in measurable outcomes while considering ethical implications, businesses can transform their operations into agile ecosystems capable of thriving in an era defined by technological innovation.

Encouraging Interdepartmental Collaboration

Encouraging interdepartmental collaboration is essential for organizations navigating the complexities of an AI-driven landscape. When departments operate in isolation, the potential of AI initiatives can be significantly constrained. Collaboration nurtures a culture of shared understanding and combined expertise, which enhances the effectiveness of AI projects. To foster this collaborative environment, organizations must establish structures and processes that promote open communication and teamwork across various teams.

One effective way to bridge departmental gaps is by forming cross-functional teams. These teams should include individuals with diverse skill sets—such as data scientists, product managers, marketing specialists, and IT professionals —who can contribute different perspectives. Take this example, when implementing a new AI tool for customer insights, bringing together marketing and analytics teams ensures that the tool is both technically robust and aligned with customer engagement strategies. This collaborative approach results in solutions that effectively meet both technical requirements and business objectives.

Regular interdepartmental workshops or brainstorming sessions focused on AI initiatives can further enhance collaboration. These gatherings provide opportunities for team members from different areas to share insights and discuss challenges they encounter in their work. Through these sessions, departments can identify overlapping goals or issues that might benefit from a collaborative solution. For example, a manufacturing team may discover that its inventory management challenges could be addressed by insights from the sales department's understanding of customer demand trends. This synergy not only improves problem-solving but also fosters relationships among team members who might not typically interact.

Technology plays a vital role in facilitating collaboration as well. Tools like Asana or Trello enable teams to track progress on joint projects in real-time while ensuring transparency about tasks and responsibilities. Communication platforms such as Slack allow for immediate discussions among team members, regardless of their physical locations. In today's increasingly remote work environment, these technologies dismantle geographical barriers and keep all stakeholders engaged.

Leadership support is crucial for promoting collaborative efforts within the organizational culture. When executives prioritize interdisciplinary projects and celebrate collaborative successes, they reinforce the value of teamwork among employees. Recognition programs that reward cross-departmental collaboration can motivate teams to seek partnerships rather than working in isolation.

Training is another critical factor in fostering interdepartmental collaboration around AI technologies. Organizations should offer training sessions that include representatives from multiple departments to ensure a unified understanding of how AI tools function and how they can be leveraged for specific departmental needs. Take this example, when the finance department adopts an AI-driven financial forecasting model, including marketing team members in the training ensures everyone comprehends how this model impacts budget allocation for campaigns.

Addressing potential challenges such as differing priorities or departmental goals is also vital for effective collaboration. Open discussions about these differences can lead to common ground or shared objectives that align with the organization's overall mission. For example, aligning sales targets with production capabilities might involve collaboration between sales and manufacturing departments on realistic forecasts based on market demand.

As organizations embrace AI-driven transformations, incorporating feedback mechanisms becomes crucial for sharing experiences related to AI implementations. Regular check-ins or feedback loops create opportunities for ongoing learning and adaptation among departments, ensuring lessons learned are disseminated throughout the organization. If one department uncovers an effective method for utilizing an AI tool, sharing that knowledge can enhance adoption across other areas of the business.

Lastly, fostering a culture of trust is essential for successful interdepartmental collaboration. When employees feel safe sharing ideas without fear of criticism or competition, creativity flourishes—leading to innovative solutions powered by AI technologies. Leadership should model this trust-building behavior by encouraging risk-taking and open discussions about both successes and failures.

In summary, promoting interdepartmental collaboration significantly enhances the effectiveness of AI initiatives by cultivating diverse expertise and shared objectives across an organization. By establishing cross-functional teams, leveraging technology for communication, supporting training initiatives, and nurturing a culture of trust and recognition, businesses can create an environment where collaboration thrives. This collective approach ultimately drives innovative solutions that align with organizational goals while advancing progress in the evolving landscape shaped by artificial intelligence.

Implementing AI Change Management Tools

Implementing AI change management tools is essential for organizations looking to effectively integrate artificial intelligence into their existing frameworks. The introduction of these technologies often leads to significant changes in operations, workflows, and even corporate culture. To facilitate a smooth transition, businesses must adopt structured approaches that address both technical and human factors involved in these transformations.

A successful implementation begins with a clear understanding of the specific needs and challenges faced by different departments. Before deploying any AI tool, organizations should conduct thorough assessments to identify which areas will benefit most from AI integration. For example, a company seeking to enhance its customer service might find that an AI chatbot can streamline responses and allow human agents to focus on more complex queries. Engaging customer service representatives early in the process can help customize the AI solution to meet both operational goals and user needs.

Once the appropriate tools are selected, training becomes crucial. Employees need to feel confident and capable when using new technologies. Tailored training programs should not only cover how to use the AI tools but also explain the underlying principles of AI that drive them. This understanding empowers employees to make informed decisions while effectively utilizing these tools. Take this example, if marketing staff are being trained on an AI-driven analytics platform, they should learn how data is sourced, processed, and interpreted. Such knowledge enhances their skills and fosters a sense of ownership over the technology.

In addition to training, establishing a feedback mechanism

is vital for adapting change management practices over time. Organizations should create channels through which employees can share their experiences with the new tools—highlighting what works well and what presents challenges. Regular check-ins or surveys enable teams to provide insights on usability and effectiveness, ultimately leading to iterative improvements in the application of AI systems.

As organizations implement change management strategies, it's important to recognize that resistance may arise at various levels within the company. Some employees might feel threatened by new technologies or uncertain about their job security in an automated environment. To address these concerns, leadership should engage in transparent communication about how AI will augment rather than replace human roles. Sharing success stories from within or outside the organization can help alleviate fears; when employees see examples of technology enhancing productivity without displacing workers, they are more likely to embrace change.

Also, integrating change management tools necessitates ongoing monitoring of both performance metrics and employee sentiment throughout the transition process. By utilizing project management software such as Monday.com or ClickUp alongside traditional performance indicators like KPIs (Key Performance Indicators), organizations can gain real-time insights into how well teams are adapting to new workflows introduced by AI systems.

Building a coalition of change champions within different departments is also crucial for facilitating smooth transitions during implementation phases. These individuals serve as liaisons between leadership and staff, helping translate technical jargon into practical applications relevant to everyday work life. By empowering these champions with authority and resources to support their colleagues during the adaptation phase, companies increase overall buy-in for change initiatives.

As teams begin to use AI tools more frequently, promoting collaborative opportunities can reinforce learning across various functions within the organization. Knowledge gained from one department can lead to breakthroughs in another; for instance, insights derived from analyzing sales data through an AI tool can inform marketing strategies aimed at improving customer engagement.

Finally, cultivating an organizational culture that embraces adaptability is fundamental during this transformative journey. Encouraging risk-taking while providing safe spaces for innovation invites employees at all levels to contribute ideas without fear of failure—a necessary element for thriving in today's rapidly evolving technological landscape.

To wrap things up, effective implementation of AI change management tools involves a multi-faceted approach that prioritizes understanding departmental needs, ensuring robust training programs for staff members, facilitating open lines of communication for feedback, engaging change advocates across teams, and regularly monitoring progress— all grounded in a commitment to fostering an adaptive culture that supports growth amid the uncertainties brought about by advancements in artificial intelligence technology.

CHAPTER 19:
CONCLUSION AND
CALL TO ACTION

Re-emphasizing Key Lessons

As professionals navigate the complexities of the AI-driven job economy, several key lessons emerge that are essential for thriving in this evolving landscape.

First and foremost, embracing a mindset of continuous learning is crucial. The rapid pace of technological advancements requires individuals to remain adaptable, constantly seeking opportunities to enhance their skills and knowledge. This dedication to lifelong learning not only positions professionals as valuable assets within their organizations but also empowers them to take control of their career trajectories.

In tandem with this commitment to learning, the importance of emotional intelligence cannot be overstated. As AI systems increasingly take over routine tasks, human qualities such as empathy, creativity, and collaboration become vital differentiators. Professionals who cultivate strong interpersonal skills are better equipped to navigate workplace dynamics and foster meaningful connections with colleagues and clients. For example, leaders must refine their abilities to inspire and motivate teams amid the ongoing changes brought about by technology.

Effective communication strategies also play a significant role in this new environment. Clearly articulating the benefits and implications of AI integration is essential for securing stakeholder buy-in. Whether presenting findings from data analyses or discussing the potential of new tools, the ability to convey complex ideas succinctly can greatly enhance individual credibility and promote a culture of openness and collaboration within organizations.

And, organizations must prioritize ethical considerations in their AI implementations. As companies leverage artificial intelligence, they bear the responsibility of ensuring that their applications uphold principles of fairness, accountability, and transparency. This commitment not only fosters trust among employees but also builds confidence among customers. Take this example, a financial institution utilizing AI for lending decisions should have clear guidelines regarding data usage and ensure that algorithms do not perpetuate bias.

Lastly, establishing a robust support network proves invaluable in navigating this transformative landscape. Engaging with mentors, peers, and professional communities creates an ecosystem where knowledge-sharing flourishes. Such networks provide insights into industry trends, best practices, and emotional support during challenging transitions.

Each of these lessons emphasizes a fundamental truth: success in the AI job economy hinges on a proactive approach to personal and professional development. By committing to continuous learning, enhancing interpersonal skills, communicating effectively, prioritizing ethics, and building supportive networks, professionals can position themselves not only to survive but also to thrive in an evolving work environment shaped by artificial intelligence. Embracing these principles will pave the way for a sustainable future where technology enhances human potential rather than replaces it.

Encouraging Continuous Learning

In the rapidly evolving landscape of the AI job economy, continuous learning stands out as a vital strategy for success. As technology advances at an unprecedented pace, professionals must actively engage in upskilling and reskilling to maintain their relevance. This commitment to lifelong learning not only enhances individual capabilities but also strengthens entire organizations against obsolescence. Take this example, a marketing professional who proactively learns about machine learning algorithms can harness data analytics to create more effective campaigns, thereby increasing their value within the company.

To foster a mindset oriented toward continuous learning, professionals should start by identifying areas for knowledge expansion. Self-assessment tools and feedback from peers or supervisors can help highlight skill gaps that are critical in an AI-driven environment. For example, a financial analyst might realize they need to improve their programming skills in languages like Python to better manipulate data sets. In response, they could enroll in targeted online courses focusing specifically on these skills. Platforms such as Coursera and edX offer structured learning paths catering to various proficiency levels, making it easier for individuals to engage with complex subjects.

Another essential aspect of promoting continuous learning is embracing new technologies and methodologies. Take this example, a project manager may find value in becoming proficient with AI-powered tools that streamline workflows and enhance team collaboration. Learning how to use software like Trello or Asana with integrated AI features can significantly boost productivity. To facilitate this process, one might participate in workshops or training sessions offered by industry leaders. Engaging directly with technology through hands-on practice solidifies understanding and builds confidence.

Networking also plays a crucial role in sustaining a culture of continuous education. By connecting with peers across different sectors—whether through online forums or local meetups—professionals can exchange insights about emerging trends and best practices. These interactions often provide valuable perspectives that extend beyond what formal education can offer. For example, attending conferences focused on AI applications allows individuals not only to learn from thought leaders but also to discuss practical implications with fellow attendees facing similar challenges.

Organizations themselves can cultivate a culture of continuous learning by prioritizing professional development. Leaders should advocate for training programs and encourage employees to pursue relevant certifications. Implementing mentorship initiatives where seasoned employees guide newer staff fosters an environment where knowledge flows freely and innovation thrives. Pairing an experienced data scientist with a junior analyst, for example, can create a dynamic exchange of ideas while empowering the latter to quickly develop essential skills.

Setting clear personal development goals is crucial for maintaining motivation and accountability throughout one's learning journey. Establishing specific milestones—such as completing a course by a certain date or applying new skills in real-world scenarios—can generate a sense of achievement that propels further growth. Tracking progress through journals or digital platforms reinforces this journey, helping individuals stay focused on their objectives.

For those constrained by work or family commitments, integrating learning into daily routines becomes essential. Micro-learning techniques—like dedicating just ten minutes each day to watch instructional videos or read articles—enable busy professionals to absorb information gradually without feeling overwhelmed. This approach not only makes learning more manageable but also promotes consistency over time.

embracing continuous learning is about fostering resilience and adaptability in an ever-changing job market shaped by AI advancements. The willingness to evolve alongside technology enhances personal career prospects while significantly contributing to organizational success. Each new skill acquired opens doors for innovation and collaboration, ensuring that professionals are equipped not just for today's challenges but also for tomorrow's opportunities.

As we navigate this transformative landscape, it becomes increasingly evident that those who prioritize ongoing education will emerge as leaders capable of guiding industries toward the ethical integration of AI technologies while driving economic growth and sustainability forward.

Fostering Collaboration and Innovation

Collaboration and innovation are becoming increasingly vital in today's AI-driven job market. The rapid pace of technological advancements demands not only individual expertise but also collective effort. When professionals unite, they can harness a range of perspectives and skills, creating an environment ripe for innovation that benefits the entire organization. For example, cross-functional teams that combine data scientists with marketers can lead to groundbreaking campaigns that are both data-driven and creatively engaging.

At the heart of effective collaboration is the establishment of open communication channels. Organizations should actively promote discussions that encourage idea-sharing and constructive feedback. Regular brainstorming sessions can create a space where employees feel comfortable voicing their thoughts, paving the way for innovative solutions. A company that holds weekly roundtable meetings, for instance, allows different departments to share insights on ongoing projects and potential challenges, fostering a culture of inclusivity where every voice is valued.

Technology plays a crucial role in enhancing collaborative efforts. Tools like Slack, Microsoft Teams, and Asana streamline communication across geographical boundaries, enabling teams to work seamlessly regardless of location. These platforms facilitate project management while supporting real-time discussions and information sharing. Take this example, a project team focused on AI-driven product development might use these tools to quickly iterate on ideas based on immediate feedback from various stakeholders, resulting in faster time-to-market and higher-quality outputs.

Innovation often flourishes when individuals with diverse backgrounds and areas of expertise come together. The idea of "diversity of thought" is invaluable as it encourages unique approaches to problem-solving. A team comprising engineers, product managers, and user experience designers is more likely to develop comprehensive solutions to complex issues than a homogeneous group would. Each member's unique perspective contributes to a more holistic understanding of the challenges at hand.

Mentorship programs can significantly enhance collaboration within organizations. Pairing less experienced employees with seasoned professionals fosters knowledge transfer and nurtures innovation. This dynamic allows junior team members to benefit from established practices while infusing fresh ideas into the conversation. For example, when a junior developer collaborates closely with a senior software architect on an AI application, they may discover novel solutions by blending traditional methods with contemporary approaches.

Recognizing and rewarding collaborative efforts can further inspire innovation within teams. Organizations should implement systems that celebrate successful collaborations—whether through formal awards or informal acknowledgments—to reinforce the value of teamwork. When individuals see their contributions recognized, they are more likely to engage in collaborative projects in the future. Creating a culture that celebrates teamwork strengthens relationships among colleagues and boosts overall morale.

The role of leadership is crucial in fostering collaboration and innovation. Leaders should set clear expectations for teamwork while providing the necessary resources for success. This includes investing in training programs that teach effective collaboration strategies and encouraging leaders at all levels to model collaborative behavior themselves. When leaders actively participate in collaborative efforts, they underscore the importance of teamwork to their teams.

To further drive innovation, organizations should embrace experimentation as part of their culture. Encouraging teams to take calculated risks fosters an environment where failure is viewed as an opportunity for learning rather than something to be avoided. Take this example, many tech companies host hackathons or innovation days where employees can explore new ideas without fear of immediate repercussions if those ideas don't succeed. Such initiatives empower employees to think creatively and pursue unconventional solutions that might otherwise remain untapped.

fostering collaboration and innovation requires a multifaceted approach that includes open communication, diverse perspectives, effective leadership, recognition of contributions, and a willingness to experiment. By prioritizing these elements, organizations build an adaptive workforce equipped not only for today's challenges but also for tomorrow's opportunities in an AI-driven landscape. This proactive stance cultivates an innovative spirit that will define successful enterprises moving forward.

As we navigate this evolution together, it becomes clear that collaboration isn't just beneficial; it's essential for survival in an increasingly complex world shaped by artificial intelligence. The synergy created through teamwork propels individual careers forward while enhancing organizational resilience in the fast-changing landscape ahead.

The Importance of Active Participation

Active participation is a cornerstone of success in today's AI-driven job economy. When individuals engage fully with their roles and contribute meaningfully to their organizations, they not only enhance their own professional trajectories but also boost the effectiveness of their teams. The advantages of active participation extend well beyond mere presence; it cultivates a culture of collaboration, innovation, and resilience.

To underscore the significance of being actively involved, let's examine how employee engagement influences problem-solving within an organization. A team member who shares ideas in meetings can ignite discussions that lead to innovative solutions. Take this example, in a tech startup developing a new AI application, an engineer might propose a novel algorithm based on personal research that could significantly improve performance metrics. This contribution can trigger a chain reaction where designers and marketers adapt their strategies based on this technical insight, ultimately resulting in a product that not only meets user needs but exceeds them.

Creating opportunities for all employees to participate actively requires intentional design within workplace culture. Organizations should foster an environment where questioning and experimentation are encouraged. This can be achieved by implementing regular feedback loops that allow team members to share insights on ongoing projects without fear of dismissal. For example, hosting monthly "idea-sharing" workshops enables employees at various levels to pitch their concepts or critiques openly. These sessions often reveal hidden talents within teams and highlight unique perspectives that might otherwise go unnoticed.

Technology plays a crucial role in facilitating active participation. Collaboration platforms allow employees to interact seamlessly, regardless of location or time zone. Tools like Trello and Miro enable teams to brainstorm and visualize projects collectively, creating an inclusive atmosphere where everyone's input is valued. In these digital spaces, individuals may find themselves inspired by others' contributions, further catalyzing engagement and idea development.

And, involving employees in decision-making processes fosters a sense of ownership. When team members feel that their opinions matter—when they have a voice—they are more likely to commit to organizational goals and strive for collective success. Take this example, inviting staff to weigh in on the direction of a new AI strategy not only garners diverse insights but also creates advocates for the chosen approach once implemented.

Encouraging active participation also promotes personal growth. Engaged professionals tend to seek learning opportunities related to their interests within the organization, whether through training programs or cross-departmental collaborations. As individuals immerse themselves in these experiences, they acquire new skills essential for navigating the complexities introduced by AI technologies. For example, someone initially focused on customer service might participate in project discussions about AI-driven customer interactions, gaining knowledge about data analytics and machine learning along the way.

Leadership plays a pivotal role in nurturing this spirit of

active participation. Leaders must model engagement by being approachable and responsive to ideas from team members at all levels. When leaders visibly value contributions—through acknowledgment during meetings or recognition programs—it reinforces the importance of participation throughout the organization.

Additionally, organizations should intentionally structure roles that promote active involvement. Creating task forces or committees focused on specific challenges encourages employees to step outside their usual duties and contribute their expertise toward solving pressing issues related to AI integration or workflow improvements. For example, forming a cross-functional team tasked with exploring the ethical implications surrounding AI usage invites diverse voices into crucial conversations, fostering inclusivity while driving innovation.

At its core, active participation transcends mere presence; it embodies engagement and investment in one's work environment. The benefits ripple outward—from individual empowerment to enhanced team dynamics and ultimately organizational success in an evolving landscape characterized by rapid technological change. By cultivating an ethos that values contributions at every level, businesses position themselves as adaptive entities ready to tackle future challenges while harnessing the transformative potential inherent in AI developments.

The imperative for professionals today is clear: embrace active participation not just as an expectation but as a proactive strategy for career advancement and organizational effectiveness. The synergy generated through collective involvement becomes vital fuel for innovation as we navigate the complexities of an increasingly interconnected workforce shaped by advancements in artificial intelligence.

Staying Informed and Proactive

Staying informed and proactive is essential in a landscape where technological advances are occurring at an unprecedented pace. As the AI job economy continues to expand, professionals must take ownership of their learning journeys to remain competitive and relevant. This goes beyond merely consuming information; it requires a dedicated effort to understand emerging trends and innovations.

Take, for example, a marketing manager who incorporates AI tools into their campaigns. By subscribing to industry newsletters, attending webinars, and engaging in forums focused on AI in marketing, they can gain valuable insights into predictive analytics, customer segmentation, and campaign automation. This commitment to continuous learning empowers them to make informed decisions that enhance campaign effectiveness. Their proactive approach not only establishes them as a thought leader within their organization but also opens doors for collaboration on innovative projects.

To stay effectively informed, professionals should cultivate a diverse information ecosystem. Relying solely on traditional news outlets can limit exposure to cutting-edge developments. Instead, they should follow blogs, podcasts, and social media channels where experts share insights on AI advancements. Take this example, tech influencers often provide real-time analysis of new tools and strategies that can significantly impact various industries. Engaging with this content fosters a comprehensive understanding of how AI technologies evolve and their implications for specific fields.

Networking plays a pivotal role in remaining proactive as well. Building relationships with peers who are equally invested in leveraging AI creates opportunities for knowledge sharing and collaboration. Participating in industry events or online communities that focus on AI applications relevant to one's profession can lead to discussions about recent breakthroughs and challenges faced in integrating AI. These interactions often result in collaborative problem-solving and the generation of new ideas.

Incorporating structured learning into your routine can further enhance your ability to stay ahead of the curve. Online courses offer tailored instruction on specific technologies or methodologies that can directly benefit your career trajectory. Platforms like Coursera or Udacity provide specialized programs in data science, machine learning, or ethical AI practices. Dedicating time each week to these courses not only helps you gain valuable skills but also signals your commitment to personal development to potential employers.

Proactivity also involves anticipating changes within one's organization and the broader industry landscape. Regularly assessing these evolving conditions allows professionals to identify potential skill gaps before they become barriers to advancement. Take this example, if you observe a growing trend toward automation in your sector, seeking training in related software or methodologies ensures that you are prepared for future demands.

And, cultivating an agile mindset is crucial when navigating the uncertainties inherent in the AI job economy. An agile professional adapts quickly to new information or changing circumstances rather than clinging rigidly to established practices. This flexibility enables individuals to pivot as needed—whether embracing new technologies or adjusting strategies based on shifting market conditions.

Feedback mechanisms within your workplace serve as another important tool for staying informed. Actively seeking performance reviews and constructive critiques from colleagues or supervisors about your approach to integrating AI solutions into projects provides clarity on areas for improvement and encourages open dialogue about future growth opportunities.

Fostering curiosity also enhances your ability to engage proactively with emerging technologies. Embracing challenges as opportunities for exploration—rather than viewing them as obstacles—encourages experimentation with new tools or processes without fear of failure. When team members creatively test different approaches using AI solutions, organizations benefit from diverse perspectives that drive innovation forward.

taking an active role in staying informed requires discipline but yields significant rewards over time—both personally and professionally. The more engaged individuals are with ongoing developments in AI technology and its applications across industries, the better equipped they become to navigate changes effectively while seizing opportunities as they arise.

In this rapidly transforming job landscape shaped by advancements in artificial intelligence, being proactive means positioning oneself not just as a reactive participant but as someone who anticipates shifts that define future success. Embrace continuous learning as part of your professional identity; through this lens of resilience amidst change will be cultivated—a defining trait for thriving careers within the dynamic realms influenced by the evolution of artificial intelligence.

Engaging with Community Initiatives

Engaging with community initiatives presents a powerful opportunity for professionals to enhance their skills while contributing to the broader discourse on AI and its implications in the workplace. This involvement nurtures a sense of belonging and purpose, linking individuals with like-minded peers who share a passion for leveraging technology for positive change.

Take, for example, a software developer who volunteers at local coding boot camps or mentorship programs. By teaching programming languages such as Python or JavaScript, they not only reinforce their own knowledge but also help close the skills gap in their community. This reciprocal relationship enhances their technical abilities while also cultivating vital soft skills—like patience, empathy, and communication—that are essential in today's collaborative work environments.

Participation in hackathons offers another dynamic way to engage with community initiatives. These events unite diverse groups—from students to seasoned professionals—to tackle real-world problems using AI technologies. A recent hackathon, for instance, focused on creating AI solutions for environmental sustainability and drew participants from various backgrounds. Over a 48-hour period, teams collaborated to develop applications aimed at predicting waste generation patterns or optimizing energy consumption in urban areas. The spirit of collaboration at such events sparks creativity and innovation, encouraging participants to think outside the box and devise practical solutions.

And, networking through community initiatives can reveal professional opportunities that might not be readily apparent in traditional job markets. By attending local tech meetups or workshops, individuals connect directly with industry leaders and innovators seeking fresh talent. Take this example, an aspiring data scientist might join a monthly meetup where experts discuss the latest advancements in machine learning. This exposure often leads to potential internships or job offers, as attendees frequently look for enthusiastic learners eager to apply new skills.

Additionally, these initiatives foster a culture of inclusivity and support within the tech community. Organizations focused on diversity, equity, and inclusion (DEI) actively seek volunteers for programs aimed at empowering underrepresented groups in technology fields. A professional involved in such efforts amplifies diverse voices while gaining insights into various perspectives on how AI can impact different populations. This engagement deepens one's ability to approach challenges with empathy—a crucial element in developing ethical AI solutions.

As professionals immerse themselves in these initiatives, they become advocates for change within their industries. Their experiences shape insights that can influence organizational practices and policies regarding AI implementation. For example, someone who has volunteered at community forums discussing the ethical implications of facial recognition technology may later play a key role in guiding their company's responsible deployment of similar technologies.

To maximize their engagement with community initiatives, individuals should actively seek out opportunities that resonate with their values and interests. Online platforms like Meetup.com or Eventbrite offer listings of relevant gatherings in one's area, while social media channels often highlight upcoming events hosted by industry organizations or local universities.

Also, forming partnerships with educational institutions can amplify the impact of community initiatives. Professionals can collaborate with schools to create programs designed to equip students with essential digital skills before they enter the workforce. Such collaborations foster early interest in tech careers while addressing skill shortages that many industries currently face.

Incorporating community involvement into one's professional journey creates a symbiotic relationship where learning flourishes alongside giving back—an essential aspect of navigating the evolving landscape shaped by AI advancements. The exchange of knowledge fosters both personal growth and collective progress within communities striving for technological empowerment.

engaging with community initiatives empowers individuals not just as participants but as active contributors who shape future narratives about technology's role in society. Through collaboration, mentorship, and advocacy, professionals position themselves at the forefront of conversations defining how AI will be integrated across various sectors—ensuring relevance while driving meaningful change along the way.

Building the Future Workforce Together

Building the future workforce is not solely the responsibility of individual organizations; it is a collective effort that necessitates collaboration among industries, educational institutions, and communities. In a landscape increasingly shaped by AI, where job roles and skill requirements are constantly evolving, fostering a shared vision becomes essential. The most effective strategies emerge when stakeholders come together to confront the challenges posed by technological advancement.

A prime example of successful collaboration can be found in partnerships between tech companies and universities. Microsoft's initiatives, such as coding boot camps and university programs designed to equip students with relevant AI skills, illustrate this approach. These collaborations provide students with hands-on experience while creating a talent pipeline that aligns with industry needs. Students gain access to cutting-edge technologies, and employers benefit from a workforce prepared to address real-world challenges from day one.

Also, businesses are increasingly recognizing the importance of internships as a vital component in nurturing young talent. Internships offer students valuable insights into corporate culture and practical applications of their studies. Take this example, Google's internship program has been instrumental in shaping future engineers and product managers well-versed in AI principles. Through these opportunities, companies can evaluate potential hires while interns receive mentorship and exposure to industry standards.

Nonprofits also play a crucial role in workforce

development by bridging the gap between education and employment. Organizations like Year Up focus on providing underrepresented youth with professional training coupled with internships at major corporations. This model not only empowers individuals through skill development but also promotes inclusivity in tech sectors striving for diversity. Participants leave these programs equipped with both technical knowledge and soft skills that enhance their employability.

Another effective strategy for preparing the next generation for an AI-centric workforce is the rise of mentorship programs. Professionals from diverse backgrounds volunteer their time to guide newcomers through the complexities of careers influenced by technology. Initiatives like Techstars' mentorship-driven accelerator programs connect aspiring entrepreneurs with experienced mentors who offer insights on everything from startup strategies to navigating ethical dilemmas in tech deployment.

Integrating AI into workforce development extends beyond hard skills; it also requires an understanding of new workplace dynamics. A significant trend is the growing emphasis on soft skills—traits such as adaptability, emotional intelligence, and teamwork—which are essential in collaborative environments shaped by AI tools. Workshops focused on enhancing these competencies are vital; they help create resilient individuals capable of thriving amidst constant change.

Communities can further enrich this effort by establishing local tech hubs or innovation centers that facilitate learning and networking opportunities for individuals at all career stages. Programs that encourage interaction among entrepreneurs, students, and professionals foster an ecosystem ripe for innovation and idea exchange. A notable example is Atlanta's Tech Village—a vibrant center where startups collaborate with established companies, generating fresh ideas that advance technology while nurturing talent.

Engaging policymakers in discussions about workforce readiness initiatives driven by AI advancements is equally important. Legislative support can lead to funding for programs aimed at addressing the skills gap present in many industries today. Advocacy efforts can drive reforms in educational curricula to better align with market demands —ensuring schools equip students with relevant knowledge while adapting swiftly to technological changes.

Involving parents in this conversation is also crucial; they significantly influence young people's career aspirations. Workshops or seminars aimed at parents about future job trends resulting from AI integration can illuminate emerging opportunities, sparking interest in fields that may have previously been overlooked or misunderstood.

As we work together to build this future workforce, it becomes evident that success relies on collective responsibility rather than isolated efforts. Each stakeholder—from educators and industry leaders to community organizers—plays an integral role in shaping pathways toward sustainable employment opportunities amid rapid technological change.

collaboration fosters resilience against disruptions caused by AI advancements—ensuring that the workforce adapts dynamically rather than merely reacting to changes over time. By cultivating an environment rooted in cooperation, we not only prepare individuals for success but also contribute positively to societal progress within our technologically advanced world. The journey ahead calls for unity; together, we can develop solutions that extend far beyond our immediate circles, inspiring generations yet unborn to embrace the possibilities brought forth by innovation.

Committing to Ethical AI Practices

Committing to ethical AI practices goes beyond merely recognizing their significance; it requires a proactive integration of ethics into all aspects of AI development and deployment. Organizations must start by establishing a clear set of ethical guidelines that dictate how AI technologies are created and utilized. These guidelines should embody core values such as fairness, accountability, transparency, and respect for user privacy. Without a solid ethical foundation, the risk of misuse rises, jeopardizing public trust in technology.

A notable example of an organization championing ethical AI is IBM. The company has instituted principles that guide its AI initiatives, emphasizing fairness and transparency in its systems. By introducing tools to identify and mitigate bias in AI models, IBM not only enhances product reliability but also bolsters customer confidence. Organizations that embrace such frameworks can stand out in a crowded market, positioning themselves as trustworthy leaders rather than mere tech providers.

Equally important is training teams on these ethical standards. Employees across all levels need a comprehensive understanding of the ethical implications of their work, particularly those involved in design and development. Regular workshops and seminars can offer insights into real-world scenarios where ethical dilemmas may arise, fostering a culture of responsibility and vigilance. Role-playing exercises, for instance, allow team members to navigate complex situations involving AI bias or data privacy concerns, equipping them with the skills needed to make informed decisions in their daily roles.

Also, organizations should actively involve diverse stakeholders in the decision-making process when developing AI systems. This inclusive approach ensures that multiple perspectives are considered, especially from historically marginalized communities that may be disproportionately affected by AI applications. Engaging ethicists, sociologists, and community representatives can illuminate potential societal impacts that technologists might overlook. For example, input from civil rights groups during the design phase of facial recognition systems can help address inherent biases and promote more equitable outcomes.

Transparency is another critical component of ethical AI practices. Organizations should communicate openly about how their AI systems operate and the data they utilize. By providing clear explanations regarding algorithms' workings and decision-making processes, companies can demystify AI technologies for end-users while alleviating concerns about "black box" systems. Initiatives like Google's "Model Cards" exemplify how transparency can enhance accountability by offering insights into model performance across various demographics.

Regulatory compliance also plays a vital role in discussions around ethical practices in AI development. Adhering to existing laws on data protection—such as GDPR in Europe—should be viewed not just as a legal requirement but as a moral obligation to protect users' rights. Compliance with these regulations not only reinforces public trust but also encourages organizations to adopt higher standards for data privacy and security.

Beyond compliance and internal policies, cultivating an organizational culture that prioritizes ethics involves creating environments where employees feel empowered to voice concerns about unethical practices or potential violations they observe. Establishing anonymous reporting mechanisms encourages individuals to speak up without fear of repercussions, fostering accountability throughout the organization.

The dialogue surrounding ethical AI must extend beyond individual organizations into broader societal discourse. Tech companies should engage with policymakers to advocate for regulations that incorporate ethical considerations while balancing innovation with public interest concerns.

Collaborating on regulatory frameworks ensures that rules evolve alongside technological advancements rather than lagging behind them.

committing to ethical AI practices means envisioning a future where technology positively serves humanity instead of merely maximizing profit margins or operational efficiency. This commitment should be holistic—integrating diverse perspectives throughout the development lifecycle while prioritizing transparency and accountability at every stage.

As we navigate this intricate landscape shaped by rapid technological advancements, our unwavering dedication to ethics will define successful organizations and foster trust between society and technological innovation. The journey ahead requires vigilance; cultivating an environment rooted in strong ethical values will help ensure that as we harness the power of artificial intelligence, it uplifts rather than undermines our shared human experience.

APPENDICES

The appendices are a vital resource hub, bringing together valuable information and tools that enhance your understanding of navigating the AI job economy. Each section serves as a practical reference, offering actionable insights and concrete steps to help you integrate AI into your career strategy.

To begin with, the Glossary of Terms provides clear definitions of key concepts within the AI landscape. By demystifying jargon that can often pose barriers to comprehension, this resource makes complex ideas more accessible. Familiarizing yourself with terms like "machine learning," "natural language processing," and "algorithmic bias" enables you to engage in informed discussions and make better decisions.

Following this, the Recommended Reading List features a curated selection of books, articles, and research papers that explore topics discussed throughout the guide. These resources not only deepen your knowledge but also introduce you to diverse viewpoints and case studies from industry leaders and scholars. Engaging with these materials can spark innovative thinking and reveal strategies you may not have previously considered.

Online Communities and Forums offer another layer of support as you navigate the complexities of AI integration. These platforms create spaces for collaboration, discussion, and advice from a diverse range of professionals across various industries. Whether you're looking for answers to specific questions or engaging in broader conversations about AI's future, connecting with community members can lead to meaningful relationships and valuable insights.

Certification Programs and Credentials are crucial for demonstrating expertise in AI-related fields. The appendices outline various recognized programs that offer specialized training in areas such as data science, machine learning, or ethical AI practices. Earning these certifications not only enhances your resume but also equips you with skills tailored to meet industry demands.

Engaging in Volunteer Opportunities for Skill Development encourages participation with local organizations or initiatives focused on technology outreach or education. By dedicating your time and expertise, you gain practical experience while building a portfolio that showcases your commitment to applying AI responsibly within community settings.

Accessing Government Resources and Grants can provide insights into funding opportunities available for individuals pursuing education or projects related to AI development. These resources can help alleviate financial burdens while fostering innovation in the field, especially for those looking to initiate their ventures.

Personal Development Plans empower individuals to create tailored roadmaps that align their career goals with emerging opportunities in the AI landscape. These plans should reflect both short-term objectives—such as completing a course—and long-term aspirations—like securing a leadership role in AI implementation.

Finally, the Guide to AI Job Boards and Application Tips consolidates essential information on where to find opportunities in this evolving job market. Knowing which platforms specialize in AI roles ensures that you maximize your search efforts while adopting strategies that resonate with hiring managers.

As we compile these resources into the appendices, remember that each element plays a unique role in enhancing your journey through the dynamic terrain shaped by artificial intelligence. Embrace these tools as part of a proactive approach to fostering continuous growth, engaging ethically with technology, and strategically developing your career within an ever-changing economic landscape.

- **Glossary of Terms**

Let's begin with "Artificial Intelligence" (AI), which refers to the simulation of human intelligence processes by machines, particularly computer systems. This encompasses learning —acquiring information and rules for its application— reasoning—applying those rules to reach conclusions—and self-correction. Understanding this definition is vital as you explore AI's applications in the workplace, providing insights into both its capabilities and limitations.

Building on that, we have "Machine Learning" (ML), a subset of AI dedicated to developing algorithms that enable computers to learn from data and make predictions. ML plays a pivotal role in modern AI systems by allowing them to enhance their performance through experience. Recognizing its significance will deepen your understanding of how data-driven decisions are made across various industries.

Another important term is "Natural Language Processing" (NLP), which focuses on enabling computers to understand, interpret, and respond to human language in meaningful ways. This technology underpins voice-activated assistants, translation applications, and sentiment analysis tools. Familiarity with NLP will enhance your appreciation of how AI interacts with users and processes large volumes of linguistic data.

In discussions around data protection, "Differential Privacy" is another critical concept. It ensures that individual privacy within a dataset is maintained while still allowing for meaningful statistical analysis. Grasping this term will empower you to participate in conversations about data ethics and individual rights amid rising concerns over privacy in our increasingly digital world.

Next is "Deep Learning," a specialized branch of machine learning that employs neural networks with multiple layers to analyze complex data patterns. This sophisticated method has led to significant advancements in areas like image and speech recognition. Familiarity with deep learning enhances your understanding of the advanced AI techniques powering many contemporary applications.

The term "Automation" refers to using technology to perform tasks without human intervention, often leading to increased efficiency and reduced labor costs. However, it is crucial to consider automation's impact on employment dynamics across various sectors. By recognizing these implications, you'll be better equipped to navigate the job market shifts influenced by AI technologies.

As we explore the evolving workforce landscape shaped by AI, "Reskilling" and "Upskilling" emerge as vital strategies. Reskilling involves training workers for new roles or tasks, while upskilling focuses on enhancing existing skills to improve job performance or adapt to new technologies. Familiarity with these concepts highlights the importance of continuous learning in today's rapidly changing job economy.

Lastly, let's discuss "Ethical AI," which encompasses the principles guiding responsible development and use of artificial intelligence technologies. This includes ensuring transparency, accountability, and fairness in AI systems. Understanding these ethical implications enables you to engage thoughtfully about how organizations can implement

AI responsibly while benefiting society as a whole.

As you familiarize yourself with these terms and their meanings, remember that they serve as tools for developing a deeper comprehension of the intricate interplay between artificial intelligence and the evolving job market. Embracing this knowledge fosters informed dialogue and strategic thinking in an era where technology reshapes not only industries but also individual careers and broader societal structures.

- **Recommended Reading List**

The recommended reading list is a thoughtfully curated collection aimed at enhancing your understanding of the AI job economy and its implications for professional growth. These resources offer diverse perspectives, methodologies, and case studies that shed light on the complexities of AI integration in the workforce.

First on the list is "The Fourth Industrial Revolution" by Klaus Schwab. This book provides a comprehensive overview of how emerging technologies, particularly AI, are reshaping industries and societies. Schwab delves into the transformative power of these innovations while addressing the challenges they present. He emphasizes the importance of adaptive strategies for navigating this new landscape, making it essential for anyone seeking to grasp AI's broader impact.

Following this, "AI Superpowers: China, Silicon Valley, and the New World Order" by Kai-Fu Lee is another critical read. Lee explores global competition in AI development, highlighting how different regions are approaching this technological frontier. His examination of the economic implications and ethical considerations surrounding AI offers readers a nuanced understanding of its role in future job markets. Personal anecdotes enrich his analysis, making this book both informative and engaging.

For those interested in practical applications of AI, "Human + Machine: Reimagining Work in the Age of AI" by H. James Wilson and Paul R. Daugherty is invaluable. The authors investigate how AI can complement human capabilities rather than replace them. Through real-world examples from various industries, they illustrate effective collaboration between humans and machines, providing actionable insights that professionals can apply in their careers.

If you're looking to enhance your soft skills amidst technological change, consider "Emotional Intelligence 2.0" by Travis Bradberry and Jean Greaves. Although not solely focused on AI, this book underscores the growing importance of emotional intelligence in the workplace—especially as automation takes over more technical tasks. The authors offer strategies for developing emotional intelligence, a crucial asset for individuals aiming to differentiate themselves in an increasingly automated environment.

Additionally, "The Lean Startup" by Eric Ries offers valuable insights into innovation and entrepreneurship within the tech space. Ries' methodology promotes iterative learning and rapid experimentation—principles that are essential when adapting to changes driven by AI technologies. This approach resonates with those looking to launch new ventures or pivot within existing organizations while leveraging AI-driven tools.

Turning to ethical considerations, "Weapons of Math Destruction" by Cathy O'Neil critiques algorithms that perpetuate inequality and bias. O'Neil's work highlights the potential dangers posed by unchecked AI applications in decision-making processes across various sectors. Understanding these ethical dilemmas is vital for anyone working with AI systems, as it emphasizes the need for responsible innovation.

To explore how education is evolving in response to AI

advancements, "Learning with Artificial Intelligence" by John O'Leary examines how educational institutions are adapting to prepare future generations for an AI-driven world. O'Leary discusses innovative teaching methods and curriculum designs that embrace technology while promoting critical thinking—a necessary combination for success in today's job economy.

Finally, "The Future of Work: Robots, AI, and Automation" by Darrell M. West provides an accessible overview of how technological advancements are transforming employment landscapes worldwide. West investigates trends such as remote work and gig economies while offering recommendations for policymakers and educators to better equip individuals for these changes.

By immersing yourself in these resources, you'll gain a well-rounded understanding of both theoretical concepts and practical strategies for navigating the complexities of an AI-driven job economy. Each title contributes uniquely to your knowledge base, equipping you with insights that will empower you to thrive in your career amidst rapid technological advancements.

- **Contact Information for Networking**

Networking plays a crucial role in navigating the AI job economy, where the right connections can significantly influence your career path. Building a strong network means reaching out to professionals across various sectors and engaging with communities that resonate with your interests and aspirations.

To begin, identify key figures in your industry—those who are at the forefront of AI innovations or shaping technology policy. Platforms like LinkedIn are invaluable for connecting with these individuals. When you reach out, personalize your messages to reflect genuine interest in their work; mention specific projects they've led or articles they've written that caught your attention. This thoughtful approach not only increases the chances of receiving a positive response but also lays the foundation for meaningful conversations.

In addition to online networking, attending industry conferences and workshops is a fantastic way to meet peers and thought leaders face-to-face. Events such as the AI Summit or local tech meetups offer opportunities to exchange insights and build relationships. Before attending, research attendees or speakers you wish to connect with; a brief introduction that highlights shared interests or mutual connections can pave the way for fruitful discussions.

However, networking doesn't end with in-person events. Join online communities like forums, social media groups, or professional associations centered on AI and technology. Actively participating in discussions shows your commitment to learning and sharing knowledge, helping you connect with like-minded individuals. Websites like Meetup.com can be excellent resources for finding local gatherings that align with your interests.

Cultivating relationships with mentors is another valuable strategy. Mentorship offers guidance and access to broader networks. Seek experienced professionals who are willing to share their expertise—whether through formal mentorship programs or informal connections made at networking events or through mutual acquaintances.

Consistency is key in your outreach efforts. Follow up on conversations initiated at events or through online platforms with personalized notes expressing gratitude for their time and insights. This practice builds goodwill and keeps you on their radar for future opportunities.

To enhance your networking efficiency, consider using tools designed for this purpose. Contact management applications can help you track interactions, set reminders for follow-ups, and categorize connections based on shared interests or potential collaborations. Free platforms like HubSpot CRM can be particularly helpful in managing these relationships effectively.

And, establishing your own presence by sharing relevant content on social media platforms such as Twitter or LinkedIn can amplify your visibility. Posting articles about recent developments in AI or commenting on industry trends not only showcases your expertise but also invites engagement from others in the field.

Lastly, don't overlook the value of existing connections within your workplace or educational institutions. Colleagues may have contacts who align closely with your career goals and can facilitate introductions that lead to valuable opportunities.

Creating a strong network is an ongoing endeavor that requires both strategy and authenticity. By consistently reaching out, engaging meaningfully, and diligently following up, you can cultivate a web of professional relationships that support your career growth amidst the evolving landscape of the AI job market.

- **Additional Resources and Tools**

In the rapidly changing landscape of the AI job market, leveraging various resources and tools is crucial for enhancing your adaptability and effectiveness. These tools not only grant access to vital knowledge but also support skill development, making them essential for anyone aspiring to excel in a technology-driven environment.

Begin by exploring online learning platforms like Coursera, Udacity, and edX. These platforms offer a wide array of courses that cater to both technical and soft skills relevant to AI. Take this example, Coursera features courses from prestigious universities, including Stanford's machine learning program. Completing these courses can deepen your understanding of AI concepts and provide certificates that enhance your resume. To maximize the benefits of these resources, establish specific learning goals; for example, aim to finish one course each month while applying your new skills in real-world projects.

In addition to formal education, gaining practical experience through hands-on projects is invaluable. Websites such as Kaggle allow you to engage in competitions or collaborate on data science challenges with peers around the globe. Participating in these activities sharpens your technical skills and familiarizes you with industry-standard tools and practices. Consider starting with a beginner-friendly competition that aligns with your interests—this approach offers both practical experience and constructive feedback from the community.

Networking within these platforms can significantly enhance your learning journey. Many offer forums or discussion boards where participants exchange insights and solutions. Actively engaging in these communities not only deepens your understanding but also raises your profile within the field. Don't hesitate to ask questions; the community is often eager to assist those who show genuine interest.

Alongside educational platforms, project management tools like Trello or Asana can be beneficial for organizing your skill development plans. These applications help you manage tasks related to your learning journey—whether it's completing an online course, reading specific books, or practicing coding exercises. By breaking larger objectives into manageable tasks and setting deadlines, you maintain momentum while effectively tracking your progress.

Additionally, subscribing to industry newsletters or podcasts can keep you informed about the latest trends and innovations in AI. Resources such as "The Data Skeptic" podcast or "AI Alignment Forum" offer insights into cutting-edge developments while allowing you to engage with expert discussions at your convenience. Regularly consuming content from diverse sources broadens your perspective and equips you with various viewpoints relevant for discussions within professional circles.

To further support this knowledge acquisition process, consider creating personalized development plans (PDPs). A well-structured PDP identifies your current competencies alongside desired skills in AI-related fields and outlines actionable steps toward bridging those gaps. This approach promotes self-awareness regarding your professional standing while mapping out clear pathways for growth.

Certification programs are equally important as they validate skills acquired through independent study or practical experience. Platforms like LinkedIn Learning provide certifications upon course completion, enhancing your credibility among potential employers or collaborators in the AI sector. Prioritize certifications that align closely with emerging technologies or frameworks relevant to your career aspirations.

Finally, don't overlook local libraries and community colleges as valuable resources for workshops and seminars focused on emerging technologies, including AI applications. Many institutions host events aimed at introducing new technologies that may be free or low-cost—offering excellent opportunities for hands-on exposure without a significant financial commitment.

By utilizing these diverse resources, you adopt a multifaceted approach to developing the skills necessary for thriving in an AI-influenced job market. Committing to continuous learning through structured platforms while engaging in community-driven experiences such as competitions and networking opportunities enables professionals to build robust strategies that keep them ahead of industry trends and foster long-term career resilience amid rapid technological changes.

INDEX

D

E

F

G

H

I

L

M

This index serves as a navigational tool for the topics discussed throughout the book. Each entry highlights key concepts that illuminate the dynamic landscape shaped by artificial intelligence. As you explore these subjects further or revisit specific sections of interest within this comprehensive resource on adapting to the evolving job economy influenced by AI.

ACKNOWLEDGMENTS

Every great endeavor is built upon the support and efforts of many individuals. This book is a testament to the collective contributions of countless people whose insights, expertise, and encouragement have shaped its journey.

I extend my deepest gratitude to the thought leaders and innovators in artificial intelligence who have generously shared their knowledge. Their willingness to engage in discussions about the ethical implications and practical applications of AI has not only enriched this book but also deepened my understanding of a rapidly evolving landscape. Their work continues to inspire others as we navigate the complexities of integrating technology into our daily lives.

I am also profoundly thankful to my mentors and colleagues who have encouraged me to think critically about the intersection of technology and humanity. Your unwavering support and insightful feedback have been invaluable, pushing me to clarify my ideas and express them more effectively. It is within these collaborative spaces that true learning occurs, reminding us that progress often emerges from dialogue and shared experiences.

And, I wish to acknowledge the stories of individuals forging their own paths in this AI-driven job economy. Each narrative reflects resilience, innovation, and adaptability in the face of change. Together, they create a rich tapestry that illustrates not only the challenges but also the triumphs across various sectors—from healthcare to education—demonstrating how diverse paths can lead to successful integration of AI.

The role of family and friends has been equally significant; your encouragement provided a strong foundation throughout the writing process. Those late nights spent drafting chapters or brainstorming ideas were made lighter by your patience and belief in this project's potential. This journey has been as much about personal growth as it has been about professional insights.

I would also like to recognize those behind the scenes—editors, designers, and publishing teams—whose dedication transformed rough ideas into polished chapters. This collaborative effort deserves acknowledgment; each person's unique talents have contributed to creating a cohesive resource for readers navigating today's job economy.

Finally, I am immensely grateful to you—the reader—for investing your time in exploring these ideas. Your curiosity drives progress, ensuring that discussions about AI evolve beyond theoretical boundaries into actionable strategies that empower professionals everywhere. Together, we are part of an exciting narrative unfolding at the extraordinary intersection of humanity and technology, crafting a future where both can thrive hand in hand.

Thank you all for being part of this journey toward not just survival but genuine flourishing in an age defined by artificial intelligence.

www.ingramcontent.com/pod-product-compliance
Lightning Source LLC
LaVergne TN
LVHW051220050326
832903LV00028B/2172